THE HEART OF THE WAR IN COLOMBIA

Constanza Ardila Galvis

LATIN
AMERICA
BUREAU

© 2000   Constanza Ardila Galvis

The right of Constanza Ardila Galvis to be identified as the author of this work has been asserted by her in accordance with the Copyright, Designs and Patents Act 1988

First published in the UK in 2000 by:

Latin America Bureau (Research and Action) Ltd
1 Amwell Street, London EC1R 1UL

Reprinted in 2002

A CIP catalogue record is available from the British Library

ISBN: 1 899365 42 7

Originally published by CedaVida in Colombia as *Guerreros Ciegos: El conflicto armado en Colombia*, 1998

Editing: Marcela López Levy
Translation: Alice Jay
Cover design: Andy Dark
Printed and bound: Russell Press, Nottingham

Contents

We all hope to see the same light at the end of the tunnel.

Introduction

To reach **The Heart of the War** took ten years. It has been a decade of building trust and listening, a process which could only come about because of a lifelong commitment to justice and change in Colombia from the author and those who have given their testimonies. The people who have shared their lives with Constanza Ardila have done so in an attempt to break out of the normality of violence in Colombia. They have looked back into history and deeply into the personal and political experiences which led them to be forcibly displaced. The opportunity to bring together their different political allegiances in an environment of trust and openness provides a complex and multifaceted view into a war which has made the violent death of civilians part of everyday life.

The right to remember, to piece together collective memory through the exchange of personal histories, is a rare process in Colombia, more so among the victims of violence. The indiscriminate terror sown by massacres and by the murders of civilians during the dirty war which has been the norm since the 1980s, has as one of its chief functions to suppress memory; to destroy collective organisation and to eliminate leaders who insist on exposing the deep divisions in Colombian society. The terror which is the precursor of displacement not only creates geographical dislocation, it also dismembers communities and families through mistrust and fear. With threats following the displaced to their place of refuge, terror becomes a permanent and internalised condition, sustained to ensure physical survival. In the telling of their lives, many reflect on the psychological costs, and upon the unbearable anguish which has at times robbed their lives of meaning.

Their engagement with the personal is not done at the cost of the political, but the aim is to complement factual accounts with in-depth perspectives into the origins and effects of violence. Putting names and life stories to some of the statistics of violence is a way of reclaiming the humanity of the victims, a recognition of each of the lives which is extinguished by the war. Marcos, one of the protagonists, puts it this way: 'we must go deeper in seeking the causes of war and displacement, not to bypass political and economic analyses which we've known about for years, but which have *overdiagnosed* the conflict.'

Ardila's aim is to reflect on the mechanisms through which ordinary people become willing and able to kill and torture and reproduce the cycles of violence in Colombia. Such reflection is particularly necessary in a country which is constantly portrayed as inhabited by a people so cruel and homicidal as to be beyond comprehension or redemption. Ardila accompanies the protagonists in dealing with the particular atrocities they have suffered, covered up or perpetrated, to reach a point where the culture of violence and how it is reproduced, within each person and collectively, becomes apparent.

Violence is most present in the social spaces of everyday life, and not on some distant battlefield. The effects in terms of the deterioration of the rule of law and of warfare, where no side respects international humanitarian law, are pervasive and implicated in the social fabric. The complexity of the war in Colombia arises from the localised nature of conflicts, within an unequal and exclusionary national economic and political system. Repression has been the method of choice used by the wealthiest to confront attempts to democratise access to resources and political power. There is nothing original in such a stance, but Colombia is remarkable in the refusal of those who have been excluded to bow down and give up. Instead they have resisted and organised in spite of all attempts to 'wipe out their seed', the expression Laura uses in her narrative to convey the widely-felt threat among the rural poor of mass killings awaiting those who demand change.

The purpose of this book is to go beyond the statistics, to portray the culture of violence which permeates Colombia and which has consistently emanated predominately from the most powerful in society and whose victims are in their majority the poor. It is not an exhaustive survey of the situation of the displaced in Colombia, nor simply an attempt to portray the harsh realities of displaced life, as those necessary stories are being told already.

The aim is to begin by recognising, as Socorro does in her testimony, that 'it is so easy to start a war, and so hard to end it', but to then to open up new ways of thinking about how to create a future without war. The protagonists of **The Heart of the War** hold that truth can provide such an opening. To attempt truth-telling is more than a mere platitude in a country where distrust is a survival technique. Everyone involved in the making of this book is seeking no less than to challenge the social and political culture of Colombia.

'Overdiagnosed' violence

Colombia has many acute observers of the political and economic antecedents for and the present conditions of the war. It is unique in having *violentólogos*, experts whose work it is to analyse violence, its perpetrators, methods, and changing strategies over time. Sadly, there is much to record, examine and denounce. The quality of research into violence within Colombia is a testament to the determination and courage of researchers who have often become the targets of threats and violence themselves. The testimonies included here are an attempt to complement the wealth of facts which exist about Colombia's war and view them through the eyes of those who live daily in the fray.

The overdiagnosed nature of the problems in Colombia becomes a hindrance to understanding when the perpetrators of the violence are known, and yet nothing changes. It is a process which engenders numbness and fatalism. Within Colombia despair is justified with recourse to history and without, by assuming a deformed Colombian national character. Neither approach provides pointers for change or hope.

The life stories plunge us into the personal realm, aspects of which would remain unintelligible without the context provided by a brief historical overview and some of the facts and figures which place the protagonists in a setting increasingly well-known to Colombians, but unfamiliar to the rest of the world. **The Heart of the War** proposes to find out how change could come about, and puts forward one way: that truth and memory can reconcile both victims and perpetrators of violence to a new beginning.

Many of the testimonies begin with the participants' childhood memories, and reach back into Colombian history at least as far as *la Violencia*, (1948-65). This period of sectarian violence between supporters of the Liberal and Conservative political parties, and the power-sharing deal they negotiated to end the civil war, provided conditions for continued strife as pacification stumbled on local confrontations. The civil strife had escalated after the murder of Jorge Eliécer Gaitán in 1948, the Liberal presidential candidate who preached the union of the people against oligarchic interests. His populist discourse revolved around themes of inclusion and exclusion in the political and economic life of the country, a recurring theme in Colombian politics. The civil war mobilised a significant proportion of the rural population, and most of the violence which survived the National Front agreement between liberals and conservatives revolved around land ownership.

Periods of comprehensive peace have been the exception rather than the rule in Colombia during the entire 20th century. The Thousand Day War (1899-1902), the first of the century, left 100,000 dead and great devastation. The continuities between periods of war and the current belligerence are not easily discernible and remain contested by historians, but the absence of peace does point to the deep unresolved social tensions which have persisted over generations.

Due to its importance in the accounts of displacement in the form of what the French sociologist, Daniel Pecaut[1] calls 'a founding historical experience' *la Violencia* provides more than an arbitrary starting point for **The Heart of the War**. The framework for memory, as it tries to make sense of personal and social experiences, is provided by this period, when two million are estimated to have been forced from their land and homes. Continuity, Pecaut argues, is expressed by Colombians between *la Violencia* and the violence of the 1990s, irrespective of the nature of the war in the intervening years, due to the centrality of displacement and the social trauma which accompanies it. In turn, the phenomena surrounding displacement, which will be examined in more depth below, are inextricably linked to the current escalation of the armed conflict in Colombia.

Other analysts argue that there are similarities beyond displacement between *la Violencia* and the present state of the conflict, in that in the 1990s a diversity of conditions reinforce each other to bring about an escalation of violence. These include the counter-agrarian reform which has been taking place due to the massive investment of drug money in land; the weakness or absence of the state from vast expanses of the country; the crisis of legitimacy of the state as it loses or cedes the monopoly on violence to the paramilitaries; and the distinct local and regional nature of conflicts.

Between the 1960s and the beginning of the 1980s, the violence was of lower intensity and more clearly demarcated, both geographically and with respect to the parties involved: on one side, the state forces of the police and the army and on the other, left-wing guerrillas. Although paramilitaries had become a legal recourse available to the armed forces in 1965, it was in the decade of the 1980s that a dirty war making extensive use of paramilitary groups became the armed forces' central strategy. With the concurrent increasing influence of drug trafficking and organised crime, the war was further de-regularised and the stages where it was played out multiplied. The rise of paramilitary groups followed the negotiations and peace accords signed between the government and a number of guerrilla groups in the early 1980s, when the armed forces clearly disavowed the agreed political reinsertion of guerrillas into civil society, but were politically constrained from continuing to wage war directly. The paramilitaries developed their own complex linkages to the drug trafficking 'new rich' and the older establishment of landowners, increasing their resources and the number of scores to settle. Private armies are not a new phenomenon in Colombia and violence has been the way in which economic élites have traditionally chosen to deal directly with social unrest, bypassing the state.

In 1997 Carlos Castaño, the notorious paramilitary leader of the Autodefensas Campesinas de Córdova y Urabá (ACCU), helped found a national coordination of paramilitary groups named the Autodefensas Unidas de Colombia (AUC). The scope of his military operations has grown in spite of the fact that paramilitaries have officially been illegal since 1989, and a bounty has been offered for Castaño's capture. He has given numerous interviews to journalists who have been led to his ranches in northwestern Colombia, and the guerrilla have attacked him, yet state forces prove unable to arrest him. This failure is one among many which discredit the government, which appears either to be cynically and tacitly in favour of paramilitarism, or too weak to control the armed forces which set up and support paramilitary activities.

There is now ample evidence of the paramilitaries' close operational connections to the armed forces, and they are currently the worst violators of human rights in the country. In 1998, of the 2,104 serious violations of international humanitarian law recorded by Justice and Peace and the *Centro de Investigación y Educación Popular*, CINEP, 1,479 were carried out by various paramilitary organisations, the different guerrilla groups account for 531 and the army were responsible for 92. In 1994 the government of President Ernesto Samper sponsored legal self-defence militias, the CONVIVIR, which reinforced the status of paramilitary groups with respect to the state. In 1999 their licences were not renewed, but the law which created them has not been revoked.

The devastation wrought by the continued presence of war in different incarnations since 1948 means Colombia suffers one of the worst conflicts of the 20th century. The overall human toll for the conflict is yet to be counted, but political violence took between 3,000 and 4,000 lives each year in the 1990s, revealing the scale of the war. The greatest proportion of deaths corresponded to targeted political killings of civilians. The Permanent Committee for the Defence of Human Rights in Colombia estimated that a conservative figure for the number of individual political assassinations, victims of social cleansing and massacres came to 3,832 people for 1998. Over the same period Justice and Peace and CINEP estimated 1,512 combatants had fallen in battle. These numbers do not include kidnappings, disappearances, threats or victims of forced displacement.

For many years the war in Colombia has continued in spite of national denial and international indifference. Colombian democracy has been widely praised as a haven of stability among the turbulence and military upsets of neighbouring countries. The economy had operated efficiently in comparison to others in the region, avoiding the severe indebtedness which has crippled other Latin American economies. In Bogotá elected politicians claimed the war involved only a few isolated armed insurgents. At the end of the century, it has become impossible to prolong the charade.

The realities of a war in which the guerrilla have a significant presence in over half of the country's municipalities – according to the government – and where paramilitaries, in the figure of Castaño, have sworn total war against the insurgents, make it increasingly untenable to downplay the conflict. Civilians too have forced the government to face reality: in 1997 nearly ten million Colombians voted for peace, demanding action from those in power. President Andrés Pastrana, who was sworn into office in 1998, made peace his central political platform. But faced with the escalation of military strength by the guerrilla and the armed forces and the impunity and unofficial support for the paramilitaries, peace talks have not been sustained.

Political problems are compounded by an economy in recession, where contraction has been so devastating that President Andrés Pastrana has called for a state of economic emergency. Official government statistics put unemployment at 15 per cent in 1999, although it is clear both unemployment and under-employment affect sectors of the population, such as the displaced, in much higher proportion. Displacement has made more acute the problems of urbanisation, and unemployment is most concentrated in the nine largest cities. The economic prospects are both worsened by the war and at the same time make more difficult a substantial settlement which would encompass the structural changes sought by the guerrilla.

Education, the most significant factor in long-term economic growth, shows how regressive the social and economic situation is in Colombia. United Nations' research found that 46 per cent of urban young people have no more schooling than their parents had. For young people in rural areas, the figures are bleaker still – 73 per cent have not achieved the level of education their parents possess, thereby not reaching the legal minimum educational standard.

Drugs production and trafficking ensure Colombia international attention, in particular from the United States, where most of the drugs are consumed. Statements by officials of a number of state departments show that the tremendous economic and logistical support provided by the US to the armed forces and the police in the 'war against drugs' is equally meant for counterinsurgency purposes. Colombia received in the region of 110 million dollars in 1998 in direct military and police aid, not including arms sales. The estimated aid for 1999 has more than doubled to 294 million dollars, making Colombia the fourth largest recipient of US military aid in the world.[2] The US provides under 10 million dollars a year for development projects to combat poverty.

In 1999 President Andrés Pastrana toured the US and Europe, seeking 3.5 billion dollars in aid 'to bring peace and activate the economy'. The Colombian government asked for 55 per cent of the aid to be used for strengthening the military – notwithstanding the grave concerns over their human rights record – and 45 per cent for economic development purposes. The response within the US has included anti-drug czar General Barry McCaffrey proposing to provide over one billion dollars, of which 92 per cent would support the armed forces.

The widespread violence engendered by drug traffickers' interests, which reached extreme forms in the late 1980s and early 1990s, provided a smokescreen to the political strife which both predated and continues. The afterlife of that violence is prolonged in the speeches of US officials who speak of 'narcoguerrillas' as the only threat to peace, when President Andrés Pastrana himself has felt the need to defend the Fuerzas Armadas Revolucionarias de Colombia, FARC, the largest guerrilla group, as a legitimate negotiating party, maintaining they do not traffic in drugs, although they do tax growers and traffickers in the areas they control. The narcoguerrilla theory provides cover for military aid agreed in the US under the auspices of the 'war against drugs' to be used for counterinsurgency purposes, while not disturbing the paramilitaries who control significant drug interests, and are acknowledged to be traffickers. The effects of drugs can be felt in the widespread corruption which has already implicated members of the armed forces and politicians in office. Drugs have become part of the violent dynamic of Colombian life, fuelling the war with its revenue. Drug money interacts with the war in the way every significant economic interest in the country cannot but be drawn into the conflict.

At the end of the decade of the 1990s, after nearly twenty years of dirty war, the main concern of those defending human rights is that they be respected by all parties. A crucial requirement is the observance of the basic principles of international humanitarian law as laid down in the Geneva Convention.

The Heart of the War gives centre stage to the people's history, which shows clearly how far the war has deteriorated, while at the same time demonstrating how civilians have grown exhausted by violence and sceptical of military solutions. These testimonies come from the rural population which has traditionally supported the war as a way of being taken into account, but who today feel the armed struggle has nothing more to offer them. The *campesinos* who speak here have been hit too hard, for too long, but instead of turning their pain into revenge and further violence, they have chosen to fight for change through peaceful means.

Displacement

By 1999 it was estimated that one and a half million Colombians had been displaced by force, according to CINEP the second most numerous victims of forced internal migration in the world. Many of the life stories which follow include displacement spanning one or more generations. The Inter-American Commission for Human Rights calls the scale of displacement in Colombia 'a humanitarian catastrophe'. It also documents how peasants are evicted to make way for powerful economic interests. In the Commission's reckoning, responsibility for displacement can be attributed in 33 per cent to paramilitaries, 20 per cent to the various guerrilla groups and 16 per cent to the armed forces and other state agents; the remaining instances cannot be attributed beyond doubt. Forced displacement violates Protocol II of the Geneva Convention.

The majority of the displaced, from the war of the Thousand Days, through *la Violencia* to the present-day crisis, are the rural poor. The current process has already proved disruptive to Colombian society, as thousands of people arrive at already insecure urban marginal areas, while employment opportunities diminish in an adverse economic climate.

Pecaut reflects that land ownership provides roots and a means of belonging. One of Colombia's long-term problems has been its pattern of land tenure, where the presence of peasants on the land has always been precarious and subject to the favour of local powerbrokers. The insecurity of land possession has reinforced the importance of agrarian reform and fuelled the war. Support for Pecaut's thesis comes from the processes of displacement which affect more than one generation and successive areas of colonisation which are described in a number of the testimonies. The experience of clearing the inhospitable land only to be moved on by violence, is recounted time and again.

All but one of the protagonists has suffered displacement for political reasons first hand. Laura expresses their predicament: 'Why had I not died in the last ambush or in the last attack? Now I'm like the wounded, merely a displaced person. In the war, people react to the wounded or the displaced with indifference or relief. As if having not died and ending up hurt or displaced were a lucky break. But to be wounded nearly always means being left mutilated, to lose limbs, senses, movement. Never again to be a complete person. They think the displaced are fortunate, when being displaced means having lost our soul, dreams, identity, home and family.'

Added to the terror of being thrown off their land, the displaced are persecuted even in their internal exile in the towns and cities. Leaders of displaced communities are accused by combatants of sympathising with the enemy or arranging displacements as a military manoeuvre, and the number kidnapped and killed has been on the increase.

According to the *Consultoría para los Derechos Humanos y el Desplazamiento*, CODHES, the number of displaced has tripled since 1995. The United Nations High Commissioner for Refugees estimates that three quarters of the displaced are women, most with children. The common theme which runs through the reports of all aid and humanitarian organisations is the overwhelming targeting of civilians in Colombia's war, who make up the highest proportion of casualties in all types of violations of human rights.

Recovering life

The process which gave life to this book was not undertaken to reach the printed page. People began to talk about their experiences primarily as a way of learning to cope with life after displacement, a life without material security and often lived out in fear of repression. Many found themselves in such hopeless situations that all their minds could hold were replays of the trauma of threats, deaths and terror which had caused them to flee.

'The world should know what we've been through and in our stories see a reflection of the lives of thousands of peasants, so history doesn't continue to repeat itself endlessly. If they can feel what we've lived through and why we expressed our most intimate needs through violence, maybe they will help us to change. We feel so insignificant, but we're a true war machine,' explains Marcos with passion.

In the process of seeking testimonies, Ardila collected over 200 life stories. The selection and writing of the testimonies to produce the final coherent account are very much her authorial responsibility, although the process of writing included returning each testimony, and the whole book, to its protagonists prior to publication for their comments and approval. The overwhelming sense they share is one of wishing their stories to make a difference to others, and for that reason, they were willing to expose themselves so starkly.

They have offered their lives here to reach to out with their experiences in the hope of changing minds and hearts about how to bring an end to the war. They appear under pseudonyms to protect their identities, as they continue to be involved in their communities, active in the daily struggle to survive and keep the faith in their internal exile.

They first came together through CedaVida, one of a number of Colombian organisations which provide material support and advocacy for the victims of displacement. It is unique, however, in its pioneering approach to dealing with trauma. The aim has been to seek the transformation of those excluded from social and political life through violence and displacement into citizens able to demand change through peaceful means. The tools for their rehabilitation work have been adapted from a range of psychological therapies, but altered beyond traditional treatment by distinct emphases: the first, to enable the traumatised individual to understand the weight of social dynamics within their personal experience, and the second, to use the healing process as a means of understanding and challenging the social context. The underlying assumption is that for the possibility of a constructive psychic life to be real, it is not the individual who should be adapted to the environment, but the context should be created for the development of the person.

CedaVida is contributing to the creation in Colombia of what Ignacio Martín Baró termed 'liberation psychology'[3]. He was a victim of a death squad in El Salvador in 1989, showing how his commitment to an engaged psychology alongside the poor unsettled the violent and powerful. It is an idea which explores the potential of psychology for collective liberation, in the way in which liberation theology sought the same through a reinterpretation of biblical teaching.

CedaVida has created a supportive space which recognises the psychological trauma of a life involved in violence. Through art therapy with children, and a variety of therapeutic tools for adults, the toll violence has exacted is examined. Support is provided to deal with how it has damaged relationships and the will to live of those who have been displaced. In the process of confronting the effects of violence on adults, what emerged were widespread patterns of violence in the home and family, in particular the prevalence of child abuse in all its forms: physical, mental and sexual. The course was charted by the displaced who began to speak of their involvement in violence and discovered their feelings took them far back in time. The importance of childhood experiences for the individuals who agreed to share their life stories, meant that the project of analysing their involvement in political violence was delayed while they came to terms with their past. Their initial reflections resulted in a book entitled *La Cosecha de la Ira* (Harvest of Wrath) published in Colombia in 1996. It was only once that process had been completed, that they felt able to face the questions posed in **The Heart of the War**, namely, how to move on from a history of violence.

To that end, they have shared with us ten complex lives which encompass violence in the home, in society, and as a means to political power. They do not claim to present the definitive explanation for the violence in Colombia, but they do underline how economic and political analyses often lack a human dimension.

The success of an approach which combines dealing with psychological trauma with political analysis is evident in the lives of those who participated in the project. Mercedes explains what it has meant to her: 'before I was displaced I wasn't allowed out of the house by my husband, and I didn't dare look anyone in the eyes; since having to deal with not only the material loss of displacement, but also the psychological mechanisms which kept me afraid and enraged, I've found it is possible to choose how I live in the midst of this violence.' She never finished primary school, but she is co-ordinating a CedaVida project to support newly displaced people, representing them before the authorities, giving them advice, accompanying them in their trauma. She has chosen to opt out of violence in a situation where none of the armed actors recognise neutrality and where threats and death are daily realities for those who defend the rights of civilians. More than 80 per cent of CedaVida's staff are displaced people themselves.

The message of those who have participated in this book is clear: we are the majority of those affected by this war without quarter. We are the rural poor who have been part of the war and who now are its most numerous victims. We no longer believe violence can solve our problems. We have changed, which means any and every Colombian is able to change. Peace will come when organised civilians, that is, civil society, is strong enough to be taken into account by those who are armed. We must insist on solutions to the violence which are inclusive of the majority of Colombians and negotiated by society as well as by the armies.

Marcela López Levy
London, 1999

[1] http://www.colombia-thema.org/pecaut.html, article published in May 1999 in the magazine *Thema*, only available through the internet.

[2] http://www.ciponline.org/ The Centre for International Policy provides a range of data on US aid to Colombia.

[3] Martín Baró, I. (1994) *Writings for a liberation psychology*, Cambridge: Harvard University Press and Caro Hollander, N. (1997) *Love in a time of hate: Liberation psychology in Latin America*, New Jersey: Rutgers University Press.

Speaking Out

It was a sweltering morning. The temperature would not give and summer's insistence showed it was not only the war which had wreaked havoc this year. One after another they arrived: Gabriela, Daniel, Mercedes, Marcos, Socorro, Laura, Antonia, Alejandra, Ana Dolores and Angela. They greeted each other with the shyness of peasants, a diffidence which clung to them still, although they had known each other for years. Some had been displaced to the same community and others had come to know each other during the rehabilitation work. It had taken them time to decide to accept the invitation to come together, as they were terrified to confront their truths stripped down to the bare bones. By coming they began to commit themselves to peace. Facing the story of their lives and presenting it in an open way was not easy. Over the years, step by step, they had looked into their feelings in greater depth: in the beginning they spoke in generalisations; then, of their small family woes; later, they changed their language from that of events to that of emotions, and in the end, with the confidence which my presence by their side had given them over the years, they opened their hearts.

Before their process of healing, life for them had been an affliction which unavoidably ended in death. Now they revealed their anguish, weaknesses, mistakes and decisions, searching for life. They wanted to break the spiral of violence they had known since their grandparents' time and in which they had participated over the years.

They had made a commitment to themselves and to history. They were going to reveal who they were and no one would try to cover anything up. Having been through an emotional recovery, they knew that only the truth could lead them to peace. Out of their history they were ready to build a collective story of the war and, through that story, to pursue paths to conciliation. It was important to know the circumstances, places, motives, facts and, above all, why they had gambled their hearts on violence. They agreed to meet because they felt proud of what they had done and because this time around they wanted to bet their life on peace.

After a brief introduction, the participants looked around the place where we were going to work. I had booked them into guest houses in the city, near this place which was located in the outskirts of the town, where the countryside's tranquillity would make them feel safe. We settled into a big room with large windows so that the light and wind of the plains could refresh us.

I gave each of them a desk, a notebook, a sharpened pencil and white paper tissues.

After the greetings and a brief conversation, we settled into our places and gave ourselves the task of establishing the ground rules of the encounter.

To start with we must be sincere; we must respect the words and circumstances of the others; have the determination to stay until the end; listen in an open way to each of the stories in silence; express opinions without judging and not take the individual story out of context.

We were going to work in a way which was true to our feelings and to our minds and we were willing to invest the time necessary to offer a new vision of the armed conflict in Colombia.

I looked at their serious faces and it seemed that I had known them all my life. We had spoken for hours, month after month, year after year. It took a long time for them to open their hearts to me and I discovered the simplicity of the war and the complexity of its causes. It was painful to understand and touch their lives and the lives of their families, to see their roots severed by a war which has many rationales and none. That was why I had called them together today. We had to do something to stop this savage killing. They were peasants, human beings who at one time or another had been at the heart of the war. They knew its causes and they had suffered its consequences. I waited for Socorro to write down the agreements on a piece of paper in large and clear letters and I said to them:

'We are going to speak here with honesty and each will reveal their truth, the reasons they had for participating in the conflict and the motives that lead them to commit to peace. My role will be to collect what is said and recount the events you examine. The majority of you have gone through a process of expressing your grief, individually, for the losses suffered not only during the armed conflict, but you have also gone back to memories of your infancy and through reflection have reconstructed emotions and feelings you had as children. For that reason, I propose we start our work there. You must not judge each other here; what we do here is between ourselves and history. My role will be to hold up a mirror in which each of you, the whole group, and the country are reflected. You all have in common that you are peasants whose land was taken from you by the war, you have seen your loved ones die and disappear, you have suffered being uprooted and most importantly, you have participated in the conflict.'

They all looked at each other. They came from different places, but they looked alike.

'We've had fifty years of war and lies. They speak of banditry, of narco-terrorism, of "violence"; of massacres, murders, disappearances and of displacement; of "the actors in the war", they mention the paramilitary, the armed forces, the guerrilla, the "dark forces", "unclear situations" and things like that; but they don't admit there's a war. That's why we are at war. They've not considered the social actors of the war. They don't want to acknowledge the war is against the people and not against a few.

'I wish I could keep you from this painful process, but it will be enriching, not only getting to know each other fully, but coming to conclusions which might stop the barbarism which surrounds us. Without your memories it's not possible to show how, when, where and why the war took place and who participated in it. Nothing done to date has been effective, be it because of the nature of the attempts or because of the ignorance of those who have tried. It seems they didn't know what it was about. As long as this is the case, the war will continue to spread. The battle is not fought in a specific place. The war is a movable feast. It is carried within each of us. You are the ones able to describe it. You have sufficient courage and love because you have suffered the war and you are the survivors. Now, it is your turn to speak.'

Part One
The War Within

Gabriela

José, and the carpenter's wife, María

Some crossed themselves, others wrung their hands and a few smiled timidly. They were their own guides and they were willing to stay together until the end and not break the rules. It was not easy to begin and so Angela, who was used to speaking out, started by saying:

'We peasants were poor, even before all this killing. I say this because of my age, not because I know the history of Colombia. I only reached level five in elementary school. We lived the same way, on rented lands or on small plots bought by a miracle, and the children grew up by our sides. The husbands worked from sun rise to sun set and we women, along with the children, took care of the animals. There was never a lack of food and coins were gathered in the savings box, on top of the mantelpiece, behind the virgin with its candle lit for the daily prayer. The boys became men through work and beatings and us girls became women by blowing on the fire and washing clothes. Our few children's games went up in smoke before we were a foot high. When we thought of the future, we thought solely about the land and the family.'

'But when men insulted each other in bars they also killed each other with machetes or openly shot each other, and they did it to show how manly they were or because they felt offended,' interrupted Gabriela. 'The political violence came after a huge slaughter which my mother lived through as a small girl,' she continued. 'It was when her town was liberal and they fought with the other town which was conservative. She told us that during Mass the priests would bless the killings of the *cachiporros*, which is what they called the liberals. The priests and the military were conservatives and they were called the *chulavitas*. At that time they said the same things about the liberals they now say about the communists, that they were atheists, they killed children and that they did not respect God or the law. But when you get to the bottom of it, it amounts to the same thing. The difference is that then they ended up killing each other for being red or blue, now it is for being on the left or right.'

'That is to say, on the right, priests and the military and on the left, atheists and communists', said Laura with sarcasm, 'and I suppose they say that they're on the right because that's the hand they use to cross themselves with and the left, because it's the useless hand. The one which can be cut off.'

'Without going any further', said Gabriela, 'I'm a child of this violence between liberals and conservatives. My mother lived it in the flesh.'

She looked around her and realised the surprise she had caused.

'How are you a daughter of the violence?' Socorro asked.

'Because of what happened to my mother during *la Violencia* which started in 1948 between liberals and conservatives. I never speak of my origins and even those who know me don't know about it. I'm the daughter of a lead *chulavita* bandit.'

'The daughter of "Blackblood" or of "Revenge"?' they shouted out.

I was surprised. In less than five minutes they had connected and were sharing their thoughts spontaneously.

'No, I'm the daughter of "The Carpenter".'

'Really? Or is this just another of your stories, Gabriela. Come on, stop messing about. You, the daughter of a bandit leader?' asked Angela.

'It's true. If you don't believe me, ask Mercedes, who knows the whole story. My mother told her about it before she died.'

'It's true. Doña Mariana, Gabriela's mother, became my friend and she told me her story in some detail. Maybe because people have certain reservations with their own children and it's difficult to speak sincerely. Especially when it means talking about their father,' said Mercedes.

'That man might be my biological father, but I don't recognise him as my father because he never looked after me. I lived with my father, Gregorio, and my mother, Marcelina, who were the ones who brought me up, along with my mother,' added Gabriela categorically.

'Gabriela, will you allow me to tell your mother's story?' asked Mercedes.

'Of course. I mentioned it because I know it will be useful to see what our parents were like and the motives surrounding the violence, not just in my life, but in those who have been its protagonists for decades.'

'With respect, I'd like to tell you the story of Mariana Montero, a woman I admired and who rests in peace after much suffering and who had a great love for her daughter, Gabriela Montero, her pride and joy,' said Mercedes.

'Mariana Montero was born in Puerto Berrío where, along with most towns in the country, the violence was taking over. One morning, during Mass and on a market Sunday, the *chulavitas* took the town. They knew that this was the day the peasants and their families came down with money to buy goods. It was the best day to kill *cachiporros* and escape with a lot of money. In other words, to kill two birds with one stone.

They came into town on horses shooting right, left and centre. People dropped what they were carrying and ran like crazy so as not to be hit by a stray bullet. That day, Mariana lost her family. She was ten years old and she had never left home except to go to market. She didn't know the town very well and she got lost among the terrified people. By the time she realised where she was, she was a long way from the town, in the countryside, and she didn't recognise anything. A woman found her and took Mariana to her house which was a big, safe farm. They waited until the following Sunday for someone to identify the girl in town. However, the following Sunday there were rumours that the town had been taken again and, to avoid danger, they didn't go to market. After two weeks in the house, bandits attacked the farm. Mariana ran away again and got lost. This time the *chulavitas* found her.

"José, there is someone over there in the shrubs."

José gestured for Onofre to be quiet and they hid behind some bushes with their guns drawn to see who was coming down the road.

"It's a girl and she's alone," whispered Onofre.

They came out and Mariana felt a hand take her by the waist and lift her into the air. She shouted, called for help and kicked the air, but this only made the group of men who had surrounded her in a flash, laugh. After they had laughed at her shouting and kicking for a while, they put her down and told her to stop screaming.

"Listen you, no one can hear you here and if you don't shut up we might get annoyed and then you'll be sorry," grunted Rosendo.

"Now stop squealing or I'll hit you," said José.

Mariana stopped shouting and began to cry softly. Her big, bright black eyes looked angrily at this man who threatened her.

He watched her and said, "She's got guts, this little girl." He took off his hat, scratched his head and went on: "We have a problem on our hands now. We're going to have to take her with us."

"Are you mad, José!" exclaimed Onofre.

"Well, it occurs to me that now she knows where we are. It seems dangerous to me to let her go back to town."

That was how, from that day on, she joined the ranks of the *chulavitas* and became one of the hunted. Later she became known as the youngest bandit of the time.

When they went out to kill and attack the Liberal towns, Mariana would stay nearby waiting for them to return to celebrate their crimes. She learnt the ways of the mountains and to live a life of hardship and wrongdoing. She saw many killed for disobedience and understood that compliance and loyalty to the leader of the group was the only possible way to survive. She became a serious, submissive and obedient girl with "The Carpenter", the leader of the group and Gabriela's father.

José was thirty-four and of medium build. Doña Mariana told me with both pride and rage that his penetrating gaze made anyone who came near him quake with fear. The Carpenter thought of himself as a strong character and a good child of the Lord. His big, bulging black eyes revealed a mix of Indian and black blood.

He looked right at you and his pallid face told of a life in the mountains which destroyed good health. They called him the Carpenter in memory of Saint Joseph, as he would take pity on the children he had turned into orphans. He never killed them even though he ran the risk that they would later recognise him. He made a show of being charitable, giving the children back the money he had stolen from their parents. He did not allow his fellow bandits to abuse Mariana, and he respected her and did not himself "make use" of her until she was fourteen years old.

Doña Mariana, blessed soul, told me that some of the aspects of life in the mountains were enjoyable for the men. They hunted, played cards and dice on their *ponchos*, ate and slept for fourteen to fifteen days at a time. They only risked their hides once or twice a month. She didn't enjoy the life because as a girl she had to cook the food, wash the clothes and dishes and do the "housework" in their outdoor home. The men learned to love and respect her. Mariana looked them straight in the eyes, she knew them like the back of her hand, knew their weaknesses and their crimes. This group of men emboldened by arms, unfeeling about death, never dared to take advantage of her. It may have been for fear that the leader would kill them or because they remembered mothers and sisters dead or lost in this war where there was no truce between God and the devil.

She slept close to José and he never tried to touch her before the day he made her his own. A few days before that happened, she had got up, as every other day, and made the fire to prepare coffee. Afterwards, she washed the potatoes, peeled the onions and started making the breakfast soup with a piece of salted meat, left over from the last animal they had stolen. Then she went to the stream for a wash, estimating she had enough time before the pot began to boil. After three years of being with them, she had begun to take to the life. She had cried so much thinking of her father and brothers that she didn't want to remember them anymore. Many nights she had thought they'd left without her on purpose, that she had got lost because they had wanted it that way and that was why they never came to look for her. In the first few days, this pain made her not want to go on living, but over time it served her well and kept her alive, as the pain became rage and then resentment. Now she didn't know if she loved or hated them, but she had decided she wouldn't go back until she was a woman in charge of her own life.

The bandits always brought her presents from their raids. Sometimes it was something useless stolen from the houses they had looted, like a shawl to wear to mass, a silver candelabra or a pair of large patent leather shoes with pointed high heels that she couldn't use in the mountains. Other times they bought or got hold of a dress the right size, shoes appropriate for the mountains, underwear or tights. She even had a lacy slip, which José had brought her from his last visit to his family, a pretty ribbon to tie up her hair and a brush with a silver handle which Onofre had acquired in an assault.

When she became a woman she relived many moments of her childhood. She became conscious of the suffering she'd lived through, remembering the thrashings her father and brothers gave her whenever she made a mistake. The shouting and humiliating words buzzed in her head like a mosquito. She wasn't sure if it would've been better if the war had never come to her town and she had stayed home with her fathers and brothers, or if she was glad to be living in the mountains with a group of bandits.

That day she went to the stream and when she took off her clothes to bathe she realised her underwear was stained with a brown paste that resembled blood. She crossed herself and cried out, Holy Virgin! She quickly put on her dress and underwear again and went back to the area where they had been camped for a month.

Her face attracted the men's attention, who were used to her songs. Although her mood sometimes changed, that morning she didn't seem the same.

"Is something wrong Mariana?" Rosendo asked.

"No, nothing," she responded.

"Look at your face first and then deny it," grumbled Milagros, one of the bandits who liked her very much.

"I already told you, nothing is wrong. Don't bother me, just leave me alone," she snapped, irritated, trying to avoid more questions.

All the men got up and as they drank hot coffee they discussed how women were definitely strange. Mariana was anxious all day. She came and went from the stream every few minutes. She had a serious face and no one heard one word from her lips that day. She was introverted, frowned and looked down, which was not her usual manner, unless she was scared.

José was surprised and asked her:

"Mariana, what are you doing with all these comings and goings to the stream? Have you lost something?"

"No, nothing José, it's just that I'm very hot."

"Woman, but it's overcast today and it's even a little cold."

"Maybe it is for you, as you don't spend the day stuck by the fire," she responded bitterly.

"All right now, girl, don't you talk to me like that, I don't like it."

That night, José came over to Mariana and said in her ear:

"Something has happened to you and you don't want to tell me. Don't you trust me?"

"Of course, but nothing has happened to me."

"I don't believe you, but have it your way, I'll wait until you tell me."

Mariana didn't sleep all night, tossing from left to right, onto her stomach, on her back again, and José was watching to see if she got up again. It was about midnight when she couldn't take the sensation of pain and wetness anymore. The worst thing was that she felt she had lost José's trust. She asked herself why she felt sick, why she didn't want to be around the men and wanted to be alone and why she wanted to cry and scream at the same time.

She was thinking all this when José moved closer to her mat and whispered softly:

"You've become a woman, haven't you?"

"What do you mean, José?"

"How can I explain it to you? When girls become women, their stomach hurts and they stain their underwear with blood. Is that it?"

"Yes José, it started this morning and now I feel like thousands of animals are stirring around in my belly and it hurts down below. Have I burst inside?"

"My María," the Carpenter said, almost to himself, in character with his nickname. His features and words were not as eloquent as his heart, but that day his origins shone through, the good, humble, Christian family he sprang from.

"I'll love you more now. María, my María, now you'll be my wife. The leader's wife. The most respected woman. You're made of the right stuff to be my wife. The wife of José, The Carpenter."

He hugged her, holding her to his chest with his arm around her and said:

"Sleep now, María. Tomorrow I'll solve your problem. My wife, my child, María," he whispered with a tenderness Mariana didn't recognise and he went to sleep murmuring her name.

From that day on he changed her name and called her María. His childhood dreams were going to come true because God, in his infinite goodness, was repaying him for the sacrifices he'd made to defend God's sacred name from the atheists. God had sent him María, his virgin, to accompany him in his sacred crusade. Mariana felt important. She was now a woman.

The next day José said to the boys:

"From now on, Mariana will be my wife. Her nickname will be María. We'll now be known as The Carpenter and the Virgin. José, The Carpenter and the Virgin's gang," he said in a heartfelt way and he believed with a faith which could move mountains. He was convinced it was a miracle, another sign of God's love.

He ordered that no one should look at her, bother her or give her orders. Only he could do that from now on. Although Mariana didn't know what it was to be a woman, she felt how from that moment they all looked at her differently. Later she found out what it meant and she didn't enjoy leaving behind her childhood.

She cried a little and then thought about nothing. The resentment towards her father grew and for the first time, she wanted revenge.

Her thoughts were confused. At times she spoke happily with the men, as if she were one of them, and at other times she hated them. Her fate seemed to have set her on a course to be always amongst men, living for them and off them. The violence had separated her from her family, but she wanted to have a family and dreamed of having her own.

Her body became more voluptuous and beautiful each day. When José was not around she attracted furtive glances. José brought her things from the raids or he sent the boys to buy her things. She was submissive in bed, but she never gave herself as he'd have liked and they began to have their first problems. José was full of suspicion. He told her off for her camaraderie with the men, even Onofre and Milagros, who were like her adoptive fathers, and he remained enraged at being a misunderstood man until they separated. Mariana kept her thoughts and feelings to herself and never shared them with anyone. No man was going to take them from her. Any man who crossed her path would pay for her father's, her brother's and José's offences. She remained strong because she didn't give away the only thing they couldn't steal: her love.

A year passed and Mariana endured José's desire with resignation and rage. He tried to be attentive, affectionate and sought to win her heart, but Mariana didn't know what love was. She had no idea how to show she was happy and contented when she was with him. The more she tried to remove herself from him so he wouldn't harass her, the more he attacked the indifference and passivity with which she protected herself. Time passed and María, the youngest *chulavita* bandit, became pregnant. José was very annoyed and pressured her to get an abortion.

"If you don't do as I say and get rid of this problem, I'll have to abandon you a long way away and then what will you do?" he said trying to play upon her fear of being alone.

She was resolute and fought to keep the baby. She learned to use all the seductive powers at her disposal, which she discovered were many. She got José to take her to his family for the pregnancy and birth; he went back to the mountains without her wifely services. José's parents and sisters finished bringing Mariana up. For a long time she'd needed a family to care of her. Gabriela was born there.

Gabriela had the same face as her mother. She was reddish, with black eyes full of mischief. They said that from birth she frowned as Mariana did to show she was unhappy and she seemed to understand she was both her mother's shackle and her liberation. Mariana didn't want to be a bandit for the rest of her life. She wanted a family, to live in peace in a room in town and to build the home she had so often dreamed of.

But again fate conspired against her. José's sisters grew fond of the child and thought the best way to take her away from her mother was to convince Mariana she belonged in the mountains, at her husband's side. This didn't work on her, so they tried it on their brother. They told him she should be serving him, that it was her duty. They would look after the child much better than Mariana, who was just a bad mannered child and if José had chosen her as his wife then he should live with her, and not allow her to bring up his children badly.

Mariana was no longer the frightened and silly girl she'd been in the first few years. She was a fifteen-year-old woman, beautiful, strong, brave and hard with a determined look, full of hate. She wasn't going to let them snatch her child away just like that. She decided to seduce José again and she convinced him the best thing would be to leave her in town with the child. She could work and support the child with his help and wait for him there. In the same way he came to town to see his family, he could also come to see her and his daughter. José always ended up agreeing to María's proposals. He was truly in love. But jealousy consumed him and Mariana used it to argue it was best for her to remain in town, a long way from his fellow bandits. After all, they were red-blooded men, there were no other women around and it was best not to risk the possibility that one day they might kill him or mutiny in order to take advantage of her.

Everything went well until jealousy reared its head again. José's youngest brother began to visit Mariana, helping her out with money and he'd stay for a few hours when José wasn't around. One of the times José came to see her, his sisters began to sow trouble:

"Do you know something, José? Efraín visits Mariana a lot at the hotel. He says he goes because she and the child need support, but I'd be careful if I were you."

"What are you insinuating, you bloody liars!"

"Nothing brother, how rude and boorish you've become. Show us some respect, we're not like her."

"I demand that you respect me. She is my wife and the mother of my child."

"If she was respectful, Efraín wouldn't be giving her nearly all of his wages."

"What do you mean all of his wages? I bring them all they need and that weakling, a coward since birth, hasn't got anything worth giving them."

From that day on, José began to treat her badly, even though Mariana tried to explain there was nothing in it. After each fight, José ended up forcing himself on her as a way of showing his dominance. His aggressive and oppressive behaviour reawakened the hate which lay latent within Mariana.

Things became difficult for José when the conservatives and the liberals negotiated peace in the capital. José and his accomplices understood that the shady dealings of the politicians in the centres of power meant they now had to be friends with their enemies. That wasn't for them. They hadn't gone to live in the mountains, sacrificed themselves, taken risks, got used to killing liberals and raping their wives and children; nor had they persecuted the devil and decapitated hundreds of atheist liberal thieves; nor learnt to exorcise the devil by ripping out the hearts of the young; nor made famous the *corbata* and *franela** deaths, for their leaders to now say they should love each other like brothers. The liberals were compatriots? Blood shouldn't be shed? What rubbish! The politicians' lies were not for them, they were clear about their mission on earth. So they had a meeting and agreed they'd continue to raid farms as it would not now be possible to attack towns. The police had orders to arrest them and attacking a town without their help would be too risky. This complicated José's visits to Mariana and he was constantly agitated.

"Bloody liberals, they're not going to confuse me. I know they tricked the idiots in the capital, but no one is going to pull the wool over my eyes," he ranted. "They'll see when the fire of God torches the liberal atheist bastards, and clears Colombia of them for good," he fulminated. "How can they ask us to greet those sons of bitches who insult our parents, covet our farms, abuse and rape our wives and our descendants?", he grumbled. "What's happening here? Can't they see how stupid this is? We're not going to become friends, not on our lives!" he repeated indignantly. What was certain was that he could go and see María less and less and his fits of jealously grew to the point where the beatings and curses of each visit became death threats and Mariana began to fear for her life.

The abuse was so bad that Mariana told him not to come back. In revenge José decided to snatch their child away. One morning when Mariana went out for milk José went into the room that was their home and took Gabriela to the mountains.

Then Mariana had to make the most important and difficult decision of her life. To get her daughter back, she and José would have go to gaol. It would mean that Gabriela would have to live with José's sisters, who hated Mariana, but at least her daughter would have a family and one day, when she had done her time, she'd be reunited with her daughter again. She weighed up forgetting Gabriela

---

* These are mutilations carried out during killings, *corbata* meaning tie, and used to describe death by slitting the throat and leaving the tongue hanging; *franela* is a commonly used sleeveless shirt, and describes the way killers cut off their enemies' arms and decapitated them. These brutal terms became common during *la Violencia* years, but made a comeback during the 1990s paramilitary violence.

against being convicted, and she chose that Gabriela should have a family and not the neglect Mariana had experienced.

For several nights she couldn't sleep, thinking about the decision she had to make and, when she had made it, she stayed up all night thinking how she would present herself to the police to report the theft of her daughter. How would she explain that she knew where the bandits' camp was and that she had lived there? What sentence would they give her? How many years would pass without her seeing her daughter? Would José's sisters make Gabriela hate her? Then she thought of Gabriela in the bandits' hands and of everything that could happen to her and she trembled with fear.

Her mind wandered and she remembered Gabriela walking in the hotel patio and heard her cry "mama" when she fell. She imagined how Gabriela would trip on the stones in the mountains, the cold she would feel sleeping outside, how she would cry of loneliness when she was older. She thought of her hands burnt from the fire, her arms gashed from carrying wood, her back aching from washing in the river. She relived all of the forgotten pain, the humiliations and the abandonment, the feelings of embarrassment, envy, jealously and confusion. The hatred grew and began to be reflected in Mariana's face. Her revived memories of hate and her love for her daughter pushed her to make the most momentous decision of her life. It wasn't her beautiful and good and indulgent feelings which gave Mariana life. These were not the feelings which had given her depth and had rendered her decisive. The feelings which helped her survive were others, ones she preferred to avoid, her dark side, which was also her most vital.

The next day, she had a bath, put on her best dress, tied her black hair in a bun and went to the police station early in the morning.

"Good morning sergeant."

"Good morning. How can I help you?"

"I've come to report the theft of my daughter Gabriela," she said it with such serenity that the disconcerted corporal thought, "she's probably mad. In this town no child has ever been stolen."

"Let's see, how was it that your daughter was stolen. Tell me."

"Well, sergeant, I have a daughter who just turned two and is called Gabriela Montero, which is my last name, although I don't have any documents because I got lost from my home in Puerto Berrío many years ago. The *chulavitas* of José, the Carpenter's gang, called me María, the Virgin, but I swear to you my name is Mariana Montero."

"Sit down," said the corporal astonished. "I'm going to take down a statement from you. Gutiérrez, come here," he called out to the secretary. "Call the sergeant to take down this report or get his authorisation to take it."

Gutiérrez got up calmly and went out. He returned shortly, having found the sergeant tucking into his breakfast at doña Gertrudis' shop, saying he authorised it and would come later to check it himself.

"All right, ma'am, we can start with your report," the corporal said, getting comfortable in his chair behind the desk as he made a gesture to Mariana to go on.

Mariana told him her story with all manner of detail. When she finished, the corporal asked: "Tell me please, why you didn't come before to denounce the group of bandits. Did you realise they were outlaws?"

"Yes, I did. I couldn't come because I was José's wife. He's the father of my daughter. He said if I reported him, I would also be imprisoned because I belonged to the gang."

"Tell me, did you participate in the taking of towns, houses, districts and did you kill anyone in these raids?"

"I never killed anyone. I had to go to the towns to gather information. I checked out how the town was guarded, how many police were in post, what the shop door was like or the door of the farm they had decided to attack, how many labourers were working in the liberal farms, what time they went home to town or if they lived on the farms, that is, everything a woman can find out by making friends or starting up a conversation with anyone."

"Now tell me, how many and which attacks did you aid in this way?"

"I don't remember, but there were lots. In this town, at least two."

"Are you willing to show us where to find this group? State if you are willing to collaborate with the law."

"Yes I'm willing to do it. I want to recover my daughter, Gabriela."

The corporal looked at her with pity and said quietly:

"Ma'am, do you know the risks your daughter will run in the attack?"

"Yes," she replied in the corporal's own intimate tone, "but I prefer to risk it and to see her dead than to leave her in the hands of those bandits. I know if she dies it will be very sad, but not as bad as what strangers might do to her." She lifted her face and looked straight into the corporal's eyes so that he understood she was determined and she wouldn't recant.

What the corporal saw in that look was what, later, during the attack, made him the first to look for the child to bring her back to her mother.

The sergeant came back at about ten o'clock and when he heard her story, he was keen to be the one who'd catch the Carpenter's group. They'd become a gang of plunderers who had disobeyed the party and continued to kill, using the excuse they were defending the Holy Cross. The sergeant had admired José and had known Onofre since he was a young man, but the war had ended and peace had been signed. The crusade was over and yet these men kept killing and living off theft, making the police's job more and more difficult. He looked forward to working on the case, as it would ingratiate him with his superiors. At about two o'clock in the afternoon, he sent someone to bring Mariana to come and talk to him. He swore to her that as soon as he had a squad of policemen ready he'd let her know and they would set out to rescue her daughter.

Mariana confirmed her determination to get Gabriela back, whatever the cost.

"Look sergeant, as I said to the corporal, I have taken the decision to rescue my daughter, dead or alive. So, you just tell me when we have to set off. The hideaway is not far, it's about two hours away and if we go very early we'll catch them asleep and it will be easier."

"Tell me Señorita, I mean Señora Montero, what's the best route to take to catch them unawares?"

"Look sergeant, lately they've become careless. They feel safe because they've been camping there for years and no one has found them. They have only one lookout on the side where they think someone could approach from. If we come upon them round the back they'll not expect it. I can draw a map for you. From here, see, they'll never expect an attack. They know that El Recodo is such a poor town that they don't even have a police station and besides, they don't expect my betrayal."

Mariana took the paper and pencil the corporal had given her and drew, as well as she could, the two towns and the exact place where the group was camped.

"Look at that," said the corporal, "they're clever, we'd never have looked there. They say the gangs base themselves near rivers or where there are various escape routes."

"This area has a lot of trees and streams. They don't need a river for water, besides there are wild animals to hunt, so they don't go hungry and they don't have to go to town for months. Although it might not seem obvious, sergeant, this area offers many places to flee to. And there are many hideaways so those who seek them nearly always get tired of looking before the band gets tired of hiding."

So, with the serenity of someone who's made a decision, Mariana participated in the organisation of the attack to rescue her daughter.

The next day, at two o'clock in the morning, the police left without her. At the last minute the sergeant said Mariana might ruin the operation for fear they would kill her daughter. He waited for her to come to the station and he left her with a guard who had express orders to not let her move until he came back. The sergeant also thought it might be a trap and to prevent her from making her own moves and escaping, it was best to leave her locked up. "If it's an ambush, she'll pay for her audacity," the sergeant said to the guard.

When they attacked the camp they took the bandits by surprise, but as they weren't novices they defended themselves for a week. There were nights when the police thought they had lost them, but once again they would pick up the trail. They were all tired when finally the bandits were cornered against a large rock and as the sergeant warned that they were willing to die, he shouted:

"Listen, José, I've arrested your wife and if you don't give yourself up, she'll pay. I know you have the child with you and I imagine you don't want her to die. If you give yourself up, we won't kill her."

When José heard this he thought of Gabriela, his daughter, who by now wasn't even crying, she seemed half dead. He thought of Mariana imprisoned and his heart made the decision, he loved her in his way, and he answered:

"All right, I'll give myself up, but on condition that you let Mariana go."

That was how they managed to get José, the Carpenter, and some men in his band to hand themselves in. Others died and four fled during the battle.

When they brought José to town with his hands tied behind his back, Mariana looked him in the eyes and very calmly said: "I had to report you because my daughter is worth more than your life or mine, do you understand?" That is how José found out she had given him up and, enraged, he muttered between his teeth: "This doesn't end here. You'll pay for this. I'll never forgive you, María. Take care, because I'll kill you, if it's the last thing I do."

Mariana opened her arms for Gabriela and the child, once held, began to cry softly. Mariana looked at the sergeant and asked him if she could leave. He nodded, looked at the corporal and said: "She's been straight with us, she's a very noble woman, hardly fit for a man like the Carpenter."

Mariana, in spite of all this, was still a naïve girl who thought life would go on as if nothing had happened. She worked for two years in a hotel, until José got out, thanks to an amnesty law. He often came to see Mariana and hit her, threatened her and abused her. Desperate, she decided to leave the town and start again alone, a long way away. The corporal, with the sergeant's permission, took her in a police car to the next town to ensure José didn't kill her on the way.'

The group, which had been listening raptly during Mercedes' narration, now started to talk in low voices. They debated whether violence, which had gone on for so many years, was inevitable. They spoke of peace, if it were possible and if they were going to keep killing each other in this armed conflict. If the problem was land, and in that case, how many were on the communists' side and how many on the army's side. If the paramilitaries were the ones who were killing people and if they were supported by the military and the landowners. The volume rose, some interrupted others, and kept them from clarifying their ideas. Mariana's life had marked a course where there was no room for lies. They calmed down and began to order the points for discussion, asking for composure. They agreed on one thing: the only way to achieve peace depended on the capacity to confront the truth, however painful it was.

Daniel

Revenge and hate are stronger than patriotism

'Will some of our children or grandchildren be able to begin anew, to reconstruct this country when all this ends?' mused Socorro.

'If one day someone decides to end this war, perhaps,' replied Laura.

'We believed everything the guerrilla told us, that they defended the truth. Who doesn't warm to being told that you deserve respect, that you should be the owners of the land, that your children have a right to education, that each district should have a clinic and each town a hospital, that services there should be free and that it's the State's duty to provide work for us? Hearing it and believing them were one and the same. Those of us who were militants made a lot of mistakes, but I still believe it was right to support the *muchachos** when they made the landowners and rich traders pay taxes.' Ana Dolores said.

Suddenly, Daniel's voice made them take notice.

'*Compañeros*, this afternoon I'd like to tell my story, but before I do I want to tell you I don't agree that the guerrilla cause the violence. My experience has brought me to the opposite conclusion. I state frankly and without fear that they've helped me a lot, as well as other peasants in San Vicente de Chucurí. They have helped us to reclaim waste lands or lands the owners had left idle and you all know land is the life of a peasant. When you're a peasant the land is everything. When you have children to bring up, feed, dress and love, what's better than a small plot of land to work and live in peace?'

He was a forty-two year-old man, malnourished, with a low, narrow forehead and big, black, lively eyes which were lost under the thick eyebrows which grew together and made a black band over his nose. When he frowned you could see the strength of his features and they in turn suggested the determination of his ideas and convictions. As Mercedes told the story of Mariana, his eyes had clouded over with tears. He showed his sensitivity every time he moved his hands, which

---

Muchachos is the familiar term used to refer to the guerrilla members.

he rubbed together at the points in Mercedes' story which had caused him most suffering.

'Look, *compañera*, I do appreciate the pain in the story you told, but at least Gabriela had a mother and father. I was left alone when I was four years old, when my mother died, may she rest in peace. My father was in gaol and I never met him. Until she died I was brought up by my mother and my stepfather, but when we came back from her funeral, he sent me and my brother to Bucaramanga, to our godparents. As my brother was ten years older than I, he went to work on a farm and I was left alone for the next three years. When I was seven, they were tired of me and found me work. I don't want to sound ungrateful, because they did send me to school. I got to the first class of primary school and when I had learnt how to read and write, they sent me to work for doña Esperanza, who had a cafeteria near the market place. She had me serving coffees from three o'clock in the morning in the market, the time when the drivers began to arrive with goods they'd brought in from the countryside. Then, from seven o'clock in the morning I served in the café until seven or eight o'clock at night. I served beers and coffees, cleaned the tables, the metal blind of the entrance, the windows, washed the crockery and ran errands.

I was very naughty. I was eight by then and at that age boys are terrible, they're always causing trouble and they just want to play. Aside from wanting to play, I wanted to eat fruit, sweets, cream tarts, white jelly, fried ants and everything in sight. One day doña Esperanza sent me to get some cumin and I went off and I stole a mandarin, and it was so sweet and so juicy I wanted another and I stole the whole box. I began to run with the box and as I ran looking behind me, I hit a mountain of rubbish piled up on a corner. They caught me and called the police.

From the day doña Esperanza had sent me to sell coffee at dawn, I'd begun to acquire bad habits. I got to know some kids who stole on the pretext that they were cleaning up the rubbish or helping a woman with her goods. They were always enticing me to sleep on the street like them and a few times I ran away. I started to smoke before I was eight years old, to steal food and to do bad things to the market women who gave us fruit.

They took me to the police station and I was there for three days. As no one came to find me, they sent me to a detention centre for minors. I didn't tell them about doña Esperanza because I was embarrassed. I didn't want her to know I was a thief, so I kept my mouth shut.

"First and last name?" they asked me.

"Daniel Argüello."

"Address where you live? Your residence?"

"The street."

"Father's name?"

"I don't have one and I never knew him."

"Mother's name?"

"Juana María Argüello. Deceased four years ago."

"Who do you live with? Who cares for you?"

"I live alone on the street. No one is responsible for me."

"Let's not waste any more time, corporal, here's another candidate for the home."

I remember it as though it were yesterday, how I came out with my short trousers and my shirt open without any buttons because when they had caught me, all the buttons had come off and the shirt was ripped. Also, I was bruised from the beating they'd given me to teach me a lesson and had a cold, because they'd washed me with a hose at dawn so the cold should rid me of the bad habit of stealing. We got to the borstal at about ten in the morning. The bigger children and the guards laughed at me because I had short trousers, a ripped shirt and was bloody and dirty. They said: "look at this beggar they've sent us from Bucaramanga. Short trousers for a mama's boy. We'll make you a man here, you'll see boy." In that moment I regretted having been naughty with doña Esperanza. In the borstal, locked up, I learnt to work hard and serve the older boys and the guards, who did things to us they wouldn't do to animals.'

His voice, choked with emotion, could no longer be heard. He couldn't find the words to express the pain of a boy who had been raped and forgotten. Tears ran down his cheeks and his brown skin went pale. He looked as if he was going to faint. Mercedes, Gabriela, Alejandra and Laura could not contain their tears. Bending over, they tried to hide the pain they felt for Daniel and for what they remembered of their own stories. They gave him a glass of water and a tissue to dry his eyes. This man, hardened by life, who had confronted the army, the paramilitary and those who had murdered his daughter with the strength of a mahogany tree, cried at the memory of his childhood agony, his lack of protection, and his misery.

The group sat and listened to him with tense necks, glassy eyes, their hands held tightly together, their lips exhausted, their faces contorted with their helplessness. Daniel looked up and was moved to see finally someone understood him and was touched by his childhood suffering. A quick glance encouraged him to continue with his story.

'As I couldn't stand that life, I decided to escape. One Sunday, when they let us play football, I gave the ball a tremendous kick and it went over the barbed wire fence, which bordered the playing field. The guard let us climb up, one on top of another, to reach it. As I was the smallest and thinnest they let me go last and I jumped down on the other side of the fence and ran like the wind. The other children, seeing how easy it was, jumped and ran after me at the speed which only terror could inject into their short legs; none of them was more than ten years old. We ran until we gasped from breath and we ended up in a field at the entrance to Rionegro, the town closest to the borstal.

We left a commotion behind us, the siren blaring. Because of the jubilant racket that went up when I jumped, the guards realised what was happening and turned it on. While they got the rest of the children back inside we gained time. As it was Sunday only half the usual number of guards were on duty and that helped our escape. I didn't wait for the other boys who jumped after me, but when we got to the town there were five of us and we climbed inside a sewer to wait for them to get tired of looking for us. At about eleven o'clock at night they went to bed. They went from house to house, to the health centre and they walked over us about four times. We had escaped at about three o'clock in the afternoon and by eleven they were bored of looking for ghosts. In fact, the ground had literally swallowed us up. They went back to the borstal leaving us free to come out and jump on the first lorry that passed.

It was a slow lorry packed high with onions. The motor groaned under the strain and as we heard it coming we stood on the dark side of the road ready to run after it, so the driver couldn't see us, because he might have reported us. We arrived at Bucaramanga hanging off the back. In the city it was going to be more difficult to find us.

We talked before each of us went our separate ways. There was a moment when we thought we could stay together and steal to survive. We would create a family because none of us wanted to go back home. They were treated badly there and most of their parents had agreed to them being sent away. They were full of hate and knew they couldn't live within the law.

I left the group and told them that I was going back to doña Esperanza because she was never mean to me and I was never going to steal again. I would have preferred that they cut off my hands before going through my experiences at the borstal again. It's the hardest thing I've endured in my whole life. I'll never be able to forget such horror, so much pain and the impotence of not even being able to kill myself.'

He dried his tears, blew his nose a few times and continued:

'I went back to doña Esperanza and told her the truth. At night, in the borstal, I'd thought a lot about this and felt sure she would be compassionate and wouldn't report me to the police. I was right. She had a good heart, cried with me and hugged me and said: "Daniel, never steal again and if you get into any trouble again, tell them to find me as I'll answer for you, my child. Don't ever let yourself be taken away again." I cried and swore to her that I would never, upon the memory of my mother, take anything that was not mine again. I tell you this story because I see most of us here are poor even though the only thing we've done is look for ways to work and nothing more.'

He sighed deeply and let a few minutes go by before he continued.

'You see *compañeros*, the guerrilla are right to fight. They're like us, they not only don't have land, but they don't own anything. Life has been hard, too many years have gone by and we haven't escaped from poverty. And it's because the revolutionaries haven't won. We fought to take lands and then they kicked us off when we had cleared the fields, planted the crops and the animals were grazing.

The landowners will always be the masters, the ones with a secure family, whose mothers don't die for lack of money or from curable diseases. Their children, although they steal, never go to a borstal. They have everything we don't have. That's why I believe in the *compañeros* of the Peasants' Association, those in the National Liberation Army and in the Revolutionary Armed Forces of Colombia. They're the ones who've shown me we have rights, dignity or at least the right to die fighting for them.'

The eyes of the man who had just been crying were now filled with fire, and looked directly at each of their faces, seeking a response. The anguish had disappeared from his face and again took up the expression of strength he normally wore when he introduced his children, saying:

"These are my children, I love them very much. It is for them that I'm going to fight for land, for them I'll work hard and for them I'm even capable of laying down my life."

But Mercedes replied rapidly, her face red with rage:

'Yes, sure, the guerrilla are good, that's why they come along and charge small farmers and settlers their tax, after we're exhausted from levelling the wilderness, attacked by mosquitoes, our skin in shreds and burnt by the sun. They're so good that when we'd prepared the land for cultivation they came to charge us their damn tax in cash, in kind, in marches, and in whatever bloody way crossed their minds. The worst was when they forced us to go out on their so-called "peasant marches". We had to leave our farms, built with such suffering, and we lost our harvests, our animals, our gardens and came back from the march to die of hunger and start all over again. They always got us to go using the lie that it was for us, for our land, but it was always to defend the guerrilla from the army. It was terrible, the revolution in Macarena. We had managed to create the only livelihood we ever had. That was why they killed my brother, who was the only one who ever protected me.' Mercedes' eyes filled with tears. Pain coursed through her body, shaking and destroying the defences she'd built up over a long time.

Everyone sat in silence, disconcerted. They were not facing a list of ideas or rights, but real human emotion, and they could not easily end the encounter with feeling running so high. Mercedes looked at them with burning eyes. Everyone respectfully retook their places to listen to her.

Mercedes

We cannot live by will alone

She had little to protect herself. From childhood, her father had shattered everything which could have given her the strength not to die of shame. Her memories went back to when she was three years old and they were clear because they had been branded on her soul. She remembered her home, with her father at the head, her older and younger brothers, a terrified and weak mother who allowed her children to be beaten and humiliated, denying for many years what went on. She was born in Vistahermosa and she had lived her childhood in the plains, at her parents' side.

For Mercedes, evil was part of her, it appeared when she was a child. Her desire to want things had made her selfish and she believed that repeating her childhood with her husband was what she deserved. She had married him through trickery. She had his sons without feeling any pleasure in their conception and took the beatings he gave her as if she had never expected anything else. These beatings heightened her buried and intense hatred of men. Without knowing why or where the love she had wanted had gone, she repeated the story of hate and abuse of her childhood, without being able to avoid it. Mercedes loved one day and disdained the person she had loved the next. She loved again and from her girlhood soul an irrepressible rage arose, a disgust and rejection of all those who wooed her.

For a long time she could not remember what had happened during her childhood, but recent events in her life had forced her to look and had made her memories sharper. She choked on her own feelings as fear returned in the form of resentment. She never had an explanation for why things happened to her and with time she settled on managing the anguish and continued to live her fate.

She felt more hate than love towards her father. Loving him a little made no difference because she herself had never felt loved. Her mind was lively and she did what she wanted even though it cost her insults and beatings. She compensated the lack of love from her father with the love of her brother, who was fifteen years older than her.

To be respected by her father, she had to grow up and earn money. Mercedes knew this before she learnt to speak. She understood from the moment in which she saw the value of money in a home full of need.

Her mother worked and served her father from before sunrise until late into the night. Pedro, her father, was not a conscientious father and husband, and he did not work hard enough to support the family. Therefore at eight at night, after a day's work in the home, Mercedes' mother went to work as a seamstress to pay for the children's schooling. As she had children from her first marriage, she could not demand anything of her husband, who took her in with her children and introduced her as his wife. She paid for that with more sacrifice and pain than she had ever thought possible to endure.

The farm, with eight well-worked hectares, a well, the house and the fields were not enough for Pedro. Mercedes was the eighth of twelve children and her mother could not give her time or love, much less look beyond the explanation the spiritual healer had given Pedro when the conflict between them became intolerable:

"Look don Pedro, the thing between you and Mercedes is that you were enemies in another life and that's why you hate her so," brother Rigoberto intoned.

"What do you mean? Explain it to me," mumbled Pedro.

"Well, how should I put it? I was able to study your life and Mercedes's. In another incarnation, you were deadly enemies and you never solved your feud. Now, in this life, you should do it or you'll continue to pass through life after life with the same hate until you work it out," the brother prophesised.

"Are you sure?" Pedro asked.

"Believe him, *mijo**, the brother is wise and if he says so, then it must be true," said Berenice, my mother.

From that day on, Pedro left Mercedes to deal with her own life in some peace. The pain of feeling rejected, the constant need for affection as well as basic things made Mercedes into an enterprising yet submissive woman.

Mercedes had calmed down and the sun had gone down. She realised that her *compañeros* were worried about her, but she could also see that most of them were tired and said:

'I think my story is going to be longer than even I thought and it would be better to continue tomorrow. Excuse me if I lost control, but we are here to express our feelings and I couldn't keep quiet.'

---

* Term of endearment used between close relatives.

'Don't worry, *compañera*,' responded Antonia, 'You'll not be the first or last who seeks to defend what they believe in, that's why we're here.'

The next day, it was a fresh morning and they arrived on time. After they had shyly greeted each other, they sat down. Mercedes was ready and asked if she could start. They all agreed by nodding their heads.

'I'm not going to say my life was marvellous because as a little girl, I suffered a lot. My father was, as any good peasant, a man of strong words and build. He treated us all badly, but he was most aggressive with the girls and the children of my mother's first marriage. But they were grown up and didn't let themselves be treated too badly. I was naughty, inquisitive and sought his affection constantly even if it cost me a thrashing. From the age of three I used to stare at my father at mealtimes. My mother served him the best of everything and we never stopped wanting to eat as he did. Every time I saw the full plate and him gulping down his food, I would cry and I couldn't control my tears. I never managed to get an affectionate look from him, only anger. One day he came back in a bad mood and threw the whole plateful of food in my face. With every blow my mother gave me that day, she shouted: "This thrashing is to stop your annoying habit of watching your father eat. I hope you cry so much you run out of tears and you never cry again."

I grew up between humiliations and I got used to being badly treated. My half-brother, who loved me very much, managed to wrest rare smiles out of me. When he came back from work I would go to him, he'd take out the guitar and we'd sing.

"Look Mercedes," he said once when we were out of the house, "I'm afraid of what my stepfather might do to you. He can't stand you. Mother doesn't have the means to prevent anything happening to you and even less to stop his brutality. I think we need to make an effort and send you away to study. You know that since your last fight with him he puts up with you less and less. He's capable of anything. I spoke to Rodrigo and between us we're going to work hard to get some money together to send you to study at a boarding school."

"All right, I'll go to a boarding school," I replied, "but only if you promise to come and visit me."

"I promise, I'll come whenever I can. Now, cheer yourself up with the thought that you're going to start afresh. In this school, the nuns insist that you have new things: bedclothes, uniform, books, shoes. When you leave there you'll be a young lady, you'll be educated and mistress of your own life."

I had fought with my father recently on a day when I was bad tempered. I saw my father lift up a machete to hit my mother. I grabbed another and confronted him.

"Damn it papa, put down that machete or I'll not be responsible for what I do."

I took too long to lift up my weapon and I felt a blow on the head and fell against the wall. Dizzy and bloody, I got up and I confronted him unarmed.

"If you hit my mother, I'll kill you," I mumbled through my teeth.

My father looked at me, surprised. The decision in my voice and my red and shining face told him that if he tried to hit my mother again, I would kill him. He put down the machete and shouted:

"This bitch, who does she think she is, does she think I'm going to put up with her impertinence? She's leaving this house right now!" He went to the room where I slept, took the box with the few clothes I had and threw it across the patio. He looked at my mother and said:

"If I find her here when I get back, you'll all pay."

"For the love of God, don't throw her out, she has nowhere to go," my mother cried, pleading with him.

"She should have thought of that before she confronted me. No woman has ever challenged me and she's not going to be the first. The person who can challenge me has not yet been born."

"Hit me or kill me once and for all Pedro, but don't force me to see my children homeless."

"Well, you should've thought of that when you raised them. You spared the rod, that's why they're so spoilt."

"Don't say that, *mijo*, you know they're good girls, what's more, they're your daughters." '

Weeping was the only sound which could be heard in the house that day. Her mother cried because she had to send her daughter away, her sister felt guilty for having provoked her father's outburst of rage and Mercedes, full of hatred, cursed her father and left.

When she went to the boarding school she thought it would free her from all the suffering, without realising it was another type of solitude. Rejecting what she had lived through did not work, she could not forget the lack of love and the homesickness. During this time she thought she would never give in, she would never submit. But life showed her that submission would be her fate.

Looking for love away from home did not work. When after six months no one had come to see her, she gave up being a studious girl and saw clearly that her will was not strong enough for life. Will was an instrument of death, but death had more subtle instruments, like hostility, physical abuse, humiliations and rape of the body and soul. She was fourteen years old and she felt dead.

'I stopped being a sweet but rebellious girl who sought to please her father and I became a woman. I would choose where and how I would live and die and I wasn't going to be cast out like a dog, a long way from my home, imprisoned inside the four walls of a convent. If I had to suffer, I would decide when, how and where I would bear it. I chose my home.

When I returned, I said to my father: "I've come home, but things have changed."

He looked at me and saw a woman who had decided to come back at any cost.

"Fine, Mercedes, come home, after all, you're my daughter and it's my obligation to take care of you."

"I'm coming back, but I'll not allow you to hit my mother or me. Things are not going to be the same. I'm going to work and will bring money home. You don't have any obligations towards me now."

"My child, I do have a duty to you, but I'm pleased you've come to help. Your mother needs you, things aren't going well."

"I'm going to work outside or on the land, as you prefer, but I'm going to contribute money. I'll see how I can help my mother with things at home. But you should be clear that as I'm going to respect you, you should do the same with me."

"Of course, my girl, of course."

"No more shouting 'bitches' at us, expecting us to be at your beck and call all day. My name is Mercedes and you're Pedro and that's how we are going to address each other. If I buy food, I'll eat it, and in addition, I'll give a little more for the household expenses and for my room. If we tolerate each other, I'll be helpful in every way I can."

Pedro looked at her astonished – what had brought about this amazing change?'

Around that time her father finally drank all of the money from the sale of the cattle, the harvests and even the sale of the chickens, ducks, turkeys and pigs. The farmhouse and the abandoned lands were all that were left and he exchanged them happily for a house in town with a bar and jukebox business. The sleazy atmosphere of the bar had steeped him in alcohol and his brutality grew. Her mother cooked, cleaned and sewed each day to support them. The older children had left home and Mercedes remained, a lost soul, seeking happiness in an unattainable love: that of her father.

At this point her sobs stopped her from going on and she ended repeating softly:

'Why couldn't he love me? Why?'

After a moment, Mercedes used the back of her hand to dry the tears from her cheeks and she continued:

'The violence killed my brother Gustavo when they forced us to leave Macarena.'

They all looked at her, surprised by the turn her story had taken. Daniel spoke, seeing the commotion Mercedes had provoked, and which had disturbed the other women:

'Listen *compañeros*, what Mercedes has recounted seems painful to me, and with that in mind, I think we should have a break and rest a little. When we return, I propose we stick to the specific theme: the problem of displacement and the armed conflict. I know how much our experiences can affect us, but if we get distracted we could begin to lose our way.'

'I don't agree with Daniel,' jumped in Alejandra. 'I think we should look at the causes of the problems which have brought us together. To talk about displacement is not as simple as recounting why we were displaced, or why each of us thinks we're victims of the violence. The subject, as I understand it, is to seek what brought us to participate in the war and why we've come together to look for peace. At least, that's what I had understood.'

A murmur ran through the room, everyone wanted to respond.

'The thing is, we should pursue deeper causes.' Marcos' voice rose above the others. 'Not to overlook the political and economic analysis we have been hearing for years, that as we know, has overdiagnosed the country. What we are trying to do here is an exercise in reflection, to examine more thoroughly our participation in the conflict. We're committed to doing it without evasions, to see what it was that led us to decide to participate in the war and what brings us now to participate in the building of peace.'

'I agree with Marcos,' Laura nodded.

'Here we go again. We had agreed to an honest discussion. If we're going to expose ourselves, if we're going to tell the truth of our lives as if we were under oath, we're not now going to dodge the issues as soon as something is painful or when something is said we don't want to hear. What we are looking for is the truth. I think we have to allow each one to tell their story, to bare their souls. Don't you think?' concluded Ana Dolores.

'The pain we're going through, our own and that of others, is exhausting and frightening. I speak for myself. Each thing you say makes me remember parts of my life. It may not be exactly the same, but fragments make me return to painful moments. This makes for double the work. The first implies an effort to be truthful before the rest of the group and the other consists in reflecting, remembering, exploring and seeking answers. I think the proposal has been very enriching and God will accompany us in this difficult and painful task. He will carry us to the right place. In his infinite mercy, He will give us enough strength,' added Socorro.

Everyone wanted to express what they thought. I agree with Ana Dolores; I with Socorro; I with Marcos, they said. They were willing to continue the task as it had been proposed, seeking the causes, the circumstances and the events which led them to participate in the armed conflict.

'We seem to have a majority agreement. I know Daniel is a democratic man and he'll accept this is what most of us want. Am I wrong?' asked Angela.

'No *compañera*, you're not mistaken, I accept,' responded Daniel.

'Then, my view is we should take a break, as Daniel proposed, and when we come back we'll continue with the search for our truth,' said Marcos.

After lunch, they came back, bound by the urge to explore what they knew, a desire which exceeded the fear of confronting it.

Socorro
She navigated a sea of violence

Socorro's attention is fixed. In her face all of the suffering has appeared as in a mirror: of Gabriela's childhood and her mother Mariana; of Mercedes and her brother, Gustavo, and of Daniel and his orphaning. She has a strong voice but sweet at the same time, not in the tone, but in the content. Her white skin and ash blonde hair give her face the sweetness of a good-hearted soul. Her direct look and unambiguous remarks reveal a tough character which does not match her features. When she moves in her seat or something she hears makes her uncomfortable her expression changes and it is easy to see what is going on in her mind.

'I want to tell you that I don't agree with what Daniel says. I know what he's talking about because I lived it and participated in the political struggle. I risked my life many times, which is less important than the fact I also risked my daughter's life, who was only a baby. I used the basket I carried her in to conceal flyers for the Patriotic Union, knowing they could kill or disappear us. That was the law in the plains. There's no such thing as the right to life and freedom of expression, or anything like it. Nothing I did with Rolando, my husband, was worth it in the end. They disappeared him and although I assume he's been dead for five years, I'll never know for sure. No money was left, not the small farm with the coca crop, not the stolen cars with legal documents, not the self-sacrificing work with the indigenous people, not a single piece of furniture was left for me after ten years of work. Money badly come by vanishes, disappears and you never know where it has gone,' she said in one go, without drawing breath.

'Pain, repentance, embarrassment, solitude and orphaned children is all I have left from a struggle of less than virtuous means. I was also left with the pain of us women who are neither widows nor married. We are half-married, half-widows, half-dead, half-alive. My children are the children of a disappeared man. They cannot talk of a dead father who they can visit on All Saints day and to whom they can pray and ask for help. They're children of a half-dead, half-alive, half-assassinated, half- disappeared man. They're children abandoned without love. I don't believe any more in the hero in camouflage gear with a gun in his hand. I consider them disloyal, more unstable than water, with closed minds and empty hearts, creators of ideologies that are like false religions and nothing more.

I have forgotten them, having loved them, because I allowed myself to be moved by the children who bleed to death, by the simple people who plough someone else's land for a pittance, by the mutilated who've lost their legs for no reason and by the tortured who have difficulty regaining their sanity. I hate those who have to use arms to teach us to obey, those who hide their miserable souls behind their patriotism.

I lived the violence of the seventies in my childhood. My father and mother went to settle the lands given by the government in Santa Rosa de Simití, in the department of Bolívar. They came from Boyacá and with other families from there and from Santander they went to settle lands near the San Lucas mountains. They got a little farm together, they worked the land until it was productive and they raised domestic animals until they managed to sustain the whole family with the sale of chickens, hens and eggs. They began to save some money from the harvest, from the sale of cattle and from the production of sugarcane to acquire other "improvements", which is what they called land which is cleared ready for cultivation.

When they achieved stability, many settlers wanted to leave because it was not as good as they expected or because their business was colonisation and then selling on. We had managed to make a living and we, the eight women of the house, spent our time working, studying and saving to be able to escape our poverty. My sisters lived a life that marked them forever, although it is painful to me that they never had what my parents were able to give me, as I was the youngest. Worst of all they had to face displacement in deplorable conditions at a very young age.

I had not turned in my mother's womb, and my breach birth was difficult for her. Troublesome and dangerous is how I've been all my life,' she smiled mischievously, more satisfied than repentant, 'I came out of the maternal womb damaging my mother's poor body, which could not give any more because the previous daughters had taken all the calcium, iron and vitamins a body can give.

Yet she gave everything she could and I was born big and strong. They say I was born purple because I was choking and I was saved by a miracle God granted my parents, who were very Catholic.

My mother was left so unwell they had to send her to the capital to recuperate and I was left in my father's care. Every day, he took me to an aunt who'd just had a baby and he collected breast milk to feed me. Then, he himself would milk a cow and give me her milk too, like a loving mother with his calf.

Don Fabián, my father, was a proud man, hard, strong, Conservative with a capital C, born Catholic and fascist by conviction. In that time the conservatives were men who were not moved by women's sensitive nonsense or daughters' sweetness, but they tell me it was a pleasure to see him rocking me or to see how proud he felt of his chubby and healthy daughter.

He headed a home of women, which was not easy for him. His arrogance made him see women as inferior, but having been my nanny when I was a baby made him act very differently with me. I always had his support and praise. To everything I did or said he would say: "it's marvellous", "you're a very intelligent girl", "you're going to be the lawyer of the house", "you speak so well", "you're very pretty, my lovely."

I was blond, with hair as fair as that of recently-born chicks. I had white skin and red cheeks. The pride of the Montoya race, my father said. He felt he had succeeded as a man in life, with the family and with the region, bringing into the world this latest child, the best of all because, for the conservatives, the white race thing was important. They held onto remnants of Hitler's ideas that came to Colombia from the Second World War. With all of his praise, I became conceited and complained when my envious sisters hit me or took something away from me. I cried about everything and my mother despaired of my whining:

"Shut up child, or I'll give you a hiding. Don't think that because your father dotes on you I'm going to stop giving you what you deserve."

As I told my father everything, she called me "telltale". I pouted and cried like a monkey until my father came and of course the first thing he asked was: "why is my lovely girl crying?" Then I would stop crying and I would tell him, sparing no detail: "Maribel took the pot I was playing with to make a lunch for you, sir"; "I was changing the flowers in your room and they pushed me so I would spill water on my dress and my mother hit me"; "I was eating some berries and they made them fall to the ground and my mother punished me" – that was how I would go on, complaining to him. Then they would pay for their snubs and rudeness because don Fabián would get furious and hit them all hard.

My childhood was marked by political violence, but really, I was a privileged girl. My father was dedicated to teaching us all to be decent and hard-working women. We were comfortably off when strange things began to happen. My sisters, who went out to place traps for the partridges came home one day, anxiously saying they had found various tins of sausages, that the fallen leaves were flattened and it seemed that a number of people had slept where the traps were laid.

Time passed and we heard they had killed the foreman of another farm, then the shopkeeper on the road and later, a number of men who were driving a train of mules with cane to the sugar mill. That's how it became customary to hear about executions in those parts. The guerrilla passed through and when the workers came for breakfast they would talk about them and we sat around eating cornmeal rolls and listened to their stories.

"Yesterday they came near the sugar mill. There were fourteen men in army uniforms and rubber boots, revolvers and machetes. We asked them if they were a group of bandits and they said they were the guerrilla."

"Juancho, why do you talk to strangers?" my mother said.

"Doña Rosario, I spoke to them because everyone is talking about them and they say they're the ones who kill the thieves who are stealing the cattle, and they're also the ones who kill the owners who mistreat their workers or steal their wages, so I wanted to get to know them, doña Rosarito," said Juancho as if to excuse himself with my mother.

"Look Juancho, speaking with those ruffians is dangerous."

"Don't worry doña Rosario, these were leaving for other parts," he looked out of the corner of his eye at the others and dared to say, "but they told me they were not bandits, but the guerrilla."

"And what is that, to be the guerrilla?" my mother asked him.

"I asked them the same thing, doña Rosario. They said they were an organisation of men who, united by the same ideals, took up arms to liberate the oppressed working class. Then I asked them what the group was called."

"We are the National Liberation Army," they replied.

"Do you belong to Colombia's army?"

"No, we are an army, but we fight against the army which protects the oligarchs, who've stolen your land and who keep you in poverty, without schooling or health."

"So, you're the ones who killed the other workers?"

"Yes, but they were not workers, they were thieves, foremen and managers who abuse poor workers like yourselves."

"So you see, doña Rosario, what they said was right. Another war has arrived, now it's not between liberals and conservatives, but against the oligarchs and the foremen," Juancho asserted.

"God help us, Juancho, to be in the presence of those murderers. You all know we're good Catholics. We listen to what the Bishop and the Mayor say and on this farm no worker has ever been badly treated. But neither do we tolerate vagrants who want to spend their lives on the mountains doing nothing," my mother said in a loud voice, to make an impression on them. She finished serving us chocolate and went out to the front room to find my father and tell him what had happened in the kitchen.

"Look, Fabián, this story of the guerrilla is going from bad to worse. The workers are talking unashamedly of this guerrilla with a tone like they know they have some one to defend them now – what do you think we can do, sir?"

"They've not harmed us, but if they come to meddle they will know what it is to deal with a proper master, a man who has worked the land with honesty and who doesn't want vagrants or delinquents around," responded my father.

"It could be dangerous, above all for the girls who now roam all over the farm."

"We must forbid them from going out. It's time they dedicated themselves to their studies and work. You must give them more tasks and then they will not go out to play."

That, simply, is how the violence came to the region where I was born and how our childhood ended.'

Daniel interrupted her and asked her:

'Tell me Socorro, what was so awful about the guerrilla, because up to now you haven't told us anything but that they killed thieves and unjust masters and I don't see anything wrong in that.'

'I'll tell you now,' she said, getting comfortable in her chair again, 'the first negative thing that happened to us was that we lost our freedom to run around outside. We had to stay in the house from that day on and it was torture. The telling offs, lashings and punishments became an everyday thing and to put an end to our habit of wandering freely, no means were enough. The most common words were: don't go out, don't run, don't play, you cannot go out and hunt birds, partridges or *chilacos*, you cannot go and walk by the river, you cannot fish, you cannot swim in the stream. The word no! was the only answer we got for a long time to everything they had previously answered yes to. A little later the men of the guerrilla appeared to speak to my father and you can imagine how don Fabián faced them.

He went out to meet them in the yard in front of the house and they came closer.

"Don Fabián, we're the law around here and we've come to offer our services to defend you from the thieves, the robbers of hens and fruit and to help you maintain order and discipline amongst the people who live in your farms," said the one who seemed to be the commander. "We know you own various farms and that you have planted sugar cane, coffee and cocoa. We also know that you process the cane at the Yellow Cane Mill, that you have cattle in Dolorosa and we've found out that your brood of hens is so large that just the sale of their eggs can support your family and pay your workers – am I wrong?" asked the leader.

"What does that mean," replied my father, "that you're better informed than I am as to what I have and earn?"

"No, don Fabián, what we know is that you are a man with money and to feel at ease, men with that much money should have someone to take care of them. We can and want to do it. You only need to pay us what you can for protecting your lands and animals."

He had not finished saying this when my father, burning with rage, with his eyes popping out of his head, made a move to take out the gun which was tucked into his belt. We held our breath, but he took back his hand back quickly, took a deep breath and answered:

"You cannot believe that I would keep idle men. Here, as you have said, there is sufficient land and work for everyone, so, if you want money and food, I offer you work."

"But, don Fabián, we already have work, we watch over the land of many farmers in the region and we want to offer you this service, that's all."

"I don't know what kind of work people are doing when they have to drag themselves around the mountains like snakes, they come out at night like the owls and kill unarmed men like bandits. If you want to work, I can offer you a job in the light of day, and of course, without weapons."

"Is that your last word don Fabián?"

"Yes."

"You'll have to live with the consequences, don Fabián. We've done what we can by offering you our services in exchange for money and food. That is how things are here now. These are the taxes in the region."

They turned around and left calmly in the direction from which they had come. My father came into the house and said to us: "Not to any of you, my daughters, nor to you, my wife, have I given things without you working for them, much less to healthy and vigorous men like those." And he thought it was the end of the matter.

That was how things were for my father, work was sacred and obedience, along with discipline, were the basic prerequisites to create a decent family. He taught us the value of money from when we were little girls and he did it with such wisdom that we never felt it could be different. For example, if we found a broody hen, the little chicks were ours once born. We had to take care of them and watch over them, and when he took them to market, he would bring us a length of material, shoes or something with the money from the sale.

This way, before we could read, we knew what it was to work, earn money and save. After the day the guerrilla threatened him he decided to take precautions to defend himself and he went to town, spoke to the army commander and offered them the farm to build a military base. Two days later a large group of soldiers arrived. They put up camp and fixed the basketball court so that a helicopter could land, which constantly brought them provisions and men with blue eyes who spoke strangely and spent periods of time there. Years later I realised those men were from the US, advisors to the army. One of them gave me a little medallion which said "made in the USA" on the back.

They were there awhile, maybe two years, according to what my father told me later, as I was too young to have a sense of time. When they disappeared Rolando, I remembered with my father how successful the army was in that era, it was the famous Operation Anorí, when they killed the Vasquez Castaño brothers. When they thought they had finished them off, they left, but shortly afterward the guerrilla came back, took the region and threatened the Montoya family with death. So my father decided to send my mother and the five eldest daughters to seek refuge in Bogotá and he was left with the three youngest who were, six, seven and eight years old. From that moment on the family began to disintegrate. Things changed so much that in two years only the façade was left of what had been a good Catholic family, with conventional ways and a strong sense of duty, with disciplined and pious women. We have kept up the farce of a united family for more than twenty years to keep my father from dying of sorrow.

My mother and sisters went to live in a neighbourhood behind the Plaza de España, where the majority of the houses were tenements. They rented two rooms and lived amongst buyers of stolen goods, thieves, prostitutes, homosexuals and all kinds of people who they were not used to being around. The little money my father sent was not enough and my eldest sisters began working as servants. My mother suffered in silence. They made a pact never to tell my father what went on. While this was going on in Bogotá the farm started to collapse. They burnt the crops, the animals were poisoned or shot in the head. No one bought the sugar and the workers began to leave. Painful things happened which I don't want to recount because they're not my experiences, but my sisters'. The decomposition of my family began then. Fate, which we thought had a good life full of hard work, unity and duty in store for us, threw us, without warning, towards a dangerous and ruinous life. We paid a high cost for not obeying the combatants and having been made to take sides. Later, ironically, as one of those tests God submits us to, I ended up being a left-wing person. It's strange that having lived through the destruction of my family, my security, of my whole life, I have gone on to help the guerrilla.'

It did not seem Socorro had touched the souls of those who listened to her. Her face was mostly serene, apparently impassive. The confidence and sincerity with which she told of her family's first displacement and the loss of her childhood world left them with a sense that, without showing sorrow or emotion, these painful events did not seem so much unfair as straightforward reality.

For them, this type of emotionless tale was surprising. She said so much in so little time, passing from her happy childhood to the total destruction of her family, but she did it as if it were normal and the group took it at face value. The disappearance of her husband and orphaning of her children left them confused, but they were more puzzled to learn how a person who was educated by the discipline of a man of don Fabián's convictions had ended up in a left-wing organisation.

They did not know how to deal with the account and, as if by tacit agreement, they let Laura speak.

Laura

To be displaced is to be mutilated

Laura has dark and vivacious eyes that show, if she allows them to, everything that goes on in her head. She is cheerful and funny and in everything and every word she looks for the risqué or the double meaning. Her body, after years of blows and contained anxiety, is never still for a minute. To be doing nothing makes her anxious and although she pays attention and seems moved by what she hears, she gets up to go to the kitchen, to the bathroom, and to change the direction of the fans which stir the warm afternoon air. A number of times she has brought sweet coffee, water and soft drinks for everyone. She attends to those in the meeting with grace and does her best not to make any noise. She has wiped the table in front of her hundreds of times in a gesture which brushes off whatever might have settled there.

Her hair, shiny and impeccably brushed back, has yet to show a single white hair. Her nails, dress, and shoes show the care she takes of herself and expects of those around her. She displays white and sparkling teeth, as if she brushes them not just every day, but every hour. Her loud giggles bring joy to the silent moments and her mocking laugh is her best defence.

Laura knows her emotions and although she has controlled them firmly for years, they are still alive. She knows that even though she has managed to become the queen of dissimulation and deception, she cannot extinguish them and they end up coming out somehow. They are intense, violent, penetrating, burning and deeply entrenched in her and she allows them only one way to come through: her work for the revolution.

She can't contain herself any longer and she decides to speak so that in her mind she is not saying again, don't be a coward, talk, express your point of view, which she considers to be the truth, the most obvious and pertinent. She does not consider she could be wrong and she cannot stand them pointing out her errors. When someone dares to, they hurt her and she returns to her childhood reactions to being punished, which arouse in her an uncontrollable hatred of her helplessness.

From the day she arrived, everyone knew that she and her family were victims of the circumstances lived in the so-called 'red zones'. She had always said how a lot of people had to leave because of pressure and threats from the army, who accused her husband of helping the guerrilla. If you ask her more she answers that the threats came because her husband was a local leader. If someone had said that Laura was an expert in the clandestine struggle, those who had known her in recent years would have laughed in disbelief. She appears to be a woman whose only concerns are to wash, iron, clean and take care of her husband and her children with the dedication her mother taught her. She had lived the last few years entrenched behind a wall of fear and of silence: I have seen nothing, I have heard nothing.

At this stage she can't stand the silence she had imposed on herself any longer. She had regained her strength and trusted herself and the group, even after what she heard the others say, when previously she would have labelled them 'counter-revolutionaries'. Now was the time to remember, to share what she had seen, heard and done. It was the moment to document her story. The fear left her and she needed to return to being who she really was. If she did not do it now, she would run the risk of disappearing from history, which for her was the same as an undignified death.

Why hadn't she died in the last ambush or in the last attack? Now she was like the wounded, a merely displaced person. In the war, people react to the wounded or the displaced with indifference or relief, as if having not died and ending up hurt or displaced was a relief, a lucky break. People don't see that to be wounded always means being left mutilated, to lose limbs, eyes, movement - to never again be a complete person. They think that the displaced are fortunate, when being displaced means having lost our soul, dreams, identity, home, and family. A displaced person doesn't bounce back to being a complete person. Laura was a case in point: ill-at-ease with everything, except her ideology, her passions, her glare and her frank words. To be displaced was the same as being mutilated or incomplete, wanting to die and cursed for having been saved.

'Yes it's true the guerrilla has displaced a lot of people from the countryside. The farmers who treat the peasants badly, the landowners, the thieves, the prostitutes and all the criminals who bleed the rural and urban poor. Do you know why?' Laura looks directly into the eyes of her friends and slides over those she is less close to, avoiding them. She doesn't want them to know how much anger she feels towards them in this moment.

'I'll tell you why. Because they're the law in those parts. They're the ones who fight to change Colombia from this unfair system in which we're living. When they come for the first time they have ideas to propose, so that the people can change, so the people can think, so they stop being lazy and drunk, but no, people don't take any notice. The landowners think they're invincible and call the army and later they don't want to deal with the consequences.' She spoke strongly, without fear of offending Socorro. The rest looked distressed because the comment was very direct and they didn't want to upset anyone. However, that was Laura's temperament and those who knew her understood it. She continued without leaving a gap for the remarks which some of her audience obviously wanted to make.

'They're so arrogant. They think they can kill us, the poor, the stupid, uneducated and unarmed, they can torture us, steal our lands and our animals, but for the rich there should be other rules.

I've suffered a lot because my childhood, as for the rest of you, was not great. I was spoiled by my father, but dear me, my mother developed a hatred for me from when I was thirteen years old the likes of which you can't imagine. From when I was very small I took care of myself because my mother worked, she was very clean and religious. Her values were sacrosanct and the family was the most important thing. She sent us to school beautifully dressed with washed, starched and ironed uniforms, to the point we always stood out in the school for cleanliness, obedience and good manners. In my house you never heard a rude word. I swear now, but I didn't learn it in my father's house. My brothers' shirts were so white they looked new and their shoes were so well polished you could look at yourself in them, like a mirror. Our notebooks were not doodled in, our bags had no scratches, our pencils were sharpened and our rubbers were not sucked on and never chewed. The rulers were marked with each name, our hankies looked as if they had been bought that day, our socks had no runs and were neatly folded over the ankles. We had tough skin from so much washing, long hair, tied up for the girls and brushed with the tufts stuck down for the boys, and our nails were clean.

My mother was a widow and the children from her first marriage suffered a lot, especially my older sister because my mother made her do all the housework and if she didn't look after us or if she looked at a man my mother hit her hard. So, poor Yolanda was up at four in the morning to mash banana for the drinks, to make the breakfast rolls and the chocolate. The rest of us woke up at five, we helped to straighten up the house until six and half an hour later they sent us to school. We were all good students and that made my mother happy and she didn't bother us. My brother Augusto was a bus driver. He gave us money for our studies and he brought us presents back from his trips: notebooks, dozens of panties, blouses and material to make dresses. He was a good son and you would never find a better brother. He was killed in an accident two years after I left home.

But not everything was agreeable. When my mother thought we girls might be interested in a man, or attracting someone's interest, we were punished with a cattle whip or a willow whip made by prisoners. She hit us so hard that our legs, torso and arms bled. She avoided hitting our faces so no one would notice.'

Laura laughs with each phrase as if the memory amuses her or she wants to avoid the pity of those present. She plays with the ring on her wedding finger which she has not taken off since the day she was married and her eyes are darting around the room, revealing her shyness.

'For my mother there was nothing as bad, no sin more horrendous, than sex. Until I was thirteen she treated me well and I was spoiled by my father. He let me to be the first to choose the clothes he bought for the family. My sisters gave me a hard time because of it, but my mother saw I was as clean and tidy as she was and with that she was satisfied. But the day came when I started to like a boy. I became infatuated with him and as my mother didn't think anyone was good enough for us, the situation became difficult. Roberto was about fourteen or fifteen and was poor. To support the family, his mother made cornmeal rolls all night and in the morning he would sell them in the stores or in the market place for the peasants' breakfasts. Compared to my family, he was poor, even though we never had much. But my father was able to bring home plenty of food, we had shoes, not sandals, and there was money to pay for our schooling.

Because of my mother's terrible habit of insulting men my sister was married in secret, although I never knew if she did it because she was in love or to escape my mother's clutches. She went off with a peasant who delivered our bananas every other day for breakfast. As he came early in the morning he saw my sister alone because she was the only one awake to meet him at that time. She offered him coffee to warm him and they decided to run off together. None of us could get married properly because my mother wouldn't have allowed it. Eventually we all ran off and that was her greatest sadness.

When I met Roberto I liked him a lot and as I've always been a strong character, I decided he was going to be my boyfriend and that was that. My mother found out and she called me one afternoon and said:

"Little Laura, you're too young to have a boyfriend and anyway this boy is not good enough for you. Look, he's lazy, he spends his time standing at the corner of the square looking at the sky, in a dream, waiting for you to come home from school, and he doesn't study or work."

"Mother, don't be like that. He does work. He helps his mother to make cornmeal rolls at night and he sells them in the morning. That's why he has time during the day. If he doesn't study, it's because his mother has no money to send him to school, but he's not lazy."

"I'm warning you, I don't like him and I forbid you from seeing or speaking to him. That's my last word and you'll bear the consequences if you disobey me." For the first time, her voice sounded threatening.

I didn't believe her. She had never hit me as she did Yolanda and I did what I liked and saw Roberto. My mother found out and that same day began to hit me. First with my father's belt, but that didn't affect me and she hit me with a *perrero*, a leather whip with a knot at the end used to herd cattle. Then she hit me with a whip she bought in the gaol, made with willow stems, which always made me bleed. As none of this stopped me seeing Roberto, she whipped me two, three and even four times a day. I became hardened, the whippings didn't worry me, the pain and the shame didn't affect me, nothing did. Stubborn as a mule, I continued meeting Roberto in secret. But this was hardly possible in a town where everyone knew us and was as small as Terán was then.

I spent my adolescence between beatings. My father didn't to try to defend me any longer because my mother's hatred was too much even for him. He preferred to pretend he didn't see, but he suffered. I saw it in his face when he came to greet me and he saw my legs and my arms bruised or bleeding because of the lashings. However, his fear of my mother was paramount and he lowered his eyes, embarrassed, and left.

Until one day, witchcraft came into it.

"Laura, do you know Roberto spends the day smoking with doña Magnolia, the witch? They told me it is to keep you under his thumb."

"I don't believe it, doña Carmen, you're telling me this because my mother told you to, aren't you?"

"No child, don't be so stubborn. See for yourself, tomorrow at about eleven in the morning, leave school under some pretext and go to the corner below the cemetery, where the witch lives and you'll see how Roberto smokes tobacco to keep you crazy for him," she replied.

I didn't reply. I entered the house softly and spent the afternoon pensive and anxious because I didn't like the sound of it at all. It might not be that I took so many beatings by choice, but because he smoked and prayed for me and I believed blindly in my love for him. Of course I myself chose to have these brutal whippings. I slept badly and got up early. I had breakfast and went to school having decided that I would leave at eleven to confirm what doña Carmen had told me. At quarter to eleven I began to complain of an intense stomach ache and put on a pained face. The sister who was teaching us religion asked me:

"Laura, what's the matter? You seem in pain!"

"Yes, sister, my stomach hurts. I think I should go home."

As I was never ill, I was always smiling and playful, the sister believed me immediately and said:

"Go on home and tell your mother to give you something because I don't have anything here for pain."

I didn't hesitate and left slowly, pretending I could barely walk. But as soon as I had turned the corner of the school, I broke into a run towards the cemetery, keeping close to the wall so I wouldn't be seen from the witch's house. It wasn't only to avoid Roberto seeing me, but also because other people we knew went there and I would get a lashing if my mother found out I'd been there. Even more so if she knew I was playing truant. A quarter of an hour went by and nothing happened, I couldn't see Roberto. Then I got angry and thought, well, I'm here now and I will not go until I know for certain. I marched into the house and came to the room where a number of people were smoking tobacco and I saw Roberto there. I tore out, ran home and went to the back patio to cry. It was the one thing I could not accept, that he practised witchcraft on me.

"What's wrong girl, why are you crying?" my mother shouted, banging hard on the patio door. "Open the door Laura, open it right now."

"Nothing is wrong with me, it's just that my stomach hurts."

"What a silly child, to lock yourself in the patio. Don't you think it would be better to lie down for a while?"

"Crying hard eases it a little," I responded.

"Stubborn, stubborn girl, if you don't come out quickly I'll send for your father and knock down the door."

"No mother, I'm coming out."

She thought something serious was wrong with me and to allay her suspicions I came out doubled over, holding my belly. She calmed down when she saw my face. I went to my room and cried bitterly for two hours. My mother brought me cinnamon water, she rubbed warm oil onto my stomach, boiled water and put it in a bottle, wrapped a towel around it and rolled it over my stomach. When she saw it didn't calm me down and I continued to cry, she went to the kitchen and said to Custodia: "the girl is lovesick."

From that day on I didn't want to see Roberto. As it was November and I ended my last year of primary school, I took advantage of the situation and told my mother that I wanted to stop studying and go to work with my godmother, to help her run her icecream shop.

"If it means you leaving that awful boyfriend, I'll even give you permission," she agreed.

I went to work at thirteen, leaving my home, my parents' protection and the comforts I had known. The icecream shop was called "The Delicacy". It was two hours away, in a larger town called Algeciras. The ice cream shop was in the central square, it had a big room and six ceiling fans which gave the place a fresh feel. It had thirty-two tables to play lottery, dominoes, chess, Chinese checkers and Parcheesi and in the afternoon there were films.

I was free from the beatings, from my obsession with Roberto, from my mother and I started to decide things for myself, even though, in truth, I had always done what I wanted. I learnt not to confront everything face on because my infatuation with Roberto had cost me dearly, thanks to my innocence. I still had the ability to get whatever I wanted. My godmother gave me a room in the ice cream shop and I slept there with another girl, Marlene, who helped serve the tables and washed the floor and plates. Aside from ice-cream cones we sold icecream in glasses, cups, berry cakes, figs with caramel spread and other fruits depending on the season. We chatted at night when my godmother went to sleep and discussed the boys who flirted with us and the girls who came to the shop. Life was wonderful for those three years. With what I earned, I bought things for my mother and kept her happy.

On Sundays when I went to see her she said: "now the happy-go-lucky girl is coming to her senses". She said my greatest defect was being a flirt, that I could start up a conversation with anyone and men didn't understand that. She kept saying that men were bad and were always after the same thing – to sleep with you and nothing more, to leave you full of children and then lose themselves in drink. I don't know where she got all these ideas about men from because my father was a reasonable man and those who knew Jorge, my siblings' father, said he was a saint.

'Well, they called them all saints, but our mothers said nothing and put up with everything' interjected Socorro, 'My mother, for example, had the same obsession. For her, virginity was sacred and she repeatedly told us, "women are like budding roses. They should keep themselves pristine until they get married, because if they allow themselves to be kissed and touched, the same thing will happen to them as to a rose when it is handled. It withers before it opens and then no one puts it in a pretty vase. In the same way, men don't take women who allowed themselves to be 'handled' to the altar." So for all of us, to lose our virginity was a shameful thing.'

'We women were naïve and the worst did happen to us. My mother didn't talk like that, but she knew that life for those who were taken to the altar or those only taken to bed, was very tough,' said Mercedes, 'in the countryside, hardly anyone is legally married. Common-law marriages are the norm and the man decides which woman is going to be the mother of his legitimate children, but it's not because he respects her. The mother is always a saint and the others, including the mothers of his other children, are bitches, whores and tramps. It is as though they needed to revenge their mothers' humiliations, for the beatings they were subjected to.'

'When one has lived a life of deprivation one cannot expect the luxury of understanding,' whispered Daniel.

'If we judge by what my mother did, I'd say men humiliate and mistreat us if we let them and if not, the coin flips the other way. In my family it's us women who rule and the men who obey. That was what my mother was like and that's what it's like in my house. It's the only way to protect ourselves, by hitting first,' explained Laura.

'And me, with five boys, how am I going to educate them, to obey orders or to issue them?' asked Antonia, who had been silent so far.

Laura's noisy laugh rang through the room. The women laughed with her and the men smiled. Laura felt calmer and said:

'Well, thinking as a mother is something else. However, I repeat that if we women demand respect then our boys will end up obeying their wives.'

'And according to you, that's best, Laura, that they obey and let themselves be bossed around by women?' asked Marcos.

'No, but it's either you or us on top and each of us chooses the life we want to live. It hurt me that my father was a coward and left us to be thrashed by our mother, but now that I live my own life and my children are rebellious and stubborn, what can I do to ensure they respect me? Nothing different from what my mother did,' said Laura.

'I'm not sure I would like to see my five boys bossed around,' Antonia returned to her question.

'That's why they do as they like. We have to stop them from succumbing to illicit and dissolute practices, to the evils which finish off family dignity. Above all, we must not forget that young people are like untamed colts and if they commit a serious mistake, we must punish them with the whip. If it is only foolishness we must slap them across the face and in no case should we loosen the reins. I learnt this on the plains when you hunt wild ponies to domesticate them,' insisted Laura.

They had broken the rules they had established. They had begun to give advice, even though they had agreed not to.

Ana Dolores reminded them:

'*Compañeros*, let's leave the advice for another time. Remember the commitment we made to respect each others' ways of being and not to give personal opinions of others' stories.'

Memories of their infancy took over as they listened to the suffering of others. Memory, which had done them a favour by keeping itself hidden, even forgotten, now reappeared, betraying the silence and with each phrase, the pain in each of them as the child inside returned anew. Why did the memories of childhood come back? Who had begun to uncover that which now had no way of sorting itself out? Why did they speak of these things? Why did they forget not to give advice? Marcos responded emphatically as if he guessed what was happening or as if he was thinking out loud:

'We forget our agreements because in this country they're flimsier than tissue, they change as quickly as the breeze and nothing is more widespread than betrayal, twisted and deformed. Ideas advance like a boat adrift, without oars to direct them, they come and go at random. We spend our lives talking of foolish fantasies, like winning the war, while the truths of daily life are like a wind which lashes at the fog of neglect. Faced with the impossibility of recovering the past, these truths clash with reality. But a sign of love, of respect or security is enough to send us back there in search of it. Love, my friends, has been buried under the tombstone of a grave which reads "rejection of feelings". That's why we ask about the truth of our childhood, because it terrifies us more than bullets.'

Everyone was quiet. They agreed. Mercedes suggested a rest and they agreed to that too. With childhood there were no half-measures, no truce, no calls to trial or war councils. Neither were there calls for the jury to be compassionate as they were the jury in this, the only judge of their victory or defeat. But there was a great relief when they managed to tell the truth. War is a major test. It is a moment of decisive choices to which any man or woman can turn to measure their fear, to discover what they are capable of when all is said and done, in short, to know if they are capable of judging themselves.

Antonia

The pain of learning to forget

When they came together to continue, Antonia had already been at her desk for some time and she seemed to be miles away. She turned a puff pastry heart round and round without taking a bite. She took long sips of water without speaking to any of her friends. She was ready for anything. She wanted to jump over this barrier of fear she had built and which had become a constant lie: her happiness. She knew she had perfected a pretence which she had repeated so many times, not only were others taken in, but she had come to believe it herself. The one way she knew she was lying was through her body, a body which had been subdued when her father forced her to forget her mother.

Antonia's words said one thing and her body contradicted her. Her happiness crashed on the wall her face had become. She did not seem asleep or awake. She was not lucky in love or well-loved, which she repeated constantly. She said she loved her children, but she treated them badly, hated them and trapped them with orders, dire warnings and doubts.

Antonia was tormented by what she felt and thought. She was imprisoned by guilt and could not remember what she had done to deserve such punishment. The body, eyes and spirit of her children, peaceful or rebellious, forced her to look back and see, with rage, her own subjugation. When they defied or disobeyed her, they reminded her that she did not rebel. It was as if they spat her greatest defeat in her face everyday, her shame, her incapacity to revolt, her cruel fate of blind obedience.

The time had come to bring everything back. To tell of the grief, the hurt, the ordeal and the torture to which she was subjected from five years of age. Although it was impossible to erase the past, she wanted to let go of it, atone for it, repair it, wipe away the results without forgetting.

The audience awaited. Antonia felt their presence, left the pastry untouched on the napkin, looked at Mercedes to give herself strength and said:

'I didn't love anyone as a child. Rather, I thought I loved my father because he gave me things and spoiled me. My mother hated me because of it and I hated her back. Only when they separated me from her I understood how much I needed her and also my love for her, because I suffered a lot.

My father was a rough man, a lot older than my mother, a man who shored up his manliness by hitting her every day, for any reason. I say that I didn't love her because I laughed when he dragged her across the yard hitting her with his belt and even with the canoe oars. I celebrated the beatings he gave her and he rewarded me by taking me to the capital and buying me things. I was happy, until one day she left while my father and I were away.

These are memories from when I was small. I was the youngest in my house. When I had just turned five, my mother left my father, tired of suffering a hard life she had been chained to for fifteen years. Most of us were born on a farm near Puerto Ospina. She had tried to leave him many times, but he had always made her come back. This time she left and came back for me two years later, two years which were my most difficult because my father subjected me to horrors so I wouldn't mention her.

I have remembered this part of my life after striving for many years to reconstruct my history. I had forgotten it not because of my young age, but because it seemed too shameful and now, at thirty-six years of age, I can begin to comprehend the magnitude of the tragedy.

When my mother left I stayed alone with my father and he didn't change his habits for me. He went out drinking every night and at other times he would disappear for weeks on end because he was working far away from home. I was a very little girl and he left me in the charge of the neighbours, but they took little or no care of me. Now I understand it wasn't possible for these women to like me when they suffered the same humiliations as my mother and I had applauded hers. So, when my father left me, the little forms of revenge began: cold soup without salt, salty meat that was nearly raw, sour milk or milk with skin and badly washed clothes. When I cried because I felt my mother's absence, there would be sarcastic comments: "You're not laughing and mocking your mother now, are you. Now say, Dad, I'm hungry, Dad, I'm tired, Dad, I'm cold, now call him to take care of you." I cried and called for my mother all day and all night and the culmination of the petty retaliations of the neighbours' was to say to my father: "Antonia misses her mother, doña Mariela, too much". With that they ensured he vented his rage on me, the only one at hand at the time.

One day he lifted me by the waist and he carried me in the air to the house, he threw me on the ground and through gritted teeth, mumbled "Antonia, although I love you, I'm not going to put up with you spending the whole day calling for your mother. That bitch left us and it is best that you understand how things are now. If you keep calling her, I will stop loving you." From then on I learnt to cry in secret, but when I was frightened, or fell, or was sad, I could not help shouting: Mum! To say Mum was instinctive.

Once my father went away for two months to work in the eastern plains. When he came back, doña Alcira, who looked after me, said to him:

"Don José María, I cannot take care of Antonia anymore. She cries all day, she doesn't eat or obey me and she calls for doña Mariela all the time. I think you should look for her and give the girl to her because she is very small and needs her mother."

"Look, *comadre*,* no one is asking you for advice, if you cannot take care of her and I will find a solution, but don't presume to send me off in search of the bad mother who abandoned her child without a backward glance."

"*Compadre*,** you know doña Mariela left when you were in Bogotá with Antonia because she knew if she waited for you to come back, she would never leave."

"Well, that's not your problem, I'll see what I do with Antonia."

He took me by the hand, which was trembling in his like a chick taken out of the nest. Tears ran down my cheeks and I was unable to stop them. When we got home, he sat me on a stool, took another one, sat down in front of me and said: "Antonia, we cannot go like this, but I want you to be very clear: you are not going back to your mother. I'm going to make you forget her, if it's the last thing I do." Not only my hands, but my whole body shook and I cried in fear, for the repressed sadness, for the ignored anguish. The breaths and hiccups sounded tragically, Mum! Mum! and I couldn't stop. The louder my sobs, the more clearly it sounded, Mum! Mum! When he heard me, my father looked at me incredulously and shouted: "Child, what can it be like when I'm not here. Cry all you like, call you mother until you're tired because from this day forth, every time you name her, the punishment will be tough and I know, for good or bad, you will stop calling her forever". I cried so much that I fell asleep on the stool and I don't know how many hours later I fell and cracked my head open. He left as soon as I began to cry and came in the morning, when the blood had stopped flowing. I woke up from the blow when I fell off the stool. It was dark and the door to the street was locked from the outside so I couldn't escape from the dismal house. I panicked. I ran through the rooms looking for my father, my siblings, my mother and they had all abandoned me. That day I felt orphaned and infinitely alone. When the sun came up, I stopped trembling. I was worried because the house was covered with blood and I ran to the kitchen to find a cleaning cloth. But there was nothing to clean up the mess I had made. I felt guilty for doing this to my father who loved me so. He was right, I was bad and did not deserve his love. I was angry with myself and I repeated to myself: "you are a stupid, stupid, bad, bad, bad, girl".

---

* Familiar term for a close friend of the family who is may be related. Feminine form.
**as above, masculine form.

With my heart crushed and a knot in my throat I cried softly repeating: "Damn you Mum, why do I call you. Damn you Mum, damn you."

The next morning he put clothes in a suitcase, took my hand and we went on a bus to Puerto López. Then we took a jeep down dusty and deserted roads for hours until we finally reached the end of the road. There, he contracted two animals. On one he put the goods, the suitcase and a bottle of gasoline and we rode on the other.

We wandered through the plains for four days. Each day I was more exhausted and I could hardly keep myself on the animal, but my father held me up against his arm. When I was awake, I looked around and I was comforted by seeing the deer run in the distance, fleeing our approach. I saw sunsets of warm colours, the silhouettes of horsemen who went past driving the cattle, bulls with enormous horns who ran threateningly or shot forward angrily on seeing our animals. The tamer ones allowed us to come close enough to touch them. They got lost in different directions towards the horizon, towards where the dry cow dung burnt, which was customary near the pastures so that the cattle could find the paddocks. We also followed the smoke and arrived at a pasture to ask for somewhere to spend the night. I was amazed to see a flock of heron flying away one after another in a perfect pattern. Eventually we arrived at an Indian hut, where a man came out to meet us and when I was passed into his arms, I realised this was my final destination.

My father had been a rubber tapper for over twenty years and knew the Witotos. He had discovered the paths, river beds and valleys with them and he had friends wherever there were streams. The Indians in the hut were shrewd and they resembled each other, as fruit does. They arrived naked offering him banana and cassava as a greeting and in palm-leaf baskets they brought my father smoked fish. Others came forward with their wives who put their right hand on their left shoulders to signal that they were married.

The Indians had different habits and I had a hard time getting used to them. I learnt to eat their food only when I fainted from hunger, but the thing I found most difficult was the nakedness. My father spoke for a long time with the chief who seemed older than Methuselah. When he finished, they sealed their friendship anew and the chief sent him to sleep with a woman who seemed to be a good friend of my father's and who was with him throughout his stay. My father spoke their language perfectly and he stayed a few days, enough for me to learn a few words so that I could get by. The day he went he said to me: "Listen to me closely, Antonia, I'm going today and I'm not coming back for you until they send for me to say you have forgotten your mother." Terrified, I watched him go, thinking I would never see him again and I cried inconsolably.

The worst part began when they initiated their treatment for forgetting. Every time I called for my mother, I had to go into the chief's house and do what he ordered.'

Antonia was choking on her tears. She coughed and breathed in deeply in a determined struggle with herself.

The moment came when she could not control her sobs and in each it seemed as if she said Mum. It was moving to see a woman of thirty-six relive the impotence of a girl of five faced with adults who abused their authority over her without the smallest mercy. The experience left her enmeshed in feelings of guilt, in the knowledge of harm permitted and condoned, and which did not allow her to be happy until three decades later she managed to remember and openly hate her tyrants. Antonia wiped away her tears, lifted her face, looked at them all and said that for the moment she could not continue with her story.

Marcos

Listen for the fox

Marcos was quiet and his small eyes reflected the anger, pity and shame he felt to be a man, at this moment. His small, wide hands with short fingers, black with glue, moved rhythmically up and down, compulsively rubbing the sticky residue from his fingers as if he wanted not only to wipe clean his hands, but also the sins of men, who today he felt were hungry wolves, predators of the love of his life: women.

Marcos was straightforward and warm once you got to know him, affectionate and affable with his children and a great friend. But his most prominent characteristic was his love for his wife, whom he admired and respected. Maybe it had not always been like this, but he had loved and respected her for so long he doubted he had ever been able to hurt her. For Marcos loving his wife and living amounted to the same thing. The children she had given him and her resilience rebuilding their destroyed home a thousand and one times was his greatest pride. Marcos felt safe at her side. The pleasant stability of a now monotonous and normal life did not bother him and much less made him yearn for the way he had lived when he was involved in the armed conflict. To strangers he gave the sense of being a bad-tempered person and extremely reserved. Those who knew him in the group did not expect him to speak enthusiastically and calmly about his life.

Marcos, son of the deceased Magnolia and the eighty year-old Justo, had been born into a poor family whose fortunes rose to the extent that together they owned a district in Caquetá. Not much time passed between Marcos' first meal and his first day's work. The combination of his parents' limited education and their belief that the only thing of value was the land, meant it never seemed important to them to educate their fourteen children. From when he was small, Marcos was very bright. His intuitive intelligence, which had not been trammelled by education, made him stand out in the jobs he had done over the years. The restlessness of his innate intellect was appeased when he could contribute his discreet courage, his cunning and his skill to the most complicated tasks the guerrilla entrusted him to carry out at a time when communications were vital.

When Marcos became a militant, he stopped suffering from his longing to overcome ignorance. He learnt everything they taught him avidly, the theory and practice, with such ease that he quickly rose to positions of responsibility which fulfilled him. When he started to speak, his tone of voice reminded everyone of the clandestine life.

'*Compañeros*, I don't agree with the two positions which have been presented here. They're radical and have not considered the circumstances surrounding the struggle in the past and at present. I believe we must carry out a deep analysis. First, I'd like to know what all of you are doing here? Why are you presenting your ideas and speaking openly about your life? The only thing I know is that we participated in the armed conflict, in one way or another, and for each of us things happened in a different way.

Aside from the reconstruction of the history of each of our lives which we are undertaking, we should look into the current conditions in the country and the changes which have taken place inside the guerrilla groups. We should try to be as dispassionate as we can and explore our support for the armed conflict and why we were attracted to it. We should also examine if it's true that we were all involved in the illegal struggle, because from what I've heard in your stories some only carried out legal jobs although the fact they were carried out in territory where the Constitution and Colombia's laws don't prevail, made them illegal.

I know you all aspire to certain ideals, in some way: the search for justice, equality and freedom, but you differ greatly in the ways in which you participated, in the methods you used and how, where and why you became part of the conflict. That's why I call upon you to think. Let's take advantage of this space we have and the experience of having suffered from displacement. Until I heard you, I could not have imagined how much and to what extent the problem of violence comes from way back and has many components. Listening to you talk of your childhood has opened up new prospects of analysis for me. Although I've not been able to consider the story of my life as you have, I recognise its importance as I've seen you change and give the best of yourselves in the search for peace, a peace which is elusive because it's being built on a lie. I'm going to respect the agreements which we've come to and although the subject that brought us together was not our childhood, its importance in analysing the war and the truth have a logic such that, I believe it's not an accident we've come back to it,' said Marcos, leaning forward.

'We were a large, poor and humble family, ten girls and four boys. My parents, who we practically illiterate, didn't consider schooling to be of any use to peasants. They applied the same brute force they had suffered, which they thought children should endure to become honest men and women. They never gave us affection, or understanding, hugs, kisses, gave us cuddles or treated us with care, but they worked hard to feed fourteen hungry mouths.

My father was convinced his greatest problem was having ten girls, because they needed a lot of attention and as they were not ugly, he couldn't even sleep properly after my mother died. He often said "I have to spend every night like a hawk: listening for the fox!", and every now and then he checked their hammocks to see they were all there. He counted them to see if the group was complete. From then on, he made us boys work harder and he taught us we should be principled. For him that meant speaking when asked to and staying quiet when not.

It was pure chance that I was the one who left the countryside. I learnt to make a living outside and it changed my life fundamentally. In the country my life was only work and deprivation and maybe that is what made me lose my connection to the land. Although at various points in my life I tried to go back to the land, to continue the family tradition, something stronger pushed me to be different and become what we call an artisan. I learnt a skill which I have lived off and thanks to which I've been able to support my family. I have enough children not to want more and a wife whom I love deeply.

I don't remember my childhood much and I would like to think it is the case that one repeats what one lived. I don't think I was treated badly in the years erased from my memory because I haven't mistreated my children much and I admire and respect my wife. I admit it hasn't always been the case and I still have residues of sexism, but in the revolutionary movement I learnt a lot and I allowed myself to see life differently and seek new horizons. Although it's not what my children have pursued, my life has given them the chance not to be peasants or skilled workers, but study to be professionals.

When I was a boy I thought my mother was a saint, but women as such, I saw as inferior, with specific functions to carry out: to be a mother, take care of and maintain the home and always obey the husband, the man. Us boys gave orders to our sisters. They served the food, sorted out the clothes and attended to us when we got back from work, tired. It was the man's duty to work and earn a living for the family. I don't think it was a coincidence that I broke with these assumptions and sought a woman who wouldn't let herself be dominated. She's been a good mother and wife and in my house we do what she wants. I learnt I was the weak one because in difficult times, when I've needed her most, she has responded with the kind of courage many men don't possess.

I haven't wanted to talk before because this war has made me careful. As I told you, they taught me to speak when spoken to and otherwise, to keep quiet. I know why I'm speaking now and it's for a reason. Everything has a cause and an effect. There are reasons for how we live, think and feel. What changes and makes us different are the circumstances surrounding us. What we have lived and learnt and brings us here at this time, is not insignificant. If you are alive, you may die and you could fall into your enemies' hands. The contradiction is that you don't want to die, but you cannot bear to be alive, either.'

One could see the fear crouched in each one of them, growing with every word Marcos spoke.

'When you feel persecuted, each minute stretches into an eternity and you remain silent, still, staring fixedly, as if you could exchange your soul with those you love and impress their features into your memory. You think of nothing but how to save yourself and you turn your back on them, convinced that they know how to defend themselves, that they can do it and they don't run any risk, but really it is treason and cowardice. Then you come back and you think it's easy to return, nothing has changed. But life is an omelette and you don't make one without breaking eggs. When you have time to reflect, many eggs are already broken and the guilt becomes a torment. We must talk about fear and cowardice, about the madness of persecution. I ask that we do this, because it may not be too late for others. It is perhaps not the right time to deal with this subject, but I wanted to raise it so we don't forget it later on.'

The silence was piercing, and their questioning looks showed they did not know how to continue. The group looked to Marcos for him to carry on. Marcos felt he had said everything there was to say that day and he remained silent.

'I think you're judging yourself too harshly. We know of fear, cowardice and abandonment, but it doesn't seem to me you abandoned your family to save your skin,' said Socorro, looking at the others who nodded their heads in agreement. 'Marcos, you're forgetting you're a human being and we all feel the same, saving our lives is a instinctive act. I don't believe you thought you were exposing your family to danger when you left them. I imagine you exposed them less by fleeing. Am I wrong?'

'You're wrong because I left them out of fear. Of course, I also did it because I thought it was worse to stay and if they raided us they might kill anybody. I'm convinced I was a coward to leave them unprotected,' answered Marcos.

'Tell me, Marcos, did they give you the chance to take them with you?' enquired Socorro.

'Of course not. What was I going to do with the children and Leonor in the mountains? It wasn't allowed. I didn't think about what might happen if something went wrong. Life gave me another chance. If I hadn't seen them again, I'd be pleading for death to take me or I would be in the thick of the war.'

'Don't you see it was not just cowardice? It's down to the circumstances,' replied Socorro.

'This is not the time to discuss it, but later, when you know my story of violence more fully, you'll understand I don't judge myself too harshly. I want to talk about it so others realise the costs. One feels very brave and tough and daring but one never knows what it means to be persecuted. If people knew, no one would go into the guerrilla.'

'That's as may be, but as you say, *compañero*, it's best to leave it for later,' said Daniel seriously.

The next day the atmosphere was tense. Those who had spoken looked better, but those whose turn was yet to come were pale and had bags under their eyes. Those who held onto more fears were lagging behind and looked down, trying to pass unnoticed. Marcos took the initiative and said:

'As no one will start, I'm going to choose someone to begin today,' he looked at Alejandra and said, '*compañera*, words are meant to be spoken, we're listening to you.'

Their bodies were stiff from sitting still for two days and their spirits were disturbed by the emotions aroused, but they focused afresh, preparing to listen to what Alejandra had to tell them.

Alejandra

She loved learning, but not through beatings

Alejandra's hard features might imply she was a rigid woman. Her thinness made her suffering more marked, but deep in her amber eyes a contrasting sparkle of tenderness glimmered. Her body already revealed the rigours of time, even though her craving for a full life, which she still sought, had not disappeared. Watching her lean, tightly crossed legs, one saw how difficult it was for Alejandra to present her life to the group. She squeezed one of Antonia's hands, who was next to her, wiped her forehead with a hankie with a nervous gesture and began:

'Well, *compañeros*, I was part of a guerrilla group. Belonging to a revolutionary army was a decision I took without much thought. I was longing to free myself from the pain of the rest of my life. I was born in a small community in the mountains of Santander where the thermal waters and cold of the region meet and heal the sick, who are drawn there from every corner of the country. They say the two things together are a blessing for health and life.

We were six children and my mother was a widow. The three youngest were my father's children. As we were very poor, we went from town to town seeking our fortune, which was elusive and avoided us constantly. Our poverty was such that my sisters had to beg in Bucaramanga to feed us. My father, faced with such responsibilities, abandoned us for a time. My mother, anxious and alone, found it impossible to quell the hunger of six mouths working as domestic help so she applied punishments, meeting our needs with the whip.

She thought she had been well trained by my grandmother and inflicted the same discipline on us. Every mistake we made got us a thrashing. Grandmother had mellowed with the years and tried to teach us as best she could so we would receive fewer beatings. She taught me how to cook when I was six and once I could do it, everyone else could go out to work. Five years went by until my mother, desperate, decided to go back to the countryside and there, I could go to school.'

She liked going to school. The two-hour trip each day flew by for her because on those paths she learnt to sing, to fly and to defend herself by attacking first. The hard life made her agile, fast, accurate, aggressive and honest. But the beatings they gave her as a child disabled her, and the results were visible as she wound her legs round each other, squeezing her hands together, perspiring copiously.

Her rebellious temperament and her struggle to not let herself be bullied surfaced in school. She loved writing and maths, colours and songs, but she did not want to learn under the threat of beatings. She never had to make any effort because she was intelligent enough to understand quickly what the teacher taught. She hated doing homework and memorising lessons, particularly after working all afternoon collecting coffee. One day she did not know the lesson and the teacher, who cuffed them habitually, hit her so hard her arm went purple. Alejandra did not want to go back to school afterwards.

The day's work started before dawn broke and ended late at night, by candlelight. Over the next seven years her routine consisted of getting up at three in the morning to light the fire and prepare breakfast and lunch quickly and then go out to work. And then:

"Aleja put on the water to boil. Aleja have you kneaded the flour to make the rolls? Aleja get up, it's already three o'clock in the morning. Aleja make the chocolate.

Aleja bring in the animals from the field. Aleja, go and wash the clothes. Aleja, don't play, Aleja, don't run, Aleja, don't be a nuisance. Aleja go and take your father his lunch. Aleja don't look, don't touch, don't laugh, don't cry."

Julia, her eldest sister, was ten years older than her and she hit Alejandra when her mother was not there. She was even tougher than her mother and she showed the little ones no mercy. She in turn was hit by her mother and stepfather with a whip, a log, kicked and smacked. She never smiled and when Alejandra laughed she got a funny feeling in her throat, and she wasn't sure if it was hatred or sadness, because it made her want to cry. Alejandra never saw her cry and admired her as much as she loathed her.

"Mum, look, Alejandra, Rosa María and Teresa are not paying attention. Today they started to play and broke the pan," said Julia one day with a calm voice as if she was saying the food was ready. Their mother, tired of washing other people's clothes, of hearing criticisms, lectures and of receiving a wage insufficient to feed her children, lost her temper.

"Alejandra, Rosa, Teresa, come here immediately."

To say they were scared would not describe the terror their mother's thrashings inspired, they felt as if she was separating the wheat from the chaff, their skin from their flesh.

'My sisters, Rosa María and Teresa, held out much longer before they started to cry. But we cried softly because otherwise my mother became angrier and it was worse for us. In spite of her, enough happy memories of childhood remain with me: skipping, hanging rope from the trees to make swings, going to the stream to swim, running, pushing each other and lighting bonfires to make sugar sweets in Chorrera. It was important for me because, back in the countryside, we all lived together again with my father and mother.

The circumstances changed, the coffee harvest was poor and the money we made gathering it was not enough to keep the house in the country. We went back to Bucaramanga to look for work. I was the youngest and they sent me to live with a family to help the lady with the housework. I had the bad luck, or maybe the good luck, to fall in love with Germán, the son of my employers. I gave myself to him for love and it was the loveliest thing I recall about that time.'

Alejandra smiles like someone who is going to admit to something personal and her cheeks redden. She makes a big effort and her features show she finds it difficult to speak of these episodes, but she wants to because they were defining moments in her adolescence.

'Everything started with a smile, then short chats which became longer when doña Hortensia went out to market. She left me making lunch and he always found a way to stay behind. Then there was a kiss on the cheek, later on the mouth, then a lot of kisses and caresses and finally a proposition to meet one night. I said no, but Germán was very insistent and one day with a flushed body and having lost my head I said:

"Tonight, Germán," and he shouted with joy and nearly gave us away.

"What's going on Germán?" asked doña Hortensia. "Why are you shouting, tonight!, what is happening tonight? Who are you talking to?"

"Nothing, Mother, I just remembered that tonight they're going to pay me a bet I won at the university and I said it out loud."

"Speaking to yourself is what crazy people do'

"It's not that bad Mother, it was just an expression of joy."

He gestured to me not to speak, to go to the kitchen and he would follow me.

"Really, tonight Aleja? Do you promise?"

"I promise, Germán."

"Oh, Aleja, I'm so happy. I will come to your room at about ten, when my mother is deeply asleep."

"I'll be waiting," I said, "I'll leave the door ajar so that it doesn't make a noise."

It took me a while to realise I had embarked on something dangerous. Then I felt a deep unease, as if I sensed a catastrophe might befall us. I spent the day like a lost soul. I didn't know if it was due to happiness or anguish because the only thing my mother said when I visited her on Sundays was: "Alejandra, don't forget you should be careful, this is not the countryside. The city is insidious and treacherous. Those who live here are not like us, they deceive us and take advantage of us. Don't ever forget it."

"Yes, mother, I won't forget it."

I felt so grown up. I was an adult now, I had had a sound upbringing and I didn't see why my mother had to go on with her same old tale: "the city is dangerous for a pretty girl."

However, the obsessive persistence with which Germán had courted and flattered me in those months worried me. I felt something forced and exaggerated in his irrepressible joy and euphoria. Often, when I wouldn't accept or return his caresses he'd be transformed into a difficult and sulky boy. I feared being made wretched by this love, that it might fail me when it mattered most. I was frightened of love. I knew nothing about love. What was it to make love? How should I behave? Was is those passionate kisses and caresses which left the private parts aching?

I'd begun to read books and newspapers again, so as not to feel so ignorant with Germán. I'd even looked for the definition of "love" in the dictionary. I had copied it onto a little piece of paper which I kept under my pillow and I read it every night to be sure of what I felt and that it was true love. The dictionary said:

"Love: a feeling which moves one to wish for the loved person to achieve what they believe is good, to ensure this wish is fulfilled and to enjoy as one's own good the knowledge that they have secured it. The sexual appetite of animals.'

The first part led me to decide to give myself to him convinced I truly loved him. The second was very familiar to me as I had known animal lust from when I was a little girl and although I always stopped to watch them, with a disturbing, if pleasant sensation in my insides, something made me reject it. This strange sensation seemed vulgar and I decided it was better to erase that part of the definition. I kept the first definition, which seemed written to appease my doubts. I repeated it night after night until I had memorised it.

I dreamt of love. In the dream, a voice said: love is much more, it's giving oneself to the beloved unselfishly and generously. I had never given myself to anyone and it frightened me to love and to start depending on someone. I understood already that love implied pain.

That night, I felt the sound of door handle turning at exactly ten o'clock. He arrived on time and brimming over with happiness. I, on the other hand, felt nervous, riddled with the guilt which had pursued me in the past months when I thought of giving myself to Germán. He came in and saw the poverty of my small room, with its badly painted walls, with no more than a lavatory and a tiny basin, a faded bedspread and a bare light bulb which hung off the wall by a wire. For the first time he was truly conscious of the difference between him and me, but he looked at my face and as always he told me how beautiful I was with my tormented child's smile and then he lifted the bedspread. My body, under a vest, lost its attractiveness and I thought he would see my fragility. He lifted up the vest, looked at me fixedly and said: "what beautiful breasts, you look like a china doll." Germán was transfixed by my softly curved hips and by my white skin which seemed to him translucent and bluish. I went red with embarrassment as he looked at me. I put my arms around him, meek and anxious to hide my torment in his neck. He embraced me and fell on me with all the repressed desire of so many months, but tenderly too. All of a sudden, I seemed so defenceless to him, so vulnerable, and he realised he could hurt me.

Germán loved me with an unfamiliar tenderness which he lavished on me every night when he swallowed his shouts of joy because of the silence imposed by the circumstances.

When I found out I was pregnant, I naively believed the joy of so many nights of love couldn't be erased and Germán would marry me. Each night he swore he loved me more and more and the relationship had been going on for a few months, but the moment I spoke of a possible pregnancy, he rejected me and his mother threw me out of the house.

"Aleja, get your suitcase ready because I'm firing you," doña Hortensia said to me one morning after everyone had left, "I don't need you to work in my house anymore. Do you hear me?"

"But, doña Hortensia, what have I done?"

"And you have the cheek to ask? Does it seem like a small thing to you, girl? This is a decent house, where one does not pursue men to cohabit."

I didn't understand what "cohabiting" meant and I dared to ask her:

"I didn't cohabit with anyone, doña Hortensia."

"Oh, no, of course not, then what's this about you sleeping with Germán and wanting to burden him with a child, when God knows whose it is."

I felt as if I had been hit, silenced and stunned.

"Hurry up, I don't want you in this house for a minute longer."

"But, doña Hortensia, I have to speak with Germán. You can't throw me out in this way."

"Of course I can!"

She ran to my room and began to throw the clothes which were hung on a nail in the wall onto the floor and she said:

"If you don't pack quickly, I'll kick you out onto the street without your things."

I didn't even cry, I was bewildered and the shock prevented me from reacting. I picked up my three sets of clothes, my shoes, sandals and washing things, I put them in the suitcase my mother had given me and went out, disoriented. Before I left, doña Hortensia put my month's wages on the table and said:

"There's what we owe you and don't ever come back or I'll have the police after you."

I was in shock. I didn't understand how being pregnant was a crime which could get me reported to the police.

I spent the whole afternoon standing on the corner next to the house, behind a dirty wall which enclosed a vacant lot, hiding from doña Hortensia and waiting for Germán. I imagined many things: Germán had told them that he was going to have a child with me and don Gerardo and doña Hortensia had screamed blue murder and had threatened to throw him out of the house and stop paying for his studies. I also imagined they had pretended to go along with him saying: "it's alright, we'll help you with this problem tomorrow", to trick him into going to university relieved, so they could throw me out and he wouldn't be able to see me again. I imagined they would invent a lie, like in the soap operas, and he, despairing, wouldn't look for me. I imagined they'd sent him to Bogotá that morning and I would never see him again. I imagined so many things that one minute I cried with love, the next with sadness and then I cried with anguish. My mind was feverish with doubt.

At about eight at night he arrived. I ran to greet him. He put a finger to his lips, frowned with an upset face and pushed me to the corner behind the lot, where I had been waiting all afternoon.

"What's wrong Alejandra? You scared me. Don't jump out at me again in the dark like a thief. I thought you would be a long way away by now."

His tone put me in my place. The truth became apparent and I started to cry. He naturally felt a bit of compassion and said to me:

"Don't cry, I'm not going to leave you alone with this problem. Come tomorrow to don Gervasio's store and we'll go to a woman who can give you an abortion and get us out of this mess. Then we can continue to see each other in secret away from my house."

Everything blurred in my mind. The hunger, anguish and standing for hours stopped me from thinking clearly and besides, he didn't ask me, he'd decided everything for me. The only thing I kept repeating to myself was: "we can continue to see each other, we can continue to see each other, we can continue to see each other." I thought, Germán loves me and I should try to do all I can for his good. So, after hearing "we can continue to see each other", I would have accepted any proposal of his, whatever it was, to kill myself if necessary. Germán loved me and wanted to continue to see me. The next day I turned up to our date at exactly two in the afternoon.

We went by taxi as the woman who was going to do the abortion lived a long way away, in a place called Chorreras, the same where I swam as a child. We came to a house which stood out in the neighbourhood as the finest. We called at the door and a girl of about nine came out and told us to come in while she shouted:

"Doña Encarnación, your visitors have arrived."

I was confused that the girl said this without asking us anything. Later I understood that only pregnant women went there.

Germán was holding my sweaty hand and he pressed my head into his shoulder and caressed my cheek to console and encourage me. Doña Encarnación came out in an apron stained with food, which she undid as she greeted us.

"So young man, what can I do for you?"

"Look, doña Encarnación, I come on the recommendation of Rodolfo Gómez, a medical student at the University who knows you. I have a problem with Alejandra and he said you'd be able to solve it."

"How late are you?" She looked at me, indicating with her head that I should answer.

"About two months."

"Are you sure? It's very dangerous if you're more than three, so tell me the truth."

"I'm sure. Last week I should have had it and for the second time it didn't come."

"If that's right, let's get on with it."

She indicated with her hand that I should follow her inside. I looked at Germán and he nodded his head to follow the woman. I let go of his hand with the sense that I was going to my death, and there was nothing I could do." '

Alejandra looked down. She felt embarrassed and guilty about what she had decided back then. Her light eyes darkened and hatred appeared in them. Her lips were tense and her jaw trembled, fourteen years later, thinking about what might have happened in that room where her dignity was trampled on and her innocence punished.

'I remember that it hurt a lot, but apart from making me bleed a bit, the woman couldn't get the child to come out and with a surly face she said to me:

"You're not co-operating, you're closing your legs and squeezing the vagina in such a way I can't do a good job. Besides, I think you lied and you are three or four months gone."

"No Ma'am, I haven't lied, but it's too painful and the fear makes me close my legs."

She went out and said to Germán:

"It's four thousand pesos. I'm charging you half because I can't guarantee it's worked. I think she doesn't want to lose it. Anyway, with what I've done she should expel it this afternoon or tonight."

Alejandra had a stifled voice and she could not contain her weeping.

'So, to cut a painful story short, I can tell you the abortion didn't work and seven months later my daughter was born. I remember that after the "operation" at doña Encarnación's, Germán gave me money for the journey back to my mother's, a thousand pesos for sanitary towels and aspirins and said to me:

"Don't call me, I'll come and find you at your mother's or if you need anything urgently leave me a message at don Gervasio's, who's agreed to cover my back."

I went back to my mother's with my head hanging with sadness and shame.

More than that, I was angry seeing how naïve and stupid I had been, believing what he had said to me in those nights of passion in my room. I felt deceived and abandoned. I grew tired of leaving him messages at don Gervasio's after the girl was born and I never bothered him again.

When my daughter was born, I didn't want her. I left her with my mother to go on working and to continue my life as if I didn't have the responsibility of a child. Now it hurts me to have treated my daughter, who loves me so, so badly. Today she's everything to me. She loves me with all her heart and she would do anything for me. It was the stupidity of youth, or rather, not youth but the maturity we acquire through blows while we're brought up. In the intense search for affection, between the fear and the unknown, giving yourself is the one thing impossible to prevent.

You, *compañeros*, already know about this, know what I'm talking about because your stories are also about the lack of love, of care. All of our stories are unique because we're different, but they're also the same: we've been abandoned by someone who we've loved, be it our father, mother, husband, or boyfriend and that makes our lives similar. Is that not true?' she looked calmly around her and the answer was evident in their faces.

'*Compañera*,' said Daniel, 'you forget a wife's abandonment. My wife abandoned me and it's even sadder, not because I'm a man, but because she abandoned her six children and they missed her dreadfully. She left us vulnerable. I loved her, but she preferred another.'

'I'm sorry Daniel, I didn't mean to remind you of your problem,' mumbled Alejandra.

'Don't worry about that. Now we must look life in the face or we'll be condemned to repeat it. I refused to recognise I was repeating it. I've made mistakes of which I'm ashamed and simply remembering them gives me the shivers. I think I'm a good man, but I don't know if I've done the right thing staying with my children. I only have the four little ones with me now because I lost my older daughters to the war and to the ignorance of not knowing I would repeat my history of abuse.'

Daniel hung his head and was quiet. Each one looked inside themselves and perhaps reflected, as Daniel was doing, on the things they had done without premeditation. So many words said without thinking, so many mistakes they now understood they had made. It was a shared pain and at the same time a shame which could not be shared. It didn't matter that they had not intended to hurt anybody, as each of them knew that knowingly or unknowingly, they had hurt other human beings. Now they were conscious of the abuse and damage, of having been victims and tyrants. They were conscious of having been mutilated and of having wounded the body or soul of their children. They were conscious of having been born to die and having killed others before they had completed their cycle of loving, looking for love and having hated before finding it.

Alejandra waited for Daniel to sit down and picked up the thread of her story:

'To end with, I want to say I don't agree that supporting the guerrilla has necessarily brought us better opportunities. I fought in the guerrilla and believed my sacrifices in the mountains were going to free others like me and my entire country, but now I understand I wanted more than anything to be a heroine and to be recognised by my parents, my siblings and my lovers. I also wanted a way to deal with my helplessness, my anger and my frustration with life. Life had not given me anything good and to lose it was easy, dying was not difficult. The struggle is beautiful when you think you're fighting for your country and when you can develop that spirit of commitment to others, which is so strongly inculcated into us women. But I never fully understood the *muchachos'* politics. I think the majority of us who fought wanted to ward off poverty and reacted against the humiliations we had suffered, but bitterness is not enough to justify the struggle. All of us, in some way, sought happiness and it took some time until we saw clearly that happiness was not to be found dressed in camouflage and rubber boots, eating a disgusting pasta soup you could stand your spoon in.

Love takes women out of the guerrilla and pregnancies, although they're forbidden, are frequently used to escape. But behind every love under the canvas sheeting, every forbidden pregnancy, every dead child, every sick mother, is the repressed wish to be happy. It is also what the men most long for. They want to run away from the hell of sleeping standing on watch and obeying a lout called "commander', who gives orders in the same way the jumped-up farm peasant called "the superintendent" or "foreman" used to. He wants to control your dreams, your stomach, your smiles, every hair on your head and your desire to shout: "I hate this bloody life!"

'I'm sorry *compañeros* for my plain speaking, but we have to tell it as it is. Let's stop lying, when we talk about the change we want for future generations, feeling altruistic and generous, what we really want is change, but for ourselves. We're so frightened of saying it that we hide behind a story of a struggle for others, for our compatriots. In war everything happens, except change. The problems of sexism, privilege, irrational orders, degradation, obedience and not being able to express our feelings, continue. In the name of our country and our people, the war provokes and justifies lies and brutality and when we're in it, it doesn't seem dirty and shameful. The war sanitises our perceptions: a crime becomes an act of bravery, a murderer is a hero, a torturer is a patriot and the perverted sexists, the masters of the immense power of war, these are the good men, brave, strong men of honour.

'What they teach is not change, how could it be change! What they want is to be in the place of those they hate, to take away their power with the same dirty tricks. The war makes us identical to our enemies, who might be our friends tomorrow. What might differentiate us would be our not wanting to be like them in any way, so that even if they mix us up, the differences would be clear. Like water and oil always separate. But it's not the case. On both sides lie armies. What they don't say is that they have the same need for power, the same passions; the guerrilla imitate the army and justify everything. That's why we've come to see the atrocities we have all witnessed.'

The horrors she had seen came out like an unstoppable vomit. The fear was gone and she spoke as if no one else was present. Her intelligence shone in all its splendour and the aggressiveness, which everyone had feared, came through, but with thoughts which, those who knew her, never supposed she would have uttered. The aggressive and disparaging fighter who had caused such trouble on other occasions now showed other facets.

'Let's look at how we talk about the ranks of the guerrilla: "the *muchachos* are here!" It's all about the *muchachos*! The same sexism, as if us women didn't participate. As if this war could have been carried on without the unconditional dedication of thousands of women. They don't acknowledge us either. In the mountains we're equal at the time of combat or death, but in victory or when they speak with respect of the heroes, they only mention men. What displaced persons' neighbourhood has been given the name of a woman killed in combat? What front carries the name of one of our heroines? They remain sexist and violent. They've not suddenly become more violent, but perhaps now they don't mind abusing everyone, rich and poor alike, to collect the war tax. In the war, only the commanders benefit from what's been achieved over the years. Every day, they repeated to us: "Who are the indispensable ones?" and we, the stupid foot soldiers, replied, "those who fight all their lives". But, who fights all their life? The commanders who get used to the power, the money, the privileges, the foreign trips, the women to dominate and the children they can keep and support away from this miserable war. Us, the "guerrilla" the "*muchachos*", "the grassroots," can't have children or families and much less sustain them with our work in the war. We don't go on foreign trips and at the end of the day, we lack a country to call our own because our families run away threatened if they don't agree to their children being in the guerrilla or because the army or the paramilitary persecutes them.

'They claim they protect the people, but at a very high cost, because they take our children. They don't care how much a mother suffers when they take away her son or daughter. They simply say: "Señora, you should feel proud that your son or daughter will serve their country, the liberation, the revolution." Later a paper arrives which informs you of their death, if you're lucky enough to be told. Being the mother of a fighter bestows no rights, not even to know where they died and much less, where they were buried.

'I don't deny I maintain my friendship with them. It's better for me that they respect me a little, which makes it more difficult for them to take away one of my children. I am thirty-five well-lived and well-suffered years old, I can't give them much, but I know my children are important to them. I'm not going to allow them to involve my children in a war which, unfortunately, has left us nothing but pain.'

The emotions were intense and they felt more exhausted than if they had walked for days in the mountains. They were people who were used to hunger and cold, to suffering the severity of the jungle, where the scorpion and the snake were tame compared to the mosquitoes, the serpents or the piranhas. They were used to malaria, but not to the ailments of the soul.

Ana Dolores put up her hand asking to speak and looked at Angela, who was the other person who had not yet spoken. Angela made a gesture of agreement and Ana Dolores began.

Ana Dolores

Her tenderness leaves an aroma of hot guava jam

When Ana Dolores was born, her mother had been through so many births that she knew she would not be frightened by the ordeal. She knew about birth and death. Her husband, after years of love and disaffection, with occasional desires and ten children, did not feel great excitement for this last child, one more consequence of poverty, pain and ignorance.

That day his wife said: "It seems the time has come", and she lay down on the hard old bed. In less than two hours Ana Dolores came into the world to a mother exhausted by giving birth and bringing up children and who knew this would be her last birth as Pedro did not desire her as before. They lived in a small plot of land on the banks of the Magdalena river, in Tolima Grande.

Her mother, Marta, took Ana Dolores in her arms, looked at her and said: "my daughter, you were born from the last throes of desire, therefore you will always love as if it were for the last time." From that moment on Ana Dolores has always loved everything and everyone as if it were her dying wish. Perhaps this is why her tenderness leaves an aroma of hot, guava jam, of warm ripe fruit. She avoids looking into people's eyes not from fear, but out of love. Her eyes are small and astute like a squirrel's, and in the same way it stores food, she hoards the will to live in the midst of war.

She realises few can know her. Behind her kind face they would never imagine the strength she possesses, her capacity for withstanding humiliations and pain with such love that people are baffled, thinking she is foolish.

'I spent my childhood in the Magdalena meadows, where the abundance of land contrasts with the poverty of those of us who live on it. The rapids of the river have carried away the truth of so many dead. Its strength has survived the bodies it has carried, the ones which can never climb its banks. Those dead who floated by without leaving a trace are the only ones who could tell us the secrets of the river of life and death. When we were small, my siblings and I thought death was inevitable, that it shocked when it came as a surprise and you never knew where it came from or where it was going.

When I was three hundred and sixty days old, I learnt what it was to be abandoned. You won't believe me, but I remember the day my father left us and now I've cried for my childhood, I know what losing him meant. He went without looking back, he didn't want to see our anguish and kept his eyes straight ahead. For me it was as if he'd died.

With other children, I ran to school through the meadows by the river. I rested in crags in the path which the river left rounded and smooth to the touch. I remember we could study, we were free and healthy like the sparrows and innocent like children everywhere.'

She grew up and became a woman in and around a canoe. There were so many trips by river that her imagination overflowed during the endless hours afloat and Ana Dolores felt she was more water than land, more breeze than breath. When she came to an island which formed a fork in the Magdalena and she met Juan, there was not much to understand or desire. The water clinging to his hands and feet, the smell of fish and sweat were his and what they called falling in love was as simple for Ana Dolores as having been born, having been abandoned, or existing.

Ana Dolores did not feel she lived and loved. But she sensed distant longings as yet not fulfilled, desires which slipped away unexamined, until the day her brother spoke of justice and freedom. Things began to change the day the guerrilla began to come by regularly. When the *muchachos* arrived they shouted greetings in a jovial tone:

"How are you *compañeras*, good morning."

Five pairs of Tolima women's black eyes rested on a group of young men who came to the pigsty and put down their guns at the door. They looked at each other and calmly went out to meet the visitors.

"Good day, how can we help you?"

It was Ana Dolores' quiet voice from inside the house, shaken and unsure for the first time. She put her hands on her belly, softly prominent with a new pregnancy, and felt a flapping of butterflies warning her.

"We'd like you to sell us a hen, make us some soup and give us something to drink."

Her response was so quick it seemed she had not thought it through.

"Do go on through to the patio. Matilde, Rosa, go get some stools for them to sit on. I only have four big stools and two small ones for the girls, the rest of you can sit on the ground, which is clean."

She went into the kitchen pushing the older ones inside, who seemed transfixed by the appearance of the young men. The smaller ones stayed leaning against the wall with their chins pressed into their chests looking up occasionally, as they did in front of people they did not know.

"Come on girls, don't be silly. Go and fetch your father, who should be arriving at the beach with the canoe, and tell him what's happening."

She went to the yard and caught the oldest hen. She clucked to call the hen towards her, and it came over trustingly. She took the fowl by its feet in a quick and round movement and went into the kitchen, while it shrieked, fearing death. She held it firmly by the wings and put it under her left arm, freeing up her right hand. She then ably twisted the neck, cut the jugular with a knife and waited for the blood to run into the mug she'd put on the floor. She gazed into space so as not to watch how the animal struggled in the throes of death. She did it as quickly as she could and said to her girls in a slow voice:

"Hurry up and peel, chop and wash everything because the *muchachos* must be in a hurry."

As the pot started to boil, Juan arrived with his shirt open, his face sweating and a grimace she knew and which appeared on his weather beaten face when he did not understand what was going on. Juan understood little. He couldn't read nor write and was not interested in knowing anything through words. It was enough for him to know the width of the river, the reality of his trade, the unfairness of the world and that nothing would change, because nothing had changed from the day he was born.

"Hello there," was his only greeting before going into the kitchen searching for his wife's face, while his girls, leaning against the wall, stared at the group who were talking excitedly on the patio.

"What's going on *mija*?"

"The *muchachos* asked me to make them a soup, they'll pay."

"They're armed."

"Of course, *mijo*, can't you see they're guerrillas."

"And what do you think about that?"

"I don't think anything different from what Gonzalo told me the other day. The same as you already know, that they fight for justice and freedom, for the poor peasants."

"So it seems."

A smile appeared on his lips, dried by the sun and breeze. Ana Dolores looked at him and thought maybe Juan finally wanted something.

Poverty, closer to destitution than to life, had made him a quiet, hard and uncommunicative man. Perhaps he spoke with the river and with the fish. Perhaps there, he cried and laughed, or maybe the turbulent waters carried his wishes to other latitudes and he could never reach them, or, rather, he never wanted to wish again for what was not possible, and so little was possible. The clearest thing in his mind was the life of the fish, their essence, their naturalness. He knew them well enough to never mistake the place where he went fishing. When he got them ready he did it with such skill that if someone sat down to watch it, they would be transfixed by the precision of his hands.

As sharecroppers, the only title Ana Dolores and Juan had in life, they had few privileges. They were satisfied when someone gave them the opportunity to clear some land, cultivate it and build a hut for shelter. It was not much, but more than they would have in the years to come. Not much time passed between the arrival of the guerrilla and the appearance of bodies in the waters of the Magdalena, the same as when Ana Dolores was small.

In the beginning, the girls shouted and pointed, but then they got used to watching them go by. Now they were only interested because of the numbers they learnt at school: "that's six, that's seven, that's eight, nine, ten, eleven, that makes a dozen." '

The days went by and life became more difficult for the peasants. Each time a body went down river, they would get a visit from the army or other armed groups like "the Macetos," the "MAS," who claim to kill kidnappers, or simply the "paramilitary" or the "paras" as they were known because they committed massacres with the complicity of the army. They nearly always killed unarmed peasants who were in the fields working. You never saw them confronting other armed groups.

The massacre in Caño Baul was the culmination of this first phase. Ana Dolores knew that in future those known to be left-wing activists or militants would be affected. The time had come to pay for having wanted something as ambitious as justice and freedom. It was common to hear talk of deaths, massacres, persecutions, threats and displacement. Amongst her daily chores she included readying a change of clothes for each child and a pack of fresh food to flee if necessary.

The peasants met as night fell and spoke of death and the course it was taking. Juan, who had never wanted to know anything aside from the creatures of the water, began to participate in the organisation of the party and found he was also good at that. What he had to offer was courage, the desire to no longer bow his head and the resentment stored up in his heart for so many years. He made use of it when confronted by the enemy.

Fear made its appearance in Ana Dolores when she noticed her eldest daughter saw the world with the intensity of someone who has already tasted desire. She knew Matilde did not want a man yet, although she was twelve years old, the age when girls begin to seek their destiny. Her future would not be far removed from that of her mother, her grandmother or other women around her. She knew Matilde had a fierce longing burning inside her and it was the desire for freedom.

'My daughter Matilde, through suffering, not crying, taking care of her sisters, helping me and accompanying her father on long working days, listened when she needed to and understood what she needed to understand, nothing more and nothing less. Everything led her directly to sacrifice. To her it seemed simple and all she could think about was how to avoid the suffering, the pain, how to seek something new and save the family from deprivation. To Matilde, the enemy was not poverty, it was those who didn't let her to go to school without crawling like a snake. The enemy stopped her from laughing loudly and running along the paths, playing hide and seek. What tormented her was not being able to feel like a normal peasant girl.

Things came to a head and we fled one night, leaving everything behind. We went from the cattle farm to the mountains where the humidity killed children and animals alike. I remember a very sad and hard Christmas when Juan wasn't with us because he was hiding for a while and my belly was growing. The rumour went round that they were coming for the guerrillas' families.

It wasn't fear of death which took Juan and all the men over thirteen and under fifty. What made them run was the rumour that they were torturing to get information or to get us to say anything at all. The hunt was on, not for those who put their chests in the way of the bullets, but for those who put their heads together to develop ideas. They hid because it was dangerous to talk, to speak of rights, to dream of change. Juan decided to lie low to prevent us from suffering the horror of knowing he'd died under torture.

In 1982, some families abandoned our makeshift shelters of wood and palm, to sleep rough. That Christmas, the threat of bombings in the zone we had escaped to led us to hide in the mouth of a swamp where no one would think human beings could live. Water squelched underfoot, the children cried constantly and fever was the only thing which calmed their sobs because it made them sleep.

Fear stopped us speaking. We heard nothing but the sounds of nature. We gagged the children so their cries wouldn't give us away and we let them cry until the handkerchiefs were soaked and them we changed them so they wouldn't choke. We communicated with gestures. We seemed a community of prehistoric people, without spoken language. Our food consisted of birds, herons, mountain boars and any wild animal we could catch. The children became more and more unruly. They ran silently, seeking anything to relieve their hunger. Their eyes got used to the dark and the dilated pupils in the undergrowth were not mountain animals, but our children crouching, waiting for death.'

On New Year's Eve, Ana Dolores sent her eldest girl to run an errand.

"Matilde, go carefully into town and buy two batteries so we can turn the radio on tonight."

'That night we listened to the radio so the children could hear music and not lose their minds. I made fritters and custard and the children smiled. That day the children knew we loved them, I heard their hearts beat with the reassuring sound a stone makes when you throw it into a well and it echoes from the bottom. I felt as a tree must feel, when its hard and rough bark shows new shoots. The birds sang and it felt good to hear them and the noise of the trees rocking in the breeze lulled us to sleep. Beauty was not only in nature, but everywhere. That night I felt free to hate those who put us through such misery.

We left the swamp at the beginning of 1983 and went to the mountains. We covered our tracks so they couldn't find us and kill us. We lived in the mountains and to be able to go to school, the children learnt to live a clandestine life. A few families put a school together and a very young teacher took the risk of giving them classes. The children arrived with their clothes black with mud, but with their hearts pounding with excitement. Each day they had to feel the threat of death to be able to learn the alphabet, the colours of the flag and the national anthem of their country.

My children's characters were formed amidst rumours, escapes, bombings, the dead and my company. They were no more than seven, eight, nine and twelve years old and they behaved as if they were guerrillas. They knew all the paths, the shortcuts, the twists and turns of the clear streams, the sound of every mountain animal and the strange and constant sounds of nature. And when they met city people they thought they would be as true as nature, not realising people are false.

One day we decided to protest. Persecution had cleared a number of villages and death had taken the youngest and the most vigorous. More than one hundred families came together from San Lorenzo, Barbacoa, La Ganadera and Chucurí to protest at the Palace of Justice, in the capital city of red soil, of fire in the air and a smell of resin. I wondered whether in the city they would take any notice of us, and I knew the truth presents itself in two ways: how it really is and how it is convenient to believe it is. There and then I felt I was lying to myself, which felt untenable, as I'm guided by desire and intuition. In spite of everything, we all marched and endured days of sun, weariness and anxiety, fearing we might be murdered together. Finally some minimal commitments were signed. The other families went back to the ravaged countryside, with thinner children, convinced they'd been tricked again.

I didn't want to go back. My children needed to study, to know life could be different. I stayed with my brother who had come to live in the city because they were persecuting him. Gonzalo and Gustavo, my brothers, were activists in the Communist Party and were willing to be true to the cause unto death.

When we were at the Palace of Justice, Gonzalo was straight with us:

"Look Ana Dolores, you and Juan should know one cannot join a party which doesn't defend the poor," he said with the face of some one who feels they speak the truth.

"But Gonzalo, what can we do if they push us off our land and the swamp and I only know how to fish," responded Juan who didn't speak of absolute truth, but of the truths he had known in his life.

"Look man, I think you can build a shelter here on this land, put the children in school and you can learn another trade. In the meantime Ana Dolores can work with a family or washing clothes. The important thing is that they don't kill you and you don't bow your head."

Juan looked at Ana Dolores and realised there was nothing to be done, the decision was taken. He would have to learn another trade or go back to the river alone. Solitude had always been his friend, but the taste of life with Ana Dolores had taught him there was another way of existing. He was thirty-four years old, with a severe, coarse face, dark skin and sweet black eyes, which stared wildly in a shocked daze. He was the only boy in his family, after six girls. All he knew was fishing, a trade which he enjoyed and had learnt from his father. He knew everything about the *bocachicos, bagres, nicuros, blanquillos, capaces, amarillos, capitanes, rayados, dormilones, ronchos, palometas* and *sierras.** He knew nothing of the creatures which lived out of the water, but he did not need to understand much to realise his life had changed course dramatically.

Matilde's and Ana Dolores's eyes shone. They understood politics. Matilde knew her mother had been right to prevent her from going with the guerrilla when they had invited her to join the revolutionary army. She loved her mother too much to leave her alone at this time, but it did not extinguish her longing. She reminded herself that not everything which growls is a tiger and not everything which hides is a coward. She quickly began to help her mother build a home with planks of wood and plastic sheeting, where she would sleep with her parents and siblings. The space they had was two by three meters, when previously their boundaries had been the mountains, the meadows and the river banks, but they kept their anger alight and their pride by being part of the struggle.

* Types of Colombian fish.

In the first few days the family regained a new lease on life, finally they could breathe without fear and lead a normal home life, but it was a mirage. You cannot lose so much without something giving. Juan helped to take care of the children, while Matilde left at dawn to wash clothes in a rich neighbourhood. The children went to the neighbour's lots and played, as always, at hiding. They crawled on their bellies, kept silent about their pains and cried inside out of habit. The clandestine life had taken them over so fully that it was many years before they could speak normally again and look at people in the eyes. For a long time they could not trust anybody.

Juan did not feel he had gained anything, and could not adapt to being between four planks staring at the wall. He wanted to go back to his river and the fish. He felt an acute pain in his chest remembering the death throes of the fishes on his canoe and wondered if their pain as their gills burst was the same pain searing through him. He thought that fish at least die struggling to breathe, fighting the murderous hand which has plucked them from the water. He, on the other hand, had given up and was dying in a place not his own, choking the same as the fish, but his agony was longer, his fear prolonged, making living more painful. He was no longer the man of the house. Each day he took on women's work, looking after the children, cooking the food and sweeping the earth which was packed solid from having been walked on every day. Ana Dolores also got a washing job and he stayed put.

He wanted to go back to being the head of the family, to be the breadwinner, to relieve their hunger and regain the position he had within his family. It was not being indoors, or doing housework, or the neighbours, or the army or the MAS which was killing him, it was the ignominy, the depression and the lost status as leader of his pack. The pain was intense and he did not know how to express it. The hatred churned in his stomach and was spat out against whoever was at hand.

The girls were fearful of going near him and the boy, still tiny, looked him up and down not understanding what he had done wrong. Juan's arms flung punches, his legs threw kicks, he flailed as a captured animal would and his lips insulted those he loved.

The punishments meted out to him became, by a trick of memory, soft recriminations which now tasted of sweet bread and honey. The hatred and humiliations imposed on his boyhood soul became wise and clear advice for a man in his armour. The beast within came out because the conditions permitted it.

Once Juan felt he had lost his place in the world, the only woman who had loved him and the respect of his children, he faced death again without a care. Something had broken inside him and the pieces were left scattered on the paths, in the mountains, in the meadows by the river, and at the mouth of the swamp. It was not possible to put them back together. Juan went back alone to fish, as awash with hate as the Magdalena was full of bloated bodies.

The war came with its horror, its confrontation and its own logic. Many peasants were activists in left-wing parties and supported the guerrilla. Their resentments were justified, were grouped together and were hidden under the same slogans. Injustice appeared with each death, truth in the guns, love under the canvas and death all over the place. Peasants killed other peasants for land which became more and more removed from their hands. When they recovered a gun in a battle, they no longer had any one to defend with it. The land they so yearned for, became simply a slogan: "Land for those who work it". No one works it now, only the dead lie in it and the landowners can keep it idle.

In the city poverty covers everything: the houses are yellow with dust and faded like the trees by the road. The open sewers in front of every house, the rottenness of the rubbish, the flies in the children's faces and the mosquitoes which come in clouds at five in the afternoon leaving them covered in sores.

The conditions in the city made Gonzalo decide to risk going back to his land for a few days to bring something to relieve the anguish and the hunger of his loved ones.

"Let's go to our land tomorrow," Gonzalo said to his brother.

"Why take the risk?" answered Gustavo.

"Because we can't sit around expecting Ana Dolores, Matilde and Guillermina to keep us," replied Gonzalo.

"But if we go and they kill us what will happen to your wife and daughter?"

"I don't know, but it's worse sitting around and waiting for hunger or the mosquitoes to consume us."

He took a few steps across the yard and shouted: "Guillermina, get a set of clothes ready for me, I'm going." He looked at Gustavo and said: "if we do it quickly, they won't even notice we were there." Turning his head towards the door, where Guillermina and I had appeared, he said to me:

"Ana Dolores, I leave my wife and daughter in your care until I get back."

"Don't worry, I'll take care of them," I responded. I looked at him and whispered so the neighbours wouldn't hear:

"Be careful, keep a low profile and remember people have big mouths. If they see you, there will always be someone who'll talk. They say that since we left the informers started to talk in earnest, thieves appeared and outsiders took our land. Going back there is dangerous, they're determined to do us in. Don't forget death awaits round every bend in the road and comes when one least expects it. Remember this is a war which has turned nasty. They say Remigio and Gualberto were shot in the back and they never even saw the cowards who tied them up, tortured them and castrated them like beasts."

Gonzalo and Gustavo didn't think too much so fear wouldn't overtake them and they left the next day. Nothing happened. They came back with bananas, yucca, corn and some sickly hens. They were sure no one who they did not trust had seen them and a new hope flickered, tenuously, of going back.

The days went by and there was a drought and power cuts in the cities. Hundreds of families driven out by the violence and hunger abandoned their homes and came to the shantytowns, to their relatives and friends. The blackouts and the lack of work heightened their distress in the first half of the eighties. The country's biggest oil port filled up with people who had come from all over the country. Peasants from Antioquia, Bolívar, Sucre and Santander fled the selective killings of local leaders and those suspected of supporting the guerrilla. The neighbourhoods "beyond the bridge', as the shanties were known by the people of Barrancabermeja, grew. Fifty-two neighbourhoods of mud floors, wooden walls and aluminium roofs were established and the possibility of returning faded. Unemployment was rampant. The men despaired, watching as life went by covered by a filthy, sticky sweat which did not wash off with water because it was not the sweat of work. It stuck to the body and became part of them, as laziness had overtaken their manliness, and it frightened them.

"Well, I see laziness is quickly taking over from diligence," Guillermina observed to her husband.

"No, *mija*, the truth is I pretend to be asleep to keep despair at arm's length, to thwart the hunger and the rage. So I sit here like a fool, and sleep, but my courage keeps me alert and I'm working out a way to get back to our little plot of land."

Gonzalo prepared his second trip, happy to leave a place where neither fear nor bravery were of any use. He went to get food and came back thinking things were getting better and they could return. He made another trip, full of plans, but this time he did not come back.

'Two days later we found out he had been murdered the day he arrived. We found out from a young man from the capital, Miguel Rodriguez. He was at university and was an activist in the Communist Party. He said there was gold on Gonzalo's land and confirmed this was why the violence had been so harsh in our region. They kept Miguel alive to find out about the links between the legal party and the guerrilla,' said Ana Dolores, looking around.

'It seems strange they didn't kill him,' Daniel reflected.

'We thought so too,' responded Ana Dolores, 'I think they made a mistake and the news they had him alive spread too quickly. People from the Human

Rights Committee came to find him and they were taken by surprise and couldn't disappear him.

The church social welfare office, which had been in touch since our demonstrations, knew Gonzalo was a peasant leader. So Rodriguez could trust them and asked them to investigate. They came directly to the house to confirm his story. I remember the day well:

"Hello! Good afternoon. Is there anyone home?" I heard from the door and saw it was a priest from the welfare office.

"Good afternoon father. How can I help you?"

"Well, doña Ana, tell me, did Gonzalo leave for the country?"

I hesitated a little, shocked that he knew.

"*Compañera*, you shouldn't deny it. If it's true, we have some information," said the young woman with him.

My heart jumped and I was immediately filled with anxiety.

"Did something happen to Gonzalo?," I asked, flustered.

"Yes, we're very sorry," responded the father.

"Have they captured him, killed him, where is he?"

"They killed him, according to Miguel, who was with him."

"The one from Bogotá?"

"Yes, him."

I understood then that it doesn't matter how much you run or hide, because if you lose your patience and fear you fall into the abyss, as Gonzalo had.

"Where is he, can I speak to him?"

"I'm afraid not, they're keeping him at the police station. We've already visited him and at least they can't disappear him, but they're not going to let anyone else see him until his file comes from Bogotá."

"How did they kill him?" I asked, with tears filling my eyes.

"Miguel says it was an ambush. Gonzalo tried to stop them from tying him up to save Guillermina and the girl and they killed him on the spot."

"The women, where are they?"

"We don't know yet. Miguel says they took him away to interrogate him and he only saw them taking her by the hair, then he heard a shot and he knew nothing more because they knocked him unconscious."

"Oh God, why? Why them?" I implored looking at the sky, seeking the God who seemed to have forgotten us.

"Child, bring your mother some water," the priest said to Magola, my third daughter.

They made me sit down. They gave me the glass of water and continued:

"The body was left about half an hour from the port on the farmers' main track," said the priest.

"They couldn't have killed him in the middle of the track, surely?" I said surprised.

"It seems after the ambush they moved them to the land of a man called Parmenio," said the woman who had spoken before.

I called the children to come in. When Ernesto returned from running an errand, he stayed with them, and I went to make the police report.

"Sir, I'm here to file a report," I said, trying not to cry.

"Go to the secretary," he said and sent me to a seat in front of the secretary's desk. After the official questions he asked me:

"Now, tell me what you want to report."

"I'm here to report the death of my brother, Gonzalo."

"Tell me what happened," said the secretary.

"I've been informed by neighbours from the Remanso region, that this morning some men in uniform shot him and it seems also his wife. We don't know anything about the child."

"One thing at a time, Ma'am, first, the names of the dead and tell me if you know for a fact they're dead or if it's just a rumour."

"People who were there and know him, told me."

"Names?"

"I don't know."

"Anonymous then?" he said and smiled sarcastically.

"No, they were acquaintances of my brother's. You know peasants come to the port for supplies and return quickly, on your orders."

"And what exactly do you want us to do?"

"Order an investigation and bring the body or bodies back to be buried."

"That we can't do. You know it's a red zone. It's full of guerrillas and we don't go in there."

"So what am I supposed to do?"

"Go to the port and look for the local officers and ask them to find the body. I think they will send you to get it yourself and then give you the death certificate in your village. From here we'll continue with the investigation, if you like. Of course without knowing or identifying the perpetrators it will be difficult," he paused and continued, "you're his sister? You should go to fetch the body. Blood seeks its own."

"Yes, I'll bring him back," I answered.

I left it there. My voice trembled and I didn't know if it was anger or the effort to not cry. I loved Gonzalo terribly and I couldn't understand why he had been such a fool, believed things were going to get better when they had never been good. He was so knowledgeable about politics, he learnt so much in the party, so much struggle to fall in an ambush.

I couldn't sleep that night. With my eyes open or closed, I saw his face and at dawn I was fighting against his memory. I cried without making any noise because I was scared. His death proved there were informers in our neighbourhood. They had been waiting for him.

Even after we buried him, the neighbours kept coming to pay their respects. I imagined one of them was the informer and anxiety rose in my throat, making me feel sick.'

'I feel the *compañera* has gone off the subject,' interrupted Mercedes.

'It's true,' answered Ana Dolores, 'but it wasn't my childhood which led me to take part in the war, or at least it was no different from what others have recounted. My mother was not harsh, but living in a region so rich and violent has marked me forever and I understood that's what I should talk about, am I wrong?'

'You're not wrong, but we can leave your story there and come back to it when we talk of the most significant incidents of violence,' responded Daniel.

'We're about to finish and we still have the afternoon to listen to Angela. Why don't we let Ana Dolores finish, have lunch and in the afternoon let Angela tell her story?' Socorro asked the group.

'What happened with the bodies?' asked Marcos.

'They only killed my brother. Guillermina and the girl survived and were hiding with some neighbours, friends of Gonzalo's.'

Ana Dolores realised she was able to tell the whole story and it was not so painful. She could speak without crying and most importantly, she did not clam up.

'The morning after the tragic news we went to the port to rent a motorboat for the trip there and back because we were sure no one would help us, from fear. We left at seven in the morning. The Party had a collection and they gave us money for the boat and to rent a mule, to retrieve the body from the track. We hadn't reported Guillermina's or the girl's death because we thought it would be dangerous if they were still alive. I didn't know where she was, but if they hadn't killed her, they would let her go because killing her was of no use to them. The killings were selective. They only killed the leaders.

We walked to the village to find a mule to carry the body. As we went past, everyone closed their shutters and doors, knowing it was best not to get involved, not even to hire out a mule. At the police station I asked them to help me get the body. We had already discussed how to do everything, how to inquire about

Guillermina and the girl, if they were still alive, and how we'd ask for the mule from the police post to avoid implicating friends.

I took the mule by the reins. Juan, who had arrived at dawn, was right behind me and Matilde followed him, silent and angry, brooding thoughts tinged with hate. We found the place easily because vultures flew over the body, which was decomposed, as it had been in the sun for two days. I had to put my hand over my mouth to stop myself from omiting and it was a big effort to not faint.

Before us was Gonzalo, thirty years old, with a disfigured face, his body ripped open by the birds of prey who fought over him and his hands and feet black with flies and ants devouring the young flesh. As best we could, we frightened away the insects and with Matilde's and Juan's help, I wrapped him in a sheet and put him in the black bag the police had given us. We put him on the mule and walked back to the village. There, we went through the formalities of identifying the body and receiving the death certificate. When the bureaucracy was done with we took him to the boat, arrived in Barrancabermeja, presented the death certificate, took him home and then to the cemetery. I didn't cry again for six years.'

One thousand and eight hundred days Ana Dolores lasted with her chest crushed, with those images in her memory, appearing calm, but with rage and fear inhabiting the place within her Gonzalo had occupied. After his funeral she never went back to the cemetery. She was frightened of herself, of what churned in her every time she remembered Gonzalo. That's why she kept quiet for so many years and her mourning was suspended until recently, when she thought the time had come to talk.

'Guillermina, in the middle of the confusion of the ambush, heard Gonzalo shout, "run *mija*, run," and she ran away with the girl, who she was carrying. She remembered two shots and a hand brutally grabbing her, pulling her by the hair to where they had murdered him. They took the girl away from her. Then, she heard as they beat Miguel up shouting, "You son of a bitch guerrilla, so you've came to support the guerrilla…", "where are the weapons?" Protests and more blows. Then, silence and she thought they had killed him. She trembled and cried. They asked her a few things and quickly realised she knew nothing. They gave her back the child and said: "We're going to leave your husband here to teach all the other bastards who come to help the guerrilla a lesson." Then, one of them turned around and shot Gonzalo in the face. He looked at her and said: "get lost bitch, quick, quick, quick or do want us to do the same to you?"

Guillermina lost her mind. Months went by and she was no better. She was apathetic and stayed in the house. She wouldn't take care of the girl, eat, or talk. She didn't even cry. Her vitality, which had distinguished her until the day before Gonzalo's death, had disappeared. She sat in a kind of vegetating stupor which discouraged those who tried to comfort her until, one day, without understanding what was going on, and desperate for the child, I said to her:

"Look woman, can't you see you daughter cries and needs you, come on, get up and look for work."

"I don't want to see her. I don't want to see or know anything or anyone which reminds me of Gonzalo," she said with a long face and tight lips. Her eyes were permanently opaque and distracted.

"Come on, you have to get over this and find work. I can't deal with everything alone. Let's go to the Family Welfare office and they'll say you should take care of your daughter."

"Leave me be, *comadre*, I don't want her," mumbled Guillermina.

I made her go anyway and they said that if the mother or the family didn't want her they'd give her away in adoption. Then I knew blood is thicker than water. I took the girl by the hand and decided to take care of her as my own. She was the only good thing the violence left us.'

After Gonzalo's death, Juan, who'd been going to and fro to be with her on Sundays, became delirious with the terror of being persecuted and seemed on the brink of madness. Ana Dolores did nothing to stop him from feeling afraid because it was confidence which had killed Gonzalo. She knew he suffered, but to keep him alive, she didn't try to console him.

It was one-thirty when Ana Dolores finished and they all got up silently.

They returned in better spirits. Facing their problems was working and they felt liberated. The time between beginning work and coffee lent itself to hugs and jokes and compliments. Quiet conversations in twos and threes recreated their intimacy easily.

'Now it's my turn to face the music,' Angela said seriously.

Without comment, the group took their seats.

Angela

Paths drawn at will

The silence resembled the hush in a sacred place, and indicated they were ready to listen to Angela and she began resolutely:

'My memory begins when I was seven years old. Of the previous years, I have vague memories of some episodes. I was born in the Yari Plains, at the time when farms were so large no one knew a whole one in its entirety. The Plain was considered both beautiful and terrible; my uncles said it was so huge that both radiant life and horrific death were contained in it comfortably. At that time, death didn't await one at every turn, as it does now, but it was respected by all. The Plain is frightening,' she said dramatically, her eyes widening to add drama her story, 'but fear of the Plain doesn't freeze the heart, it's a hot fear like its immense solitude, closer to the fever of its palm groves.'

Angela recounted how her grandfather sat on a stool every night at the entrance of the house. He would lift her onto his lap while the other, older children, sat on the ground to listen to the stories he told of the plains, a land he had loved wholeheartedly ever since he was introduced to it.

'My grandfather repeated the stories to us hundreds of times. He said it was a good way of learning. I remember many of the stories and to keep the tradition, I've told them to my children and they've told them to theirs. If it wasn't for the violence, all of my descendants would have known the plains in their splendour and terror.

I'll tell you what I consider to be important in this context, as they say these days, so you understand where and how we lived. My grandfather was forty-something, very tall, with Indian features, brownish-gray eyes like mine and black, shiny, curly hair. His Indian blood shone through in his copper-coloured skin, his thin lips and his agile hands for weaving straw. At about three in the afternoon, when he finished work and after a succulent lunch, he rested awhile. After his sleep, he played the guitar and when the afternoon drew in and you could see the last rays of the sun setting over the plains, he called us grandchildren and started with the stories: "Children, you must respect and care for the plain because the plain can drive you crazy. The madness of the plain is man's imagination before a wide, free land, without mountains to contain it, without boundaries in sight, without limit to hope. A good war was conceived here and the land saw its best men fall. The liberators of this country came from this land. They arrived naked at the plateau above the capital, and from there conquered the whole of the plains, which seems infinite to us. Very few know it fully. Here, on the plain, the wildest untamed colt is tamed and the bravest man is brought low. Do you know why we work on the plain from before sunrise?" "No grandfather, why?" we all shouted together. "Well, you see children, on the plain a day's work is done so the man of the plains can enjoy the heat of the afternoon in his hammock and when he opens his eyes, he can see in the distance how the dry shrub lands burn crimson when there's no water, or how the emerald green of the plant shoots sprout tender tips when the rains come.

Furthermore, we work this way because the man from the plains knows he cannot allow himself the luxury of dreaming, it would be rash to allow the soul to wander faced with a unique cow."

"What do you mean, faced with a unique cow?" asked Joselo.

"You clever boy, that's a good question. A unique cow is a special cow, of a size no one imagines is possible. Here we can still find them in the wild, but when we take them from the farm to sell them to the abattoir at the port, they say they look like buffalo and ever since I was a boy, they would say: oh yes, that's a unique cow! We call them unique, because there are none like them in any other corner of Colombia, they're singular, like the plains."

"Grandfather, how do you go mad for the better? I thought that you only went mad for the worse," asked Rosaura.

"Very good Rosaura, now you're starting to have use of your reason. You can go mad for the better when you use it to sing, to compose songs, to love with freedom, to hunt the heron and find its nest full of feathers, with which you can get rich or make the softest bed for your lover. You can go mad for the worse when you suspect everything and you use prayer and trickery to stab someone in the back; or when you keep a jealous watch over your wife with visions of adultery, or because she laughs or sings. You can go mad for the worse when the fever of money grips you and takes over everything and makes the man of the plain capable of selling his wife or giving away his children to rubber workers who make them into slaves in exchange for a miserable payment which he confuses with great wealth.

This land you see every day is ideal for enterprise and bravery. We've always dreamt of reaching the horizon and its hope. In this land all paths are drawn at will, as with life when you make it your own. Beasts are tamed to carry men and men to not be dominated by the beast within. The hens lay eggs when they come down from the *totumo* and *merecure* plants so the children who populate the palm groves grow up healthily. The partridges don't hide, but skip between the fields to feed the cowboys who work a long way from home. Everything here is kept in balance. The flock of parakeets fly by, indicating where there's a herd of guinea pigs to hunt. The marsh birds guide us with their caramel wings to find turtle eggs to extract their oil. The white herons, serene and silent, accompany us fishing, to show us where the fish are, and later, the fish, dried in the sun and salted, make us firm and strong and give us flexible wrists to show off in the *coleo*.*

The herd of young angry bulls gallop, following our shouts and the unbroken mares approach the water holes greeting the whinny of our tamed horses. That's how life beats on the plains. At night, silence reigns in the house and when there's

---

*A type of rodeo, where a man catches the cow by its tail and wrestles it to the ground.

a full moon the distance deepens. Perched on the branch of the *totumo* the cock dreams of the hawk and his cry of fear causes a commotion in the chicken coop. The dogs, asleep in the yard, lift their heads and their ears straighten when the cock crows, but when they quickly discover it was a false alarm, they put their noses back between their paws again." '

'What lovely stories, Angela,' said Ana Dolores 'your grandfather sounds wonderful, don't you think *compañeros*?'

'It's marvellous to hear how the plain used to be, its customs, before all this killing. I was remembering many things I've heard when I was growing up,' said Marcos.

'When I arrived in Macarena, I couldn't believe such a beautiful and civilised place existed. Were it not for the cocaine and the guerrilla, it would be paradise,' said Mercedes.

'I lived in paradise too but there I also found death and pain. We destroy everything which could bring us happiness and wealth. It's as though we were cursed,' murmured Socorro.

'We should let Angela continue her story,' interjected Antonia.

Angela picked up her thread again.

'My childhood was lovely, but also sad because I didn't have my mother at my side as I was born out of wedlock. Nothing worried me then, all I did was run, eat, laugh and wait for the evening to come to listen to my grandfather's stories. He ran the farm and was brave. He hunted tigers with my uncles because they killed the calves at the banks of the rivers when they came to drink water. Such was my life until the day my grandmother said to me:

"Angela, your mother has written. She wants us to take you to live with her because she wants you to go to school."

I was happy because my mother asked for me and from that moment my grandmother began to prepare our trip. My grandparents spent a month getting ready because they took advantage of the trip to fish, collect turtle-egg oil and buy goods for the next six months at the farm. My grandfather readied the canoe for our long journey. He built a cabin with sugarcane branches and palm leaves for the roof, for my grandmother and us small children to shelter from the sun and the rain. During the trip she worked, darning clothes, making hats for everyone, making pouches to store the goods and clothes and every day she shucked the corn cobs to feed the chickens and hens we brought to sell in town. On the way, we ate their eggs, if we couldn't find turtle eggs, and the rest we kept to sell at the market.

In the bends of the river we found groups of turtles to eat and we crushed their eggs to extract the oil from them. When we had a lot of them, we crushed them inside a small *potrillo*, which is what a small canoe is called. Then, we ground them, poured enough water in the canoe to cover them and left them in the sun. The next day the oil floated on the water, we collected it and fried it until it was purified. Then, we preserved it in leather pouches. Turtle oil was excellent and earned enough to pay for the household expenses for six months or longer. If we found many eggs, we sold the oil and bought clothes and goods to take back to the farm.

During the trip we also fished. We hung the salted fish on cords and dried it in the sun. We filled up sacks to sell it at market. The trips were long, busy and memorable. My brother and I ran along the beaches by the river. We killed flies, collected white, red, grey and bluish stones we liked. At night we would camp and hang the hammocks, while my uncles cleared the area around us, brought wood and my grandmother made a fire to cook on. They kept the fire going all night to frighten away the tigers. We took days to get to where my mother was waiting for me.

"*Mija*, you're so big!" she made me turn around to see me better. I felt shy, looked down and my heart thumped, making so much noise I thought my mother would notice I was embarrassed.

"Greet your mother, Angela," said my grandmother.

"Good day, mother."

"Hello, daughter."

"How are you?" my grandfather asked my mother.

"I'm well, father, and yourselves?"

"Old, but hearty," answered my grandfather.

My uncles came over after mooring the canoe, which they left with my brother Justo. My mother looked his way and waved. He waved back shyly.

"How are you?" my mother asked my uncles, Miro and Jacobo.

"Not bad, Carmenza."

"Go on to the store and drink something before unloading. Have you brought oil and animals to sell?"

"Yes, the fishing and oil collection were good this year. Etelvina has brought chickens, hens, eggs and fat guinea pigs," replied my grandfather.

"It would be best to go to bed early, get up at dawn and catch the first buyers."

"We'll unload tomorrow. We can leave the goods in the canoe and sleep there," said Jacobo.

We fetched our hammocks to hang them on the patio in my mother's house. It must have been about five o'clock in the afternoon because it was cool, although the wind was warm, which meant the sun must have been shining on the palm groves.

We rose in darkness, lit the candles, drank thick coffee to wake us up and unloaded the canoe with my uncles. We tied up the hen's feet and hung them, head down, from a long pole. The eggs went in a basket and the guinea pigs in a cage from the farm. We gave them food and water because they looked a little worse for wear from the trip and we wanted them to look good to get the best price. My mother, my uncle Jacobo and my brother Justo went first with the pouches of oil and the bags of corn, which were heaviest. My grandparents carried the animals and I carried the water in an earthen jug to keep it cool in the hot morning sun.

Once we'd sold everything, we went shopping ourselves. My grandmother told my grandfather, Agapito, to buy me two sets of good clothes:

"*Mijo*, buy Angela two sets. It might be the last thing we get her in many years."

They bought me shoes which were too large for me, and rubbed my feet because I'd only ever used espadrilles.

When my grandparents, my uncles and my brother left, I felt a little sad, but the joy of living with my mother was greater than missing them. But my happiness was briefer than the flight of a stone curlew. She had organised for me to go to a convent orphanage which educated poor girls without relatives. I didn't understand how I fitted that description when I had my grandfather, my grandmother, my uncles, Jacobo and Miro, my cousins, Rosaura, Joselo, Martin, Gabriel, James, José Luis and my uncles' wives were pregnant. Furthermore, the nuns didn't know my brother Justo existed and with him and my mother, we were a big family. Later I realised my mother hadn't lied and not having a family meant not having a father. My mother took me to the boarding school the following week because my father, who was a married man, had threatened her with taking me away with him. I didn't understand anything, but neither could I ask. My mother was a stranger even though I loved her. Many years later, when I was a young woman, I found out my father was very jealous of my mother because she was living with another man. That man was his eldest son, in other words my half-brother, who by living with my mother, ended up being my stepfather.

It took two days' travel to reach the boarding school. First we rode in a lorry to Puerto Leguizamo, then we walked twenty-five kilometres to the Ingaparana, a boat which went to Puerto Asís, where the orphanage was.

The nuns came out to meet us. They asked my mother if I'd been baptised, if she still worked mending army officers' uniforms and they told her she should come at least once a year so I wouldn't miss her too much. When she left, I felt my whole body go cold. The farewell was like her greeting, sharp and simple:

"Angela, I'm leaving you here so you'll be educated and not ignorant like me. You should obey the nuns always. They have my authority to do whatever they feel is best for you. They can punish you, hit you or leave you without food if you're bad, do you understand?"

"Yes, Ma'am."

"Whenever I can, I'll come to see you. I hope you take advantage of this opportunity that God, in his infinite mercy, has granted you."

She looked back at the nun who was seeing her off and said:

"Thank you again for the chance you're giving my daughter. May God repay you." Without giving me a hug or a kiss, she smiled at me, turned around and left. I began to pout and cry quietly so she wouldn't hear me. The nun put an arm around my shoulders and softly pushed me into the building saying:

"Angela, this is a moment of sacrifice which Our Lord Jesus Christ asks of you. In return, he will give you the opportunity to be educated in his doctrine and study to leave ignorance behind you. With these two lessons you'll become a good Christian woman. How you're treated will depend on your obedience, meekness and sacrifice. Try, as your mother said, to be good, make the most of your time in school and you'll achieve good results."

The days went by and I cried all the time: when I got up, at lunchtime, in Mass, when I helped in the bathroom or the kitchen, during study hours and when I went to sleep. The food was horrible. It was a type of Indian food made up of cassava and yucca flour which, mixed together, made us fat in no time. Time mitigated the pain and finally I was absorbed into the social life of the school. There were over two hundred girls aged between seven and fifteen. They appointed one of the older girls to "mother" me. She taught me and helped me adapt. I learnt to dress myself, to tie my shoes and to brush my hair and tie it well back. At five in the morning we left for the town's church to attend Holy Mass. Afterwards, we ate breakfast at the orphanage and at seven we had our first class. At nine we were in church again to visit the Holy One, then back to school to study. At twelve, to the church for Angelus and at night we prayed the Holy Rosary. The first Friday of every month there was another outing at the Holy Hour and between prayers, four years of my childhood passed. The discipline was rigorous and there was someone responsible for every task or activity required for the perfect running of the community.

"The girls who've joined this year should learn that here every one has their work," said the Mother Superior, "depending on the age and behaviour of each. You'll rotate all tasks, accompanied by an older girl who will teach you and be your tutor and 'mother' during your time here."

Of the twenty nuns, most were foreigners and only two Colombian. My mother visited me once, three years later. She had not been able to leave her work again after the days she had taken off to bring me in the first place. She wrote to tell the nuns the soldiers were angry with her on her return because the woman she had left in her place, doña Martina, had washed and ironed the shirts and uniforms badly. They told her if she asked for leave again, she'd have no job to come back to. So she sent me letters and the things I asked for through the boat operators.

We saw each other again when I was twelve years old. I was a good student and did as I was told, which earned me the sisters' praise. In addition, I was the only one who didn't leave for the holidays and when the rest of the girls went away, they treated me like one of them. The best food, juices, fruits, cheeses, eggs, meats and everything they ate. I even tried things from their countries and tasted, for the first time, tinned food and foreign biscuits.

When my mother came, they said they were very pleased with me and told her not to worry about leaving me over the holidays, as they would always take care of me. They wanted me to continue my studies in Pasto, where the orphanage had a secondary school. My mother went home and recounted proudly what the sisters had said. When doña Martina found out, she said:

"Doña Carmenza, they told me in the square your daughter is going to study at Pasto next year."

"Yes, doña Martina, imagine how proud I am of Angela."

"Well, if I were you, I wouldn't allow it."

"What do you mean?"

"Don't you know once those nuns offer higher education, they never let the girls go?"

"No, doña Martina, I didn't know that."

The following year, on the basis of that comment and without any other evidence, my mother took me out of school, saying she needed help with her work and she had a piece of land to build a home on. She came to fetch me from the orphanage once I was settled and happy. The year she took me away she brought my brother Justo, and put him in the boys' orphanage on the other side of the church.

In my last year, Ofelia, who was my "mother", had to leave and I felt abandoned again. When it was our turn to clean out the chicken coop, which had over a hundred hens, Ofelia didn't show up and sister Gertrudis came instead.

"Reverend sister, where's my mother?"

"Ofelia was sick last night and her uncle came for her."

"She didn't say goodbye to me. Reverend sister, do you know if she'll come back?"

"I doubt it, she's grown up now and her uncle needs her," she said ending the conversation and leaving me in tears.

With each departure, I felt more convinced no one truly loved me. My grandparents had handed me over without fighting to keep me; my mother gave me to the nuns without looking back and Ofelia had now done the same. That day I was unwell and the food made me sick. I vomited all night and my temperature went up to forty degrees for a few hours. I was delirious and I called out for Ofelia. But nothing changed and I had to go on obeying and repressing how I felt to avoid punishment. I could receive up to one hundred lashes with a studded whip they used for penance.

When my mother came to take me home we went through Puerto Ospina where some girls who'd been in the orphanage saw me and shouted:

"Angela aren't you going to come and see Ofelia and father Anastasio's son?"

"Holy Mary, what are you talking about."

"If you don't believe us, Angela, see for yourself."

I stepped off the boat and looked for my mother, who was buying special thread for the army uniforms and I asked for her permission to go and see my mother Ofelia. She said:

"Fine, go, but don't be long because the boat could leave any minute."

I ran off with my two friends from school to Ofelia's house. She was sitting in the doorway of the house on a stool with a cradle at her side and a boy sitting in it. When I reached them, I realised he was identical to father Anastasio. He had blonde hair, blue eyes and white skin. I went up to Ofelia and, full of emotion, I hugged her as she got up with her arms outstretched. After the first excitement had passed I whispered:

"What happened, Ofelia? Will you be turned into the devil's mule?"

"Oh, Angela, how young you are. You still believe everything Mother Superior tells us."

"Yes, but, Ofelia, I thought when a woman got involved with a priest, the devil put a bit on her and destroyed her mouth pulling on the reins."

"You can see it's not like that. You going home is for the best, now you won't go through what I did."

"It was in the retreat room, wasn't it?"

"Yes, little Angela, the father takes advantage when we're made to confess in the room they have for retreats. I don't think I was the first, nor do I think I'll be the last. The Mother Superior was not surprised and worked everything out quickly and secretly. A decision was made to kick me out of school as if nothing had happened."

"You know, Ofelia, father Anastasio also left and there's a new one called Gabriel."

"I hope they stop having confessional in the retreat room and leave the young girls by themselves less often."

I didn't know how babies were made and I understood even less how the sisters and the Mother Superior, who were so good, had kicked Ofelia out and forgotten about her and the boy. Especially this little boy who looked like a pure angel of God. I quickly associated her misfortune with mine and said:

"Don't worry Ofelia, I'm also a child born out of wedlock, like your son, and I've survived."

"Angela, you're so innocent," she said stroking my head, "Go to your mother and appreciate her, because you're lucky to have her. I'm telling you as an orphan. You don't know what it's like putting up with my uncle Antonio, it's worse than the suffering of Our Lord Jesus Christ. You must learn not to believe so many foolish tales of devils and penance," she smiled at me and said, "don't worry about me. I'm not going to be the slave of any devil with horns and a tail. Hell is here on earth and the devil is any man." She hugged me, kissed me on the forehead and pushed me towards the door. I went back to the boat and on the journey I remembered the nuns' four years of lessons. I felt it was too soon for everything I believed in to crumble. I didn't know it was to be the least of my troubles and after seeing Ofelia I began to understand the evil of the world and to die a little each day.'

Angela's story had been so detailed that everyone sighed when they thought she had reached the end. Her childhood appeared to be relatively good and she had not mentioned the armed conflict. It was odd to get to know Angela through stories of her childhood. A few hours earlier, no one would have bet a penny on Angela being a docile and obedient child. Now she was a brave woman, hard and aggressive. She had a personal history characteristic of a peasant leader. Everyone knew she had lost children in the war. She had not said a word about the war. She got up, went to the kitchen and poured herself a coffee. Everyone stirred in their chairs, they stretched, yawned, looked at each other and the silence was palpable. For them, Angela was a figure of authority.

She came back with her coffee and looked at them all. When she frowned, her eyebrows joined to create a warning signal. Everyone sat down automatically. Her brows parted as quickly as the flap of the wings of a hawk. She was not used to accepting sympathy from anyone and much less from her *compañeros*; she did not tolerate tenderness or anything which would make her feel weak, either. It was the way she was in response to her considerable feelings for the cause, for her dead children: to not go soft when it mattered.

She believed she had a sixth sense, and she claimed to recognise witches at a glance. The *brujeadores*, as they were known on the plains, could cause great damage and put the evil eye on children and adults. But they could not hide from each other and they never looked into each others' eyes for fear of suffering evil eye. If it was cast between *dañeros*, it could prove fatal. She had passed onto her children beliefs of all kinds. She was recognised in her community as some one who could wield the powers inherited and learnt from the Indians, and consequently she was widely respected.

Angela's superiority, her domination over others and the fear she inspired seemed to stem from being silent and guarded. It was useless trying to get a secret out of her; no one could second guess her and nobody knew her true feelings. The disconcerting silence she sometimes maintained bothered her *compañeros*. Everyone wanted to know what she thought. She spoke calmly, with a querulous voice which seemed to spring from an androgynous devil inside her. Her voice was deep, like the murmur of the jungle and sharp, like the wailing of the wind.

When she spoke of her sons, the males of her lineage, all killed in combat, her voice was a plaintive wail. She seemed to hear their pitiful cries, calling for her in the midst of battle.

'I don't think we can invalidate the armed struggle, comrades,' she said with her authoritative voice, 'my sons can't have died in combat without their sacrifice being of some use. As a woman, a mother and comrade I won't accept it. My children were rebels and wanted to live as warriors and they died as heroes die, in combat. I spent my best years bringing them up and I taught them my ideals. I participated with them and also fought to build a better world for everyone. It didn't work out. Now that I'm an old woman, I don't have anything to offer the struggle. My pain is constant, for the death of my sons, for the orphaning of my grandchildren, for my husbands' betrayals and for the constant injustice against my class. It's hard for me to admit we've worked and died each day and each night to achieve nothing. I continue to be convinced we must keep dying, giving birth and bringing up soldiers for the revolution.

I'm too old to change my principles. Maybe I'm here to see if I can continue fighting with other means, not because I want to, but because I cannot go on fleeing, hiding, and participating shoulder to shoulder with the young people. My muscles are no longer supple enough to run, my eyes cannot see with the sharpness of a mountain cat and my nose can no longer smell danger as the palm grove dogs can. But my mind and my heart are strong and my anger has never waned. The injustices committed against my children and remembering those who shot my son in the back keep the pain alive and that's enough to seek to change my world.'

No one dared interrupt her. Her voice had the weight of absolute truth. Having handed over her sons to be sacrificed, without arguing, she deserved the silence with which everyone offered their recognition, but their looks said more. You could easily see in their faces the decision to continue the next day.

Part Two
This is the War

Gabriela

Death is not one, but many

They took the weekend off to rest before continuing the work. They returned with smiles on their faces, longing to accomplish the proposed challenge. Now they would examine the violence which had displaced them and explain their participation in the war. They had reflected and were ready to give the best of themselves and between them, to seek the path to reconciliation.

Gabriela asked Mercedes to finish the story her mother had told her. Mercedes took up the story again to Gabriela's adolescence:

'Gabriela spent two years in her grandfather's care. Mariana, who was proud of her daughter, decided to look for him to confront him with all her repressed hatred. She was seeking an explanation for her childhood neglect. Her father, now a grandfather, with the guilt weighing heavier than his years, decided to give Gabriela the care he had dreamed of giving Mariana after she disappeared. She wanted to understand the explanations he gave her, but she never forgave him for his unsuccessful search. Every caress her father bestowed upon Gabriela was a blow to Mariana, as the bitterness she had cultivated over the years remained.

"I'm going to find work and I'm taking the girl with me," she said to her father one morning.

"But, Mariana, you can't leave so soon after arriving. Please don't take Gabriela."

"She's coming with me because children should never be abandoned," she said pointedly.

"You're right, but why don't you work here. This is your home and your family is here."

"No, father, this is not my home, I'm independent and I've been alone since I was a girl, don't you remember?"

"Yes I know, but if you don't want to work here, at least let the girl stay, so she doesn't wander as you had to. We'll take care of her and you can send money when you can."

Mariana went to a nearby town and took Gabriela with her. The work ran out as quickly as her resentment for her father and she returned to his house and left the girl there. She went to the city to find work. It was the first time Mariana had been away from Gabriela and her pain showed in the bags under her eyes, in her lack of appetite and in the sadness which enveloped her. When people asked her about her sorrow and she retold the story of her life, she saw her childhood repeated in her daughter and felt embittered.

Mariana was so responsible and diligent in her work that the possibility of bringing Gabriela to live with her soon became a reality. The years they spent together made Gabriela learn to love her and consider her her guardian angel. When Gabriela went to school, Mariana realised the money she earned was enough to cover their physical needs, but was not sufficient for the needs of the soul. Mariana found a paradoxical way to alleviate those needs: selling her body on the road leading to the port where other women lined up to fill their stomachs. She realised she was capable of anything to give Gabriela the chance of a better life. She left doña Marcelina's house and Gabriela in her care. She found her place under cover of the night; darkness was her friend and accomplice, from the days living rough on the mountains, to the present half-light of the hotel room. She knew how to suppress her most intimate needs so it was not painful for her to live in the place where men buy love with money. To her that was all men's love consisted of: a moan in the dark, a payment for each groan, whisper or false caress. For years she saw the girl to bring her presents, books, sweets. It was the only way Mariana knew of showing her love.'

Gabriela interrupted Mercedes and said:

'I'll carry on from here,' she said with a frown. Her round face seemed severe and determined; she ran her long fingers with their short, polished nails through her hair in a nervous gesture. She thanked Mercedes for her kindness in telling the story, got comfortable in her seat and continued.

'Everything was fine until I started sixth grade. It was June and the holidays were coming up, when, in a playground fight, some one said sarcastically in front of my other classmates:

"I bet you don't know where Gabriela's mum works."

"Where, where?" they shouted.

"On the road to the port, where the whores are."

I felt my heart was going to explode, right there and I thought I would die of shame and anger.

"That's not true, you bloody Indian! If you speak badly of my mother again I'll punch your face in!" I reacted very badly when someone offended me.

"Ask around, or look for her and you'll see I'm not lying and neither is my mother. She saw her go into a café at the port."

I punched her twice and ran home choking back my tears. I wanted to die, to be far away from everyone. I didn't know what I had done for Mary to have humiliated me so. I was conceited, but nothing could justify her viciousness.

I was so upset when I got home that doña Marcelina, who was almost a mother to me, confirmed what Mary had shouted. I cried and waited in anguish for the day I was supposed to meet my mother. I was anxious to see her, and yet I also never wanted to see her again. I wanted my image of her as my protector untouched, I wanted to live without a care, all to appease the stupid pride of a spoilt adolescent.

That day I had to recall my grandfather's affection to overcome my murderous instincts. I wanted to kill my mother, to see her face smashed up. I wanted to see Mary with her legs and back marked by the thrashing I gave her in my imagination. I wanted her to plead for forgiveness for having insulted my mother. I discovered hatred and the monster hidden in my heart. I remembered my father was one of those macho bandits and, for the first time, I yearned for him. Near him, no one would dare insult me.

Time passed and Mariana didn't come. She tried to overcome her fear of confronting Gabriela. When she thought she was ready, shame paralysed her and her courage abandoned her. The more effort she put into getting a grip of herself, the more her courage seeped out of her, her mind became a black hole and she was petrified of Gabriela looking at her.

Gabriela decided to look for her mother without telling anyone. She walked up and down the road to the port looking at the houses, examining them closely. Most of them were in ruins, with metal nets over the windows to keep the mosquitoes from the nakedness of sex. They had rusted windows, chipped walls and signs promising pleasure. The red light bulbs, filthy and covered with flies, caught Gabriela's attention more than the tired and lazy inhabitants, depressed by memories of lost dreams.

The women looked at her strangely. Many must have thought she was a new victim who had come to exchange her virginity for cash and others thought she was lost. But no one said anything to her and she walked up and down the road three times without daring to ask for Mariana. It wouldn't have helped anyway, as Mariana was known as Ester and hardly anyone knew her story. One of the few who did was the owner of the house where she worked. They had become friends and she understood Mariana, but did not agree with her way of protecting her daughter. Gabriela waited for a miracle and Rosaura made it happen. She was a young girl, not even eighteen, and she remembered Ester was always talking about her daughter and once she had shown her a photo. She went to the house where Ester slept and said:

"Doña Ester, I think your daughter is out there looking for you. Go and get her because men are lying in wait and this is definitely not the place for her!"

"It will never be her place!" Mariana answered in a pained voice, but stayed put.

"Well, go on then, or you'll have no one to blame but yourself," Rosaura spat out as she left, frustrated by the passive response and mumbled to herself, "that's what I get for trying to help..."

"Mariana!" chided María Isabel, the owner of the house, "Rosaura is right, you have to go out and confront her or it will be too late. This is no place for girl like your daughter."

Mariana ventured forth nervously and she could not utter a sound when she saw Gabriela. She took her by the arm and led her to the house where María Isabel welcomed her calmly and Mariana withdrew embarrassed.

I looked at doña María and without any great formality, she said to me:

"*Mija*, may I call you that?" I looked at her in silence and agreed by nodding my head, "what has brought you here?"

"I've come to talk to my mother, Mariana. I've found out what she does and I want to know why she lied to me."

"It's very simple, Gabriela, because you could not understand it before. Now you're a grown woman and you know what prostitution is, but you don't know you can sell your body here and preserve your soul. Your mother gave herself to this work, not because of hunger, like the rest of them, but for you. So you never have to sell yourself and you can be a lady. She dreams you'll be like her mother, your grandmother, a respectable woman."

"They insulted me so badly at school," I said to her, "I'm not going back to study, I can't bear it."

"You shouldn't be embarrassed, girl. You should be more concerned about your schooling, otherwise what's the point of the sacrifice Mariana is making for you?"

"How am I going to show my face again? I'm never going back," I insisted, and began to cry.

Mariana, who had been listening behind the door, came out to confront her daughter, her face red with shame, but resolute in her intention to change Gabriela's decision.

"Look, *mija*, I never wanted this to happen. If I had my way, you would never have known. I wanted to protect you, but it wasn't possible. I have to tell you about my life to explain why I ended up in the port," she ran her hand through her hair, trying to wipe the sweat away from her forehead and throat, "I didn't become a prostitute because I'm lazy. It was the only way to earn enough money to pay for your schooling so you wouldn't have to go from town to town and house to house as a servant. I didn't want you to be like the hundreds of women who lose everything in the violence and end up selling themselves for a piece of bread. It was my decision and I don't regret it. I want to prevent you from living this tragedy. I want to have a family through you and live with my grandchildren in a house shaded by acacias on the banks of a river. You can't throw away my sacrifice as if it were nothing, because my life would become meaningless the moment you did that. But if you give me the satisfaction of becoming an honest woman, educated, a good mother, I'll never say the nightly pain wasn't worth it. Look, *mija*, go back to where you belong. If you prefer, I won't come near you so nobody recognises me. If you want to change school, do it, although in this bloody town it's hard for people not to know who you are. But please don't tell me my life has been wasted and all I achieved was shaming you. Don't tell me I've thrown away my life, the one I rescued from the harsh conditions of my childhood."

Gabriela stared at her amazed. She never thought her mother would speak to her like this, raw and distressed as she was now. She had instilled so much virtue in her, spoken to her so much of purity, filled her head with so much rubbish and now they wanted her to accept you can sell your body and retain the integrity of the soul. So much praying and repenting, to now, all of a sudden, find out no one is as good as they say and God forgives everything, if it's done with good intentions. It was not easy for her to believe the opposite of what they had taught her for the thirteen years of her life. The simplicity of her girlhood soul could not understand the complexities of adults and the incomprehensibility of the divine. Bad woman, low life, prostitute, temptation of honest men! They had shouted at her referring to a good woman like her mother, the same woman she had placed on a pedestal, the same who had sacrificed herself for her, she who had never done anything to deserve it.

"I don't understand anything mother, it hurts, I feel ashamed and I won't go back to school. At least, not to that school. I don't mind walking a long way, but I can't face the girls, I would die of shame. I want to work and live with you, where I belong, and go somewhere else to study. How does that sound to you?" '

Before Gabriela had finished speaking, Mariana was already crying. Finally her daughter had understood her, although she said the opposite. She was racked by sobs which came from a suffering which seemed a hundred years old. She did not need to hide any longer, she could watch her grow and live with her when work was done. There would be no more avoiding her daughter, no more lying on Sundays, no more candies sweetened by cowardice and the fear of being found out and rejected. Her suffering ended there, the resignation and patience were bearing their fruits. Life now brought her good fortune and she would walk hand in hand with her daughter.

'My life changed completely that day,' continued Gabriela, 'years went by and I had a man and a daughter and I was happy. My first love didn't last very long, but I found happiness again soon after, and my other sons were born, big and strong, with brawny bodies and black eyes. They take after my mother. I built the home she had yearned for for so long and I behaved like a lady. I fulfilled my mother's wishes and was a good wife to my husband, and a conscientious mother to my children.'

Everything seemed to go smoothly. The children grew up between caresses and beatings, in the age-old way, and Gabriela and her husband lived between love and fights. The years passed quickly through the front door of their rented house. The children were still small and it seemed a sweet lethargy enveloped their lives, until, one hot May afternoon, they heard a burst of machine-gun fire.

'I began to shout, Holy Virgin! Holy Virgin, protect us! When the shooting stopped I waited a moment and went to the window to see what was happening. I saw everyone was running towards the bar and I had a bad premonition. I took the children by the hand, led them into the house and told them not to open the door until I came back. Then I left immediately.

I joined the crowd which was growing by the minute. People came out of the houses and shops asking "what happened?" "who have they killed?" No one answered and the questions were repeated on every street until I bumped into my friend José Alfonso, who seemed worried.

"*Mija*, there's nothing to be done." I didn't understand what he meant, but in seconds I realised Ramiro was dead.

"What's going on?" I asked, "What do you mean nothing can be done? What are you trying to say?" I shouted, trying to deny what I already suspected, as my feet kept moving forward.

The police had cordoned off the bar and people shouted, cried and pleaded, pushing at the cordon which obstructed the entrance.

"Ma'am, you can't come in, stop pushing," a young policeman said to me.

"Officer, please, I beg you, let me in, my husband is in there!" and the policeman beckoned me through.

I went to the middle of the bar and saw blood splattered on tables, chairs and walls. On the floor there were bloody footprints. I felt someone was breathing and shouted.

"An ambulance, please, a doctor, my God, someone help me!"

But no one moved. My friend managed to get in and he grabbed me by the shoulders:

"There's nothing we can do, *comadre*, Ramiro is dead."

"No, no, no! My God! Why? Why him?" I cried and shouted and through my tears I saw the blurred figures of soldiers who wouldn't let me go near him. "He's alive, I can feel his breathing, he's alive!"

"No, *comadre*, he's dead, I swear," my friend insisted as he led me towards the door. I turned around with every step and repeated:

"He's alive, I know he's alive, please do something!"

I couldn't take it, I became hysterical. The heat was unbearable, the smell of blood made me gag and flies made the bodies their own, riddled as they were with bullets, showing three, seven, up to ten bullet holes, pouring with blood.

The children watched me arrive back at the house, leaning on José Alfonso. They gaped at me, silently. I sat on the edge of the bed and I hugged them through my tears. I didn't want to scare them. "Maribel, they've killed your father!" was all I said to them. They cried too, without making any noise, without showing any vestige of understanding, but feeling my pain. Within the hour, the house had filled with people: neighbours, friends and relations. The news had spread rapidly. They could talk of nothing but the massacre, reinforcing my anguish:

"It was a slaughter! Brains splattered everywhere! From blocks away the stink of death is nauseating…" They say they were alive and they left them to die without mercy! My godson, who's a soldier, says he touched a hand and it was still warm! They told me a few groaned and they kicked them so they would shut up!" I felt fury and horror. My God, I asked myself, why could they not be granted a peaceful death like grandfather's, who died in old age, in his coffin surrounded by candles and flowers and relatives and friends? Why did I have to live the horror of this violent and unexpected death?'

Gabriela was angry with God. A minute ago she was thirty years old and now she felt ancient. From that day on she did not believe in anything, not in God, nor in the Virgin, nor in the Saints, nor in guardian angels, nor in men.

'God doesn't exist, neither do the virgin or the saints she repeated to herself, men exist, but it would be better if they didn't because they're bad, they're worse than animals. Animals only kill to defend themselves, to eat, not like men who go and shoot fathers, brothers and sons without concern.'

Ten years later, Gabriela was finally able to cry and be her age again. She should have understood it was a war, not let herself surrender to depression, but it was difficult to go on without support and without someone to lean on.

'The family wants to provide everything, but they don't know how. They think it's best to talk of resignation, enhancing the feelings of guilt. They distract the children hoping they'll forget, as if by ignoring what's going on, we could change anything. A child of four or five who's used to the noises of a helicopter and guns, hears them as if it were any normal sound, like rain. For my children, the sound of shooting is the sound of death. They don't say anything, they go silent. I understood how much his father's death had affected John when I heard him talking of his father in the present tense, five years after his death. In adolescence he needed him again to support him and accompany him. If I couldn't understand the effects of death on myself, I understood even less the harm it did to the children. Because they were small, I believed it hadn't affected them.

Children of war are intelligent, they're special. They're quiet and you think they don't understand, but if you enter their world you know it's not true. When you see how they react to strangers, how they distrust adults and how they look at uniforms, we can understand the effects violence has on them.

Death is not one, but many. I want to live indefinitely to build not one, but many homes and to love not just one, but many children,' concluded Gabriela, stretching, eager to start a new life which she could be in charge of.'

It was midday and they wanted to rest. They had reached the moment of truth: why had they participated in the armed conflict? How had the decision marked them? The first day was always the hardest, and tensions began to mount.

'Your husband's death affected you a great deal, but we don't know if he participated in the armed struggle' queried Mercedes, raising her painted eyebrows, trying to understand.

'He was a Patriotic Union activist and everyone knew it. His death came before it was clear there was an extermination campaign against the party. He collaborated, amongst other reasons, because he was a lorry driver and he travelled to areas controlled by the guerrilla. All I know is that they stopped him and he had to help them. In the beginning he was scared, but he became closer to them and although I never saw him with a gun, I'd say he gladly helped them.'

'Had they threatened him?' asked Angela.

'Not that I know of.'

'Did he trust you sufficiently to tell you of his involvement?' asked Daniel, as if he were insinuating something.

'*Compañero*,' Marcos quickly intervened 'you know they prohibit us from implicating our wives. If Ramiro loved her, he'd have told her as little as possible. I'm sure he never went further than telling her he helped them on the road.'

'When I asked him to tell me what he did, he told me it was best I shouldn't know in case something happened to him. He always said to me: "I don't have meetings in the house so no harm will come to you." His activism went beyond meetings. The rumour was they found a stash of arms in the bar where they killed him.'

'Gabriela, do you have any idea who ordered their deaths?' asked Alejandra with the forceful tone which she adopted when she spoke of acts of violence.

'My only lead is that the night before, the group had met in the same place, the army had gone by, asked for everyone's identity papers and insulted the men. The next day, the killers were dressed as civilians. Ramiro and the others were accused of being guerrillas at the time of the massacre. The press came to my house and the priest advised me not to say anything. I didn't know better and I didn't say a thing. When we were holding the wake, the engineer who managed the company's drivers arrived and I introduced him to a journalist. He behaved very formally and when the journalist asked him what Ramiro was like he answered: "a serious and honest worker".'

'What happened after the funeral?' asked Socorro with doubt written all over her face.

'We held wakes in the houses and two days later we had a collective funeral. A lot of people came. I didn't want to stay in the neighbourhood, so I went to my mother's and stayed with her for six months. I felt despondent and couldn't accept I had to rebuild my life alone.' Gabriela spoke with the certainty and security of someone who has managed to get on. Her big, black eyes move over the faces calmly and they don't show signs of anguish. She had cried while telling the story, but she is not distressed and is able to answer the questions serenely.

'It would be best to follow the rules of the game, at the end we can comment, we can talk about what happened next and how we solved our problems, then the discussion will be richer,' Ana Dolores reminded them.

Daniel

A soul destroyed by enduring injustice

At two in the afternoon they came back. They came one by one and began to talk about the importance of knowing the facts of the violence from the mouths of the protagonists. They were not going to leave anything out because the details illuminated what each of them had lived. Now it was Daniel's turn, as they had agreed to follow the same order they had used in retelling their childhood. They looked at me as they talked and I continued in my assigned role as guide. There were moments when the strength of their feelings made them forget I was present, but when their feelings were less heightened they remembered I was taking notes and recording their interventions. Daniel got comfortable in his chair and began:

'It's not that I didn't approve of what my daughters did. I was happy they had chosen the revolutionary path, even though I was hurt by how some of them went about it. When my wife and I got involved in land occupations, the *compañeros* supported us and we managed to build a little house and cultivate our plot of land to feed one, two, three and up to the nine children we had. I've never been so happy in my life. I had my home and my children, a young, pretty, and brave wife, whose heart I lost through the years of unattended births and mistakes I couldn't prevent. I worked all the hours necessary and more. I organised people to defend occupations of waste land which we made productive with the sweat of our brows. It took us more than eight years to achieve what we had and in a few months we lost everything. We moved there in 1982 and in 1990, the army arrived with a bulldozer and destroyed it all. They got tired of evicting us in a mountainous and remote area which is impossible to control. The last time they came to take us away we occupied San Vicente and cut off communications. Some of you here may remember it. There were forty of us inside the small room of the town's telephone exchange. They took us to speak to the Mayor, but we weren't stupid and we moved in groups big enough to keep up the pressure. The Mayor promised us land titles if we went back peacefully and didn't help the guerrilla.

We fell into the trap, like everyone else. We never got any proof of ownership beyond our feet planted firmly on our cultivated land. Then the violence arrived. The *muchachos*, the guerrilla, roamed the lands and dropped in to the houses as any friend would, and we not only admired them, we obeyed them too because they were the law. Nothing important was done without consulting them, they punished civilians when it was necessary and they ruled according to their principles. They had the authority of those who fight for their people. So when problems started with Inés María, my wife, she went to the *compañeros* and I was punished. I complied, hoping they would listen to me and understand what was happening. Unfortunately, I lost Inés María's love and my children were left half-orphaned, which upset me. She went off with another *compañero* of the guerrilla and although I had orders to split my plot of land and the children with her, I disobeyed. I said to them: *compañeros*, I can divide the land with Inés because we've worked it together, but the children can't be split up like the land or a herd of cattle, they should stay together. So they ended up staying with me.

My older girls left home around then, with *muchachos* who had wooed them into the struggle. The eldest was left a widow before she was twenty and she never got over the pain of losing Fabio, who was a good man. She left military life malnourished and broken from having seen such injustice and cruelty. The second girl was in the struggle for more than ten years and the third was killed in combat, she died on her own terms. Yet I suffered most, not from their involvement, but because of the cruelty of the military after her death.

When I found out my eldest daughter was sick and in hospital, I set out by bus, risking my life, but determined to confirm the news. I wanted to help her recuperate, as I had nothing else to offer her. I left one early morning, before sunrise. I reached the first military checkpoint at about six in the morning and felt terribly uneasy. My premonition was so strong I told my young son, who was with me, that he should keep going in this bus or on the next into town. There, he should tell his mother to look for María in the hospital, they should get her out and help her, as it was possible I would'nt be going any further. They had looked for me a few times at home and I'd always managed to escape. They never found anything to confirm I supported the guerrilla and much less that my daughters had gone off to join them. When I stepped off the bus and handed over my identity papers, I felt sure something serious would happen.

The lieutenant came back with his squad of soldiers, gave the documents back to the passengers and ordered me and another man to go to the sentry post to ask us some questions. Whilst they were studying the documents, I found the driver of the other bus and I asked him to take my son. When the boy left, I lost my courage. My unease increased and I couldn't control my fear.

"Daniel Argüello, is that you?" asked the one who seemed to be conducting the interrogation.

"Yes, sir," I answered.

"Yes, Captain, you son of a bitch!" he shouted at me.

"Yes, Captain," I answered.

"Let's see, you bastard, tell me about your contact with and support for the guerrilla."

"Me, Captain?"

"Of course you, you stupid bastard, son of a bitch, or are you not Daniel Argüello?"

"Yes, Captain, but I don't support the guerrilla."

"Let's see if you know this girl who we killed in combat. The photo was published in the press," he passed me a newspaper cutting in which she appeared, my daughter, naked, shot, her little face swollen and her eyes open as if she were looking to heaven. I began to shake even more, but I didn't cry and I said:

"She's not my daughter. I only have six children and they're still small," I wanted to be convincing to protect my other girls.

"Well you'll be glad to know she wasn't your daughter," he said looking me in the face and then he turned around and looked at the soldiers who were at the door, "isn't that true boys? Because the girl in the photo was raped by thirty soldiers after her death. She was a bitch, a dog who deserved that and much worse. Naked, as she is in the photo, the whole battalion had her," the soldiers laughed and the Captain looked at my face to see if my expression gave me away.

I trembled, felt my heart was pounding so loudly everyone could hear it and my pallor was not just visible, you could touch it. Everything around me turned white, I didn't know if I was going to faint or if the rage was killing me.

"Let's see Argüello, stop being so macho and admit she's your daughter. I'll show you your other daughter, too, who we've also killed. She was older, wasn't she?" he said passing me a photo of a girl with a group of dead guerrillas. I didn't want to look at it, but he took my face and turned it, saying in a menacing voice, "when I order you to look, you do it, you lying bastard."

I looked at the photo, it wasn't María or Edna. I felt a brief moment of relief and thought, if I make them believe she's my daughter then I'll save her from being persecuted.

"That's my daughter," I whispered.

The Captain left with the soldiers. My muscles were tense, my face was as pale as death and my eyes were shining from the tears held back. The Captain came back and turned me around:

"Don't look around, bastard," he said pushing me.

A little later I felt a hand on my shoulder and a voice said to me:

"Don Argüello, why are denying your daughters? Are you going to tell me they're not yours, when you showed such pleasure in their work for their country, when the guerrilla went by?" Although he tried to disguise his voice, I recognised it and quickly understood what was going on. Now I couldn't lie because the man behind me, with his hand on my shoulder, was Jacinto, the one who had seduced my third daughter. It was him, only he could confirm with such certainty who was my daughter. The world changed colour, everything turned red, hatred burned in me and fear left me. The game was up, it was impossible to deny anything now her own partner had betrayed her. He made me sick.

No sound came out of his mouth, his sticky and bitter tongue felt swollen, as if it had been stung by bees. His twisted jaw revealed a man distraught by rage and helplessness. He did not know where his strength came from. He thought his best revenge was to get out of their hands and struggle and avenge his daughters by saving the little ones. Only seconds went by, but it was enough time for him to clear his head and control his emotions. All his suffering had to be for something. It was not possible that a man who had been raped and abandoned could not control himself enough to play with them with the same cynicism and cruelty with which they played with him.

"Listen, Jacinto, why don't you tell your bosses how you wormed your way into my daughter's heart, when you were a guerrilla. Tell them how I opposed her going. Tell them how you took her at night, like a thief, so I wouldn't realise. Lieutenant! Sorry, Captain! You know no one can fight against love. My poor daughter was only fourteen and she believed the heroic tale this creep told her and he only used her. Look Captain how she ended up." I took a breath and continued, "Come on, tell your commander the truth, Jacinto, tell him honestly if there's any way a poor peasant like me can oppose what the guerrilla want or what their children want. Explain to him what happens to us if we resist."

"Look Daniel, don't be the fool and talk, like you talked to those sons of bitches guerrillas. It was all smiles when they arrived."

"You know perfectly well one obeys their commands and if you don't, you're in trouble. They're the law as long as the army don't appear. They do as they please, they rule and issue orders and we do as we're told, we obey and let ourselves be judged without a word."

"But you never showed disgust, be honest Argüello. You know where they are now, how to contact them and who has joined up," responded Jacinto.

"You should know better than me, you lived with them. You mean you walked the trails at their side for months and they didn't show you the way?" I said pretending not to understand.

"Don't take the piss," he whispered in my ear, "you don't know what I'm capable of."

"Oh yes, I have a good idea of what a bastard you are, but I'm telling the truth, aren't I?"

"Look Argüello, it's better to cooperate, don't get killed for no reason. Think of your other children at home. I know you must still be taking supplies to the front and they trust you."

"It's a long time since I've heard from them. Since you took my daughter, they've not been back because there's no one else to steal from me, the others are still young."

He moved away and spoke to the Captain. Then, the Captain came back alone, allowed me to turn around and said to me:

"Argüello, it's best to cooperate, don't you see," he took out a wad of bills and waved them in my face, "this will be yours if you do what we say. It's a million pesos, you'll be able to go far away with the children if everything goes well and the commanders are caught. If you think about it calmly, you'll see it was they who allowed your girls to join the guerrilla so young and, in the end, they're responsible for their deaths. If everything goes according to plan, the front in your area will never fight again. We'll give you more money when they're destroyed and we'll help you leave the region."

"Captain, I'd love to earn those millions and leave this region now my girls have died here and their mother has left me. So, what more could I wish for, but I don't know where they are. As I told you, it's a long time since they came by the house."

"Oh Daniel, little Daniel, so you prefer to be shot and left for the vultures to feed off?"

"No, Captain I don't want that, but if it's the price I have to pay because I know nothing, well, it's God's will. If I lie to you to save my skin, you'll check it out and kill me like dog, and you might kill my children. If I lie, I'm only putting off my death, so it's better not to lie. If I have to die because I don't know anything or because I didn't know how to be a stricter father and prevent my daughters from going off with them, well, then kill me, Captain." Fear had totally left me and the pain of seeing my daughter dead and raped meant nothing mattered to me.

"Fine, Argüello, I'm going to give you another chance. Go back to your house and try to make contact. Do as they say and we'll send some one over to you. He will tell us what you know and that's that. The offer of the money still stands and if you want to, you can leave the region. What do you say?"

"I accept, Captain. I'll try and make contact and I'll pass on everything I know."

They untied my hands, told me to get on the first bus and continued interrogating the other man. When I left, it was nearly ten and the sun beat down on me. I waited for ages for the next bus and I went to San Vicente wondering whether my María was really in hospital and anxious because of the danger if they found her. As they thought she was dead, they wouldn't look for her, but if they found her in the hospital, she ran the risk that they would disappear her. We knew many *compañeros* had been taken from there. I spent the morning walking around town, trying to lose anyone who might have followed me. At about one in the afternoon, taking advantage of a moment when no one was near, I went into the hospital and asked for her. María was not registered under her name. I pretended I'd made a mistake and, in a moment when the nurse was not looking, I went inside to look for her by bed by bed.

In the third bed of the fourth room, I found her. Her black eyes were distant. Her face was so pale it made me sad, her previously glowing, lively skin was a greenish colour, like avocados left in the sun too long. The energy, the vigour of her youth and her strong character, so like her mother's, were no longer with her. When she saw me, she began to cry silently and she quickly rubbed the back of her hand over her cheeks, angrily rejecting the tears running down them.

I was alarmed because her face and her evident weakness showed she was in a critical state. I went to her, stroked her head, as I used to do when she was small and, trying to smile, I said:

"*Mija*, how are you?"

"In a bad way, father. What are you doing here? Who told you?"

"The *muchachos* sent a message with Justiniano. What's wrong with you? Why are you in hospital? Are you wounded?"

"No, father. I'm anaemic and malnourished. It seems this last operation and the bad food did me in. At the front we've had problems with supplies and very little meat arrives. We've had to survive on flour and tins. The mosquitoes were vicious during the long summer and cooking over a wood fire has wrecked my lungs." She spoke so softly I could hardly hear her.

"Don't worry, *mija*, I'm here now and I'm going to help you because the authorities are near. On my way here, the army detained me and it's a miracle I'm alive. Jacinto has become an informer. I think he was a spy already. That's why I was so against him taking Edna, not jealousy, as everyone thought," she looked at me with a "don't start that again" look but I continued, "I always distrusted him, because each time he came round, he threw down his gun and his rucksack as if they were a nuisance, not his life. He was never alert, of course, why would he be, if he knew nothing would happen in the days he was doing his spying. I wasn't told he had deserted and betrayed Edna. Your sister is dead," tears ran uncontrollably down my cheeks, "They're going to pay for it, on my life. Today I escaped unharmed, but I won't risk it again, I must make them pay for her life. Listen María, they think you're dead too. As that swine didn't know you, I went along with a story that a girl in their photo was you. But here in the hospital you're in danger. Tell me, *mija*, what are the doctors like? Do you think they would help us?"

"Yes, father. At least I'm sure the director would."

"I'm going to talk to him to see how your health is and if we can take you elsewhere. The army is too close," I said to her, holding her hand and left.

I looked for the director, but he was out having lunch. I sat on a bench to wait for him. I was restless with anguish so I wandered out to the street. I decided to look for him in the restaurants. Suddenly, I saw the soldiers again, the same who had interrogated me. I thought of hiding, but realised they had already seen me and it would be an admission of fear and guilt. So I walked past them as calmly as I could. I felt like thousands of animals were doing somersaults in my stomach and I couldn't stop myself from going pale. I walked on, but my legs were like rag dolls, the knot in my throat was choking me and my eyes were watering. I managed to go past them and even waved at them. I continued to the first café I saw, went in, and almost collapsed.

"A strong coffee please," I said and I didn't recognise my trembling and shaky voice. The waitress looked at me and asked:

"Is something wrong, are you alright?" and she crouched down to look closely into my face.

"Nothing is wrong with me, thanks," I answered.

She looked at me and smiled as if she knew what I was going through. After taking my order she drifted towards the doorway and said to no one in particular:

"This town is deserted today. Not a soul around."

I breathed deeply. I waited for her to bring me my coffee and wiped my sweaty hands on my shirt. She brought me my coffee and said:

"Would you like anything else?"

"No, thank you very much for everything," thanking her also for the intelligence that the army had moved on.

I finished my coffee, paid and left. I went to the church, then to the telephone exchange. I went to see a friend who had nothing to do with politics and at about three in the afternoon, I went back to the hospital to look for the director.

"Good afternoon, are you the director?" I said to the young man in a white coat who was standing in front of the door marked "Director".

"Yes, sir, how can I help you?" he asked.

"Look, doctor, I need to have a few words with you in private." He looked at me strangely and finally I got the courage to gesture with my head to go into his consulting room. He understood and we went in.

"Tell me, how can I help you?" he said closing the door behind us.

"You see, doctor, I've a daughter in hospital here, but she's in danger." He raised his eyebrows. "It's not her care, but because of the army," I said, looking at him to see if he understood me, "you know these days, children take little notice of their parents and from when they're small, they do what they like. She married one of the *muchachos*," I said looking him in the eyes to see if he followed me, and as he nodded his head in affirmation, I continued: "Being here could cost her her life. The army is all over the place. They stopped me today and they think she's dead which is reassuring, but if they come around here and find her, they might kill her."

"What's your name?" he asked me.

"Daniel Argüello, doctor."

"What's your daughter called?"

"Well, you see, she's not registered under her real name because of the risk she runs, you understand?"

"Yes, of course, but tell me what name she's using, so we can work out if we can let her go."

"I don't know. I found her by looking through every room, but if you like I'll show you where she is. They've told her she has anaemia and she is very thin."

"Let's see what we can do."

We went out and I took him to María's room. She looked even worse than before with the news of her sister's death and because she knew the danger she was in with the army nearby. When she saw me come in, tears ran down her cheeks again and the doctor was very moved to see her sadness.

"Now, now, don't cry. We'll work something out and see if you can go with your father."

On hearing the doctor she began to cry in earnest, trying to control the sobs which shook her like a paper boat in a huge lake. She was so thin, pale and defenceless, the living image of neglect. I stroked her head with my callused hand and I began to cry myself. The doctor put his hand on my shoulder and said:

"Señor Argüello, don't worry. I think you can probably care for her at home. Although you must comply exactly with the treatment prescribed. You must give her the food we recommend because she's very sick. The anaemia could become something more serious. Her lungs are in bad shape," he looked at me firmly to see if I understood how critical María's state was.

"Yes, doctor, we'll do everything you say, just let me go and find her mother who lives nearby."

"Go on, señor Argüello and may God protect you."

"May God repay your goodness, doctor," I said to him knowing he was one of us.

I made another long detour round town in case they were following me and eventually arrived at Inés María's house, running the risk of meeting her new partner, José. I banged on the green door which they told me was where she lived. I heard whispers and shouted: "It's me, Daniel."

I heard a child's footsteps and I remembered I'd sent my son there that morning. With so many problems, I'd forgotten about him. He opened the door slowly and I saw his half-open eyes through the crack. He looked to see if I was alone or with soldiers which incensed me. When he saw I was alone, he flung the door wide open and threw himself into my arms. "Daddy! Daddy!", he said and ran his hands over me as if to make sure I was really there. It seemed he found it hard to believe I was real, and he looked again and touched me anxiously. His mother came out when she heard him say Daddy and made a furtive gesture for me to come in.

"Come in quickly. They may have seen you," said Inés María, with her black hair tied up.

"How are you?" I asked.

"I'm fine, but Rodrigo and I thought they had murdered you. We nearly died of shock when you knocked. He told me María is in hospital. I'm waiting for José to arrive to go and get her."

"How could you think I'd betray you," I said, irritated, "No, Inés, even with everything you've done to me, I wouldn't put the army on to you."

"Alright, don't take it so badly. We know how they extract information and even the bravest end up talking. These days, informing is frequent and you know they offer very kind of reward.'

"That's true, but I'm a loyal comrade, don't forget it.'

Without moving from the entrance and looking her straight in the eyes, I said:

"We have to get María out of the hospital immediately. The army thinks she's dead but if they find her …" then I remembered Edna, looked at Inés with tears in my eyes I said suddenly, "they killed Edna."

Inés stumbled as if she'd been hit. I thought she was going to fall. The boy managed to call out, Mum! and stepped towards her to hold her up, but she was stronger than I'd thought and holding her head she mumbled: "Holy Mary!" She went to the kitchen and sat on a stool, held her head in her hands and said nothing for a while.

"No, no it's not possible. Damn them, damn the bastards!" she ground her teeth and I thought she was going to have a fit.

"Rodrigo, get your mother a glass of water," I said to the boy. He went to the water jug, filled a cup and gave it to her.

As she drank she looked at me as if she wanted to say something. I didn't know whether to reproach her again for leaving us or shout at her it was her fault they had gone down that path. We had lost them without realising when or how, and all I managed was to bow my head for a while. I realised with a start that Rodrigo didn't know about his sister's death and Edna had been a mother to the little ones for a long time. I lifted my head to look at him. The expression of cold hate I saw in his face frightened me.'

His son was rotting from the inside. It wasn't the look of a child. His innocence, lost long ago, changed his little body into a man's. Hate was destroying him with each decaying corpse, with our dead, with those of other people, or the ones who were simply named on the radio and television. Daniel remembered the borstal and sadness filled his soul. He felt he was not a good father, he had not saved his children from nurturing hatred, he had not managed to keep them safe and with his sins out in the open, their tender hearts were corrupted.

'I opened my arms, called him to me and held him:

"Son, my son!" I said. His rigid body rejected my embrace. Then I burst out: "don't let these pigs get their way!" I was frightened that Rodrigo's resentment would lead him to meet death by taking up the gun also.

"No, *mijo*," I said, "I have to free you from this hell to beat the army. If they kill us all then your sister's struggle and her death will be in vain. We must survive."

The boy looked at me defiantly, his chin up, with rage in his eyes under his frown. I understood then how by conceiving them at all, Inés and I had made them participants of the war.'

Daniel breathed, drank a glass of water and continued:

'In the end, I continued doing the same work, but with more anger because of my daughter. We were well organised and every time the army arrived, we were warned and hid in the mountains. They found only children who were trained to say nothing. Once I left so quickly I left my papers behind. The patrol went through the house but didn't find them. I became careless after that, and the next time they came, I didn't hide. I stayed in the house and went through another bitter experience. They played psychological games with my children – and then they want us to not hate them!'

'*Compañero*, do you think this new event is important?' Socorro asked.

'Yes, it's very important for the debate,' answered Daniel seriously.

'Go on then,' Angela suggested.

'When the army arrived, they took the youngest boy who was only seven years old, they wrapped a green towel around his head and they carried him off with his arms tied behind his back. I pleaded with them not to take him and the other children cried. Nothing moved them. They said: "tell us, you son of a bitch, where are the guerrilla?" I don't know, I responded. "Let's see if you talk after we smash your son's head in!" I insisted I knew nothing, told them to kill me, if that's what it took, but to let my son go. They took me to the front yard and in front of the children, they pulled down my trousers and the lieutenant took out a dagger and said: "what this lying bastard wants is for us to cut off his balls!" All the soldiers laughed with him. He grabbed my balls and made as if to castrate me a few times. I was shaking like a leaf. When he saw it was not enough to make me talk, he put a gun to my head and he fired blanks time and again, and on the third shot, I knew he was not going to kill me.' Daniel looked very pale and was silent for a few minutes. No one in the group knew what to say and you could see the indignation in their faces.

'I stood my ground and as time wore on, I became more angry. I asked them again to leave the boy alone, but they'd decided to force him to show them where a local leader they were searching for lived. I was forced to walk behind them and they wouldn't let me see anyone, which made me think they were going to disappear me. I couldn't hear what they said and I couldn't see the boy. At about four in the afternoon, after forcing us to walk around all day, they led us back towards the house. When they left me they told me they had killed the boy. I panicked, but realised I hadn't heard a shot, although they could have strangled or beat him to death. They left me between two large rocks so I couldn't see anything and they started to talk as if it was an interrogation. One came close and said: "yes it's him, he's the one who put us up." Then the Lieutenant came forward and put the gun in my mouth again, forcing it between my teeth and shouted: "Now, your time has come, you bastard," he pretended to fire and I fell back as if the shot had really knocked me to the ground, but the gun wasn't loaded. Again it was an intimidation tactic. They finally returned me to the house and I saw the children in a huddle, including the little one and felt a huge surge of relief.

They had detained three other *compañeros* from the farms around. No one had talked and they were extremely angry as a result. They said to my friend Elías that they were going to take him and me to the barracks and the methods there would make us talk. "You'll get at least twenty years," the Lieutenant said to me; he sent for some one to get food because it was a long way. My friend told them he had some money and he wanted to leave it with his boys. They counted it in front of us and gave it back to him saying it would be better for him to keep it because he wouldn't be coming back in years. In the end, they only took my friend Elías and they killed him six kilometres away to steal his money.

From that day on, every time my children see a soldier, they look as if they're going to faint. I reported the soldiers even though they threatened that if I did they would disappear me and the children. I had to abandon my land, lose eight years' work and come and live as a displaced person in abject misery.'

The afternoon came to an end and the intense pain they all felt listening to Daniel's story showed in their tight lips, in the silence and in the amount of coffee they drank. They needed to have their hands occupied so as not to cry like children. The ripped papers and chewed pencils of some, the twisted legs and the tense necks of others were a clear demonstration of what they were feeling. Daniel's eyes had a strange glow. They left in silence. I saw them walk towards the road and I knew it would be a long night for them and for me.

Mercedes

We cried while we marched

The next day a rainstorm flooded the streets of the town and the traffic jams began to resemble those in the big cities. At about nine in the morning Laura arrived. She was freezing cold from the seasonal rain and wind which battered the plains.

'Good morning, has no one arrived yet?' she asked, confirming what her eyes took in.

'No, the rain must have delayed them,' I said.

'I'm glad to find you alone. How do you feel the work is progressing?'

'How does it seem to you? You seemed quite nervous and cautious with the others when we began.' I prompted.

'I think it's going well. The *compañeros* are all very special and although we're not all on the same side, I appreciate their sincerity. I respect anyone who defends their ideas. I've learnt a lot since I've worked legally. Now I respect others. Before,' she laughed nervously, 'I would've thrown them to the lions. In my eyes a few of them would have been counter-revolutionaries. But when you hear the story of their lives and what they suffered, you understand much more.'

They arrived in dribs and drabs, commenting on the number of cars stuck on the roads.

The previous day, when someone spoke well of the guerrilla, Mercedes had arched her eyebrows and drummed her fingers on the table, leaving no doubt of her scepticism. Now was her opportunity to put her views across:

'My story is different. The violent event which changed my life and displaced me was caused by the guerrilla.' She knew she was going to be at odds with the majority, but she wasn't afraid and continued. 'When I was nineteen years old I married Fausto, thinking I don't know what. I liked his toughness, his authority and only now I realise he was exactly like my father. I ran a café and I lied to him and said it was mine, when in reality it was my brother Rodrigo's. Poverty had stuck to me, hunger and neediness were part of my life. It was a life where, however hard I worked, it never got better and with Fausto it stayed the same. Rodrigo had gone to Guayabero to settle a good patch of land. He came to town once and invited the whole family to work together and improve our lot. My generation signed up for the adventure and we left with a few clothes and a longing to escape from the brutal poverty which had surrounded our childhood and youth. In Guayabero, he gave each couple some land. The coca plants were already about ten centimetres high and the first harvest could be collected soon. We also had animals, we would pick coca on our sections and begin to clear more land to enlarge the farm.

By the time we'd been married for a month, Fausto had already hit me. I knew if life didn't improve, especially our economic situation, this was going to be worse than with my father. So I worked like mad to improve it. I got up at four in the morning and went to pick coca on other farms until six in the morning. Then I'd come home and cook for the workers, all seventy of them; I'd peel yucca and bananas, put the huge pots on for lunch and dinner, which nearly always included chickpeas or beans and had to be left on the boil for hours; I'd kill the animals which went in the two main meals. I then fed the hens, cleaned the pig pen, threw them the leftovers from breakfast and collected the eggs. I cleaned the breakfast dishes and cleaned the house. At midday, I served lunch, left the kitchen in order and carried on preparing dinner. In the afternoon I'd go to the stream to wash our clothes and other people's to earn a few pennies. By about six thirty, I'd clean the kitchen again and prepare breakfast to be able to pick coca in the early morning. At eight thirty, I'd climb into bed to comply with my wifely duties and, with hate, frustration and anxiety weighing on me, I slept,' said Mercedes in a rush to get the story over and done with.

'Fausto and I overcame many hardships. We had a daughter and built a wood cabin on our piece of land. We raised animals, cultivated yucca, banana, and peas, the basics to survive and save a bit of money. We decided to wait until the girl was six to go back to town with a little bit of money and put her in school. I put up with Fausto's jealousy, and imprisoned on my plot of land, I resigned myself to solitude and beatings which got worse by the day. They made me remember what I had suffered as a girl when my father hit me with a whip or with the iron's lead and when he pulled me along the ground by my hair, kicking me.

We had enough to eat and the girl was big and healthy. One day the guerrilla visited us, doing the rounds – they were the law in those parts. They told us the army had decided to come into the area and we were in danger. They said the best thing to do to defend ourselves was to hold a protest march to San José del Guaviare and stay there until the government negotiated the departure of the troops with us. Hundreds of settlers went, taking our children, and stayed away for forty-five days. We put up with the sun, the rain, the bad food and we risked our lives. The army killed some men and the protest became a huge battle. We had nothing with which to defend ourselves and the guerrilla fired back, we were the human shield and we panicked. The death of those peasants forced a negotiation. We went back to our plot of land and the army left the zone.

During our time in San José, we lost the harvest which was our sustenance and some animals died. The food for the protest had been taken from our farms. So we came back tired, burnt by the sun, our bodies tormented by nights of sleeping on the ground under the elements and we found the disaster of neglect. The army, at that point, didn't persecute us because of our coca growing, but because of the guerrilla who had mobilised us so the army wouldn't come in to their stronghold. Coca was an accepted crop amongst us and no one who grew it consumed cocaine. It was 1983. We didn't get rich from our earnings, we didn't have laboratories and they only paid us by the hectare and for picking the leaves.' Mercedes spoke excitedly without leaving gaps for interruptions.

'Growing the crop is easy, but the picking is tough. Your hands are destroyed and your back hurts day and night. Anyway, we managed to save. We dreamt we'd leave behind the misery we'd endured since childhood. I remember I raised a sow with such hope. She was ready to give birth and I could sell her for a good price and keep the litter, but the marches were so frequent I had nothing else to give. So, I had to lose her, give her to the cause. We were tired of suffering and in April 1986, my brother brought the local farmers together and we decided to oppose a new march. They communicated this to the guerrilla and we agreed we'd send food for those who went. That peasant march lasted two months and every day we had to send boats full of bananas, yucca, hens and pigs and again it ruined us. They forbade us from going to town to buy supplies. The lard, salt and sugar ran out and we went hungry. The children cried all day. The women breastfed their own and others' children, but it wasn't enough as the bigger ones needed solid food and there wasn't any. We had to eat mountain animals and chop and grind sugarcane to give them drinks. We even stole lard and salt from the houses of those who had gone on the march, we were so desperate.

Just as the situation was becoming critical, the march ended and death cast its shadow upon us. I remember the morning the first marchers arrived and the rumour spread that they were going to execute those who had not been on the march. I ran with our girl to tell Fausto what they were saying and we went to Rodrigo's farm. He called all of the farmers and pickers together, more than seventy people in total. We thought if we faced death together, we'd be less scared. We knew we could do nothing against a machine gun spitting out thirty or forty bullets a minute. For hours, we discussed whether we should split up and try and save ourselves, everyone for themselves, or die all together so the massacre would move the country and our deaths wouldn't be forgotten.

Finally we stayed together. Some hung their hammocks in the porch of the big house, others "slept" on the ground. I say "slept" because I didn't sleep a wink and neither did anybody else as we were terrified. We knew that if the guerrilla ordered something and if it wasn't done, a punishment was meted out, the most severe of which was death. I've never heard as many noises as I did that night: footsteps trampling on the undergrowth and the leaves on the trees moving, it was the longest night of my life. At one point I thought they would never kill so many children and the next minute I thought they would separate them from us and they'd be left orphaned.

The atmosphere was tense, the anxiety and everyone's fear became almost tangible. I found myself reviewing my whole life. In a few hours, I covered the ulcers, welts, scratches and scars my twenty-five years of life had left me with and I didn't feel sorry for myself. Instead, I searched for where and when it was I had lost love and affection.

I remembered my grandfather's abuse and how, since I was eight, even though my mother was there, I'd suffered because my father called me lazy, a tramp and a flirt. I thought how my daughter could end up in the hands of a pervert and my heart skipped a beat. There was nothing to do but pray and so I spent the rest of the night asking the Virgin Mary and Our Lord Jesus Christ to take pity on the children and save our lives.

Dawn broke, dull and faint because it was winter and they still hadn't executed us. At about six in the morning we saw a group coming and on the porch you couldn't hear a pin drop. We held our breath and you could say each of us died a little as we watched them coming.

They spoke to us: "Gather what you have," said the one who seemed to be the commander, "you are leaving these lands forever. It's the decision we have reached to spare your lives. You will not go through the port by boat, you'll have to walk through the mountains and if we see you here again, you should know the order is to kill you. Those who don't obey are sentenced to death," he turned around and left.

They couldn't let us go through the port because the communities by the river would see us and would know we had disobeyed. They ordered us to go through the mountains to Macarena. The march was long and tough. The children, about fifty of them, cried with hunger and us women carried them. My arms could not take any more and my legs wouldn't respond. The men carried heavy bundles, trying to save anything, a set of clothes, kitchen utensils or some piece of furniture. We had to leave the harvest to rot after two years of sacrifice. We cried as we marched.

The journey took three days and our dreams were left along the way. In their place we carried pain and resentment which weighed on us for years. We used those lost years of our youth to survive what befell us: being displaced without anything but our hands and our characteristic resilience, despite hunger and disillusionment.'

The group began to discuss the problem of authority. They realised that authority which relies on violence, be it by the guerrilla or the army, easily becomes authoritarianism. Authority without reason is the beginning of violence. If there had to be a hierarchy in life, the positions should be earned so authority is not a menace. For them authority had equalled arms, arms meant force, and force caused oppression and, where had oppression led them?

'To war, to violence and to death,' some of them said as if trying to fix it in their minds.

'Do you see how these things follow from each other?' Mercedes pointed out.

Whichever way they looked at it, they reached similar outcomes: hatred, from hatred to revenge, from revenge to force, from force to arms, from arms to a distorted concept of authority. Mercedes looked around her and as no one disagreed with her, she continued:

'We lost everything except our lives. My brother's departure affected more than twelve people directly as he was supporting my parents and my younger siblings who, along with our grandparents and some nephews, lived off what he sent from the farm. For the first time, I saw my father gaunt with anxiety on seeing us back in his house with all our bundles under the hammocks. The children ran around, shouting during the day and crying at night. The latrine was blocked even though we put off going for as long as we could. The two fires in the kitchen were not enough to make food for more than thirty people and we had to take turns.'

They wanted to leave, but they didn't have anywhere to go as the five eldest siblings had put their all into settling the land. Mercedes wanted to die, but she knew one doesn't die when one wants to and at the time her desperation was such she couldn't take her life. In town they lived daily humiliations; they'd lost the war against poverty and servitude. The war in the Guayabero had not devastated them as badly as the eternal postponement, deferment and subjugation of their needs. They had fought so hard since they were children, yet all that survived was their anger.

'My brother's father-in-law, who'd gone on the march, managed to bring some cattle and sell them; he also sold the land for ten times less than it was worth to a relative of a guerrilla. The agrarian reform they go on about, they carry out themselves, through violence. Where the army or the paramilitary win, they keep the lands and where the guerrilla is in charge, it's their people who take over the land of the evicted. Anyway, we, the poor, those who don't obey and refuse to resign ourselves to misery, are the ones who lose out. This war is no one's and everyone's, a war of changing sides where today's winners may be tomorrow's losers.'

The family moved into tin and wooden huts or small, dark, smelly rooms in the shanty towns rented to pariahs like them. Without references and keeping silent about what had happened to them, they built a life around fear. The dead, the disappeared and the wretched filled their dream world. Without any authority to defend them, there was no insecurity they didn't feel or blow they didn't endure, resigned. They were willing to shoulder the shame which suggested they were cowards and cowards could not aspire to more than living like rats, hidden, treading carefully, stealing food and bringing up their children as they were brought up, amidst humiliations and beatings.

Tears ran down her face and the furrows of premature lines showed the severity of what Mercedes had lived and felt. Despite her effort to win the game against misfortune, her soul showed that, faced with the memories, it had lost. She didn't know how she had come to so much neglect, and less, how she had been able to live a life where her arms, of a woman, of a lover, were superfluous.

Socorro

Both sides at war consider it a job

Socorro had expressive coffee coloured eyes. Her hair had darkened with the years, but it retained golden strands which showed she had once been blonde. Her hands moved and crossed when she talked, like priest's do. Her closeness to the church gave her very characteristic mannerisms. She mentioned God every other minute, she invoked him when she was anxious and she crossed herself when she heard something improper or cruel. She could also maintain an amazing stillness, but she was a sensitive person. When she spoke of herself she revealed a control which surprised everyone in the group. She started her story in this way:

'I understand Gabriela's passion for life. I lived my relationship with my partner intensely and before I lost Rolando I thought I'd tried everything. But I'd forgotten about death, the agony of being and not being at the same time, the feeling of being incomplete.

I left home when I was sixteen and I was still a virgin. My life was full of contradictions and I survived them. I fell madly in love with an older man; I felt that if he stopped breathing, I would suffocate, if he closed his eyes, I wouldn't see. So I decided to leave home and I promised myself I would build a proper home and I'd recreate the family security I had had as a child. This remained my vision, which I fought for in every way, legal and illegal. The day I went, I left my parents a letter saying: "I leave my home a young lady and if I don't return as a married woman I will never come back to live in it." I wanted them to know I was a virgin, that I was not leaving on a whim, that I wasn't forced to leave by circumstances, but because I loved him more than my own life. I was not hiding anything, I was going to give my body and soul to Rolando, who I hoped to love until the end of my days. It was a mature relationship. He knew of my religious beliefs and wanted me to fulfil my desire to be a virgin until I had a home. So, the first night we slept in a hotel, we kissed and hugged, but I left as I had come in, a virgin. I gave myself to him when we slept in the room where I set up my home, on a double bed which took us in lovingly, between white, cotton sheets, between which we sealed our commitment.

Rolando loved me so much that for years he hid his true needs. He was a thirty-four year-old man who had a talent for deception. He was able to carry out the most crooked business and appear an angel. He was able to transform dross into gold and my love was so great I ended up accepting his angelic side and not questioning his dark side. The story of my life is soiled by papers of stolen cars, tons of contraband and an emerald green coca farm in the plain, which had been lovingly cared for by our own hands. I knew my life appeared proper to others and in the incorrect, immoral and risky acts of my life at his side, I saw only my desire to work for my family.

We lived in many cities, places where it was possible to launder the papers of cars stolen in Venezuela, to change their chassis, to bribe transport officials and sell them to naïve people, who paid for the dream of having a car which they couldn't normally afford. Our house was filled with electrical goods, but we had them one day and the next, they might be pawned to start another business. Rolando stopped at nothing when he saw the possibility of a juicy profit. His passion was risk and that's how we achieved so much and also how we lost it all, including his life,' said Socorro in a sincere, passionate voice.

She didn't know in what dark recess she had hidden her principles. She still doesn't know what happened to her, or what he did to her so she would work side by side with him in all his robberies, scams and frauds. She thought she had done it for love, with a blind passion and the longing to be recognised and respected which had stayed with her since they had lost everything in the Bolívar mountains.

'The men who worked for Rolando would say to each other, "Don't look at doña Socorro, because the boss will kill you". That made me feel important and respected, the boss's wife and not any old boss's wife, but the wife who was respected above all else; he was even capable of killing for me.

I loved him more than my principles, more than my own life. I depended on his glances, his breathing, his strength, as if I would die in his absence. Those were the best years of our lives. Our daughter was born at the height of our involvement in coca and she completed our happiness. He loved her so much that, when she was sick, he wouldn't allow anyone else to care for her. He cried as he watched her sleep and he was capable of travelling for days without rest to carry out a promise he had made to her. We took her everywhere with us and many times, her innocent face was the accomplice to our trade in illegal documents. The life in the plains was wonderful, far away from civilisation, on the farm with the Indians and the coca pickers. It wasn't easy to love it. I had to get used to cooking on wooden fires, washing the blackened pots on the river banks, sleeping in a badly equipped house, walking in the undergrowth waiting for snakes and bathing in the streams, fearing I'd tread on a sting ray which would slice through my foot. In the beginning I suffered from all this. Rolando consoled me and he went to the stream and washed the pots and pans. At four in the morning he brought me coffee in bed and helped me as I prepared breakfast, supporting me in this new life which, once we had adapted to it, was a gateway to paradise.'

Once past Puerto López, Socorro felt free. When they caught sight of the Viciada river with its clean waters, the white and brown herons and all the other birds, when the smiling men and women with tender hearts met her at the farm, she thanked God for having sent her to paradise with the man she loved. It was hard for Rolando also. He had to leave behind his life on the streets, the parties, the alcohol, the prostitutes and drugs. She did not yet know that when he was away from home he sought these stimulants and she gave herself to the happiness conferred on her by the noble, kind and strong man who lived at her side at the ends of the earth.

'I never asked myself if coca production was right or wrong. The work was hard and in between, I enjoyed the jungle and the laughter of the Indians when I taught them to read, to write, to put on make-up or do their hair. The crop entailed hard labour but I'd been brought up to work and bring up my family. Everything was marvellous, including feeling protected by the guerrilla. I adored being a leader and the fact the peasants, the harvest workers, the activists and the Indians loved me. I went to all the meetings to teach them what I knew and I quickly earned their trust. They gave me a motorbike to get around on the paths and when the bike could not go down the steep terrain, they saddled up an animal and I looked after them. I cured spots, cleaned wounds, prepared purgatives, treated the asthmatics and set up a dispensary. Rolando was delighted to be important again without having to leave his old business of fixing stolen cars. Feeling master of the land seemed to him to be a more stable proposition. He lived happily and without worries.

We were constantly travelling from the city to the farm bringing tools, medicine, clothes, food and cars, which in that far-off place didn't need legal papers. In the end, Rolando chose not to buy the agricultural supplies to process the coca in the countryside and instead, decided to start a business bringing them in for ourselves and the other farmers. This was dangerous, but as I didn't want to be separated from him, I made the risky trips too. The happier I was, the more I depended on him and the greater my part was in his crooked deals.

My leadership became more committed, they nicknamed me "the monkey" and they allowed me to be a catechist. I kept deceiving myself that I was doing Christ's work, when what I did was serve the guerrilla's interests without realising it. Rolando got to know more people and he started to hear rumours: "They're going to ask 'the monkey' to join up as a member of the armed organisation. If she does they'll never let her out again." This frightened him and he decided to pull me out of paradise. I suffered when I went back to the city because I loved that life and I would never have wanted to leave it,' she said sighing.

'When I pleaded, he would sometimes let me go down to the plains. I learnt to bring in propaganda, arms and agricultural tools to extract the paste from the coca leaves, as well as notebooks and books so that the people of the area could combat ignorance. I remember one trip where we carried enough money to buy off all of the agents on the way. We were carrying "salt", as the sulphuric acid and permanganate were commonly called. We'd gone through the known control posts and we had some money left so we decided to buy mattocks, spades, picks and a fumigator so we wouldn't have to make another trip, as things were getting fraught. We left and twenty-five minutes before Puerto Gaitán, some DAS* agents took us by surprise.

"Good afternoon, where are these supplies going?" the agent with a trim moustache asked.

"To Cumaribo," answered Rolando, calmly.

"What are you carrying in the sacks?"

"Cement," said Rolando smiling. To check they stabbed the sacks and there was no way to deny what we were carrying.

"And this?" the man said to my husband. He smiled and answered,

"It's salt," and we were kept there until two in the morning. I cried and Rolando avoided me, because he always said before we left, "remember, if they stop us, you have nothing to do with me. You go back or you go on, you're clean. We are only travelling together because we are both going to Cumaribo," and this was the moment to obey him.

I knew it was to protect me, but I couldn't stop looking at him, guardedly. At dawn, Rolando, desperate from hearing me cry, said to the group commander, "let us go, you're not allowed to keep us for so long." That annoyed the commander and he ordered for us to be taken immediately to the port.

We were held because, after the purchases, we didn't have a peso left to bribe them with. I had the baby in a makeshift crib and I had my own gun under her along with Patriotic Union flyers. The DAS men kept cooing over the girl, because she was gorgeous, fat and white, with red cheeks. She was calm and they never suspected what was underneath her. However, they stripped the car completely. Every time they came near me I trembled and thought I was going to faint, but no one noticed. God, whose mercy is great, never forgot us. The commander in the

---

* The DAS is the Administrative Department of Security, a plain-clothes police force which reports directly to the executive branch of government.

port turned out to be a friend of Rolando's. They had worked together in the DAS in Cali. After they embraced, he began to ask questions to find out why we were detained:

"Rolando, old man, you were always a crook," and he started to laugh.

"*Compadre* Bolaños, please let us go, we don't have any cash," but friendship was not enough and Bolaños answered:

"I can't, my friend, the agents know what you're carrying and you have to pay, it's the same law for everyone."

In the end, they struck a deal. We left some sacks of salt as a guarantee and we came back with the money for the bribe. To lose them so late in the game, after fourteen hours on the road and when we had nearly got there was too costly. It was better to pay than lose the goods. When I remember that I was carrying a weapon and I'm sure I'd have used it to save my family, I cross myself and think about what might have happened if things had got complicated,' she crossed herself indicating with the emphatic gesture the dangers and atrocities from which God had saved her.

'The plains are a divided territory. The police, the DAS, the army and the paramilitaries control one part and the guerrilla another. Each side knows where the other is and respects their territory, but outside of those boundaries, on the road, on the paths and in the towns every type of revenge and outrage is committed. Us women have to let them search us as they like. They touch our breasts and our bodies as many times as they feel like it. They're also such brutes they cut the palms of the Indian's hands slowly, each nerve, each tendon, each muscle, each finger until they say where the guerrilla is. They were so cruel that once a sergeant arrived and hung the Indians by the hands over a well with piranhas in it and lowered them slowly so that the fish ate them bit by bit until they talked. He was such a brute of a man that he didn't know they only spoke their own language and he wanted them to give him information about the guerrilla in Spanish. Fortunately, the army ordered his capture and it seems that they committed him to a few years in prison.

And all of these barbarities, for what? To avoid having to confront each other. We even saw how the guerrilla camped on one side of the river and the army on the other. Each washed on its banks, but they didn't attack each other. Each side considers the war a job to be done and if they're not forced to fight, they prefer not to risk their lives. One side charge for the crops, the other charge for the tolls, if one side charges the war tax, the others charge custom duties. Both want us, the people, to offer them our services and when we serve on one side, the other side kills us and vice versa. At that time I remembered the bible: you cannot serve two masters.'

Socorro always referred to the bible and the gospels. She took a phrase from a sermon or crossed herself with every painful memory.

'Before the army crossed the river, the guerrilla imposed their justice,' Socorro continued, remembering those early times.

"You, *compañero*, come over here, we have to talk," a guerrilla commander would say.

"Yes, commander, at your service," answered the one who had committed the crime.

"We've found out you're paying your workers badly."

"No sir, they're lazy and don't work hard."

"Look *compañero*, the complaints are frequent, which is why we've taken up the case. If you don't pay them fairly you'll have to go. You have been warned," and without listening to the response, he turned around and left. That was the first warning. The second came with a stronger threat:

"Señor Bedoya, see here, we've told you not to steal from the workers and to treat them properly, but you don't seem to take any notice. If you cannot live within the law here, you'll have to leave."

The third time it was a curt order:

"Señor Bedoya, you have three days to leave."

If anyone disobeyed, they were disappeared and no one asked what had happened to them. Everyone accepted the guerrillas' justice. We also knew we had to give them ten per cent of the paste processed from the harvest or the equivalent in cash. No one ignores the guerrillas' rules. Those of us who had farms and sold coca also knew the laws of the other side. If you want to get the paste through you have to pay ten per cent and if you have to get chemicals in, there's another tax, which is why coca is so expensive. They're each doing their job, the struggle is a lie, or at least, it's not the principal reason for the war. Real confrontation takes place when they're pressured or because someone has overstepped the mark.

It's as though there were two countries inside Colombia. If you're in one territory you should follow the laws and they're not that different on either side: obey and serve. One ends up committed to one side or the other. The coca-farm owners were on the guerrilla's side because the army couldn't protect us due to the illegality of the work. I also enjoyed being with them because I could offer the Indians my support, I felt I was serving Christ. For me too, it was a job. I don't want to justify myself because I also backed the violence, I bribed with cash and smiles, I used all sorts of tricks to carry Patriotic Union propaganda and I felt like a true leader.

I put my daughter at risk many times. I knew that if we were caught and identified whoever detained us wrongly, we were signing our death sentence. To make the wrong move could cost lives.

What I'm about to say may sound strange, but in the Vichada, to be a member of the Patriotic Union was forbidden, it was worse than being a guerrilla. Legality is a myth, as is the lie about respecting indigenous people. They respect strength, anyone who holds a weapon. The peace accords amount to nothing – they killed all Patriotic Union activists.'

'We believe you, Socorro, the surprise is that it should be you who's telling us,' responded Daniel.

'Why are you surprised?'

'Because you're so religious and always talk about God. If anybody heard you, they'd think you were a communist. Isn't that true *compañeros*?' Daniel asked.

'Absolutely,' said Laura raising her eyebrows to show her surprise.

'I'm not so taken aback,' remarked Alejandra. 'Socorro has shown herself as she is, sincere. Her testimony is valuable precisely because we cannot say she is left-wing because of her training. It's exciting to see how we are opening our hearts to find a solution.'

'If all of you have been brave enough to tell me your stories, when I know you find it hard to trust me and my approach is rather different to yours, the least I can do is be straight with you. I feel I'm confessing my sins, I'm truly penitent. I always thought if I ever told anyone, it would be to repair and move on from I'd done. Now is the time to talk about the violence I lived with and to seek new ways to build peace.'

Socorro's eyes were brimming for the first time. She hadn't cried in the most painful parts of her story and now, faced with the possibility of committing herself to peace, she was moved.

'I'm going to continue, I think my story can contribute other elements. As I was telling you, Rolando and I had tried many crooked ways, but we never managed to consolidate our wealth and the farm with its coca crop seemed a more torturous, but more stable path. We were wrong, things were changing. Pressured by the surplus of coca, Villavicencio became a centre for traffickers. Money was flowing and the order came to dismantle the laboratories. The army was forced to cross the river and all hell was let loose. With the fighting, the bombings and the burning of crops and laboratories, the business became nearly impossible. Every time they announced the army was coming into the area, we had to take the chemicals and dismantle the house. The Indians carried large barrels of gasoline on their backs a long way from the house and buried them. We waited for the crops to be burnt and then we planted again. One harvest would be lost, the next would be planted, I would dig up the buried products and work on the paste, then we'd have to hide again because the army was coming and we'd escape to the mountains and wait for them to go.

Everything became difficult for us. We had invested all the money from the cars and we had to protect our patrimony in any way we could. With all of the army incursions the chemicals became scarce and an unqualified chemist told Rolando that if we planted Peruvian coca, he could bring the price down by making the paste with cement. This coca plant, unlike the bitter or the sweet, took longer to cultivate, but it was no problem to get cement. According to him, he could get us eighteen grams for each *arroba**, which was an excellent percentage and we got involved. We worked hard and processed with cement, but it only gave us an eight per cent return and we couldn't even pay the workers. I remember how we cried in the doorway to the house calculating how much we had lost.

We went to Villavicencio, without saying anything, to sell the paste and pay the pickers and those who had pressed the crop, but we didn't even get enough money to do that. While we were selling the paste, we found out the guerrilla were looking for us to kill us because we hadn't given them their percentage. We didn't understand why until we were told the sham chemist, to make himself look better, had said the harvest had rendered eighteen per cent and it wasn't true, so we couldn't pay. Rolando decided to confront them:

"Socorro," he said to me, "if I don't come back in three days it's because I'm dead." He gave me a kiss and left.

Five days went by and he wasn't back. I decided to look for him and I went off in a rented car without knowing how to get to where the guerrilla were. I cried the whole way. I came to a town called El Viento, on the border of Meta and Vichada and there I found him drinking beer with the guerrillas, celebrating the deal they'd made: he would give them a car instead of the percentage.

Our adventure with coca ended there and to make some money, we became traffickers. It's a risky part of the business because you carry a lot of money and the chemicals and also take the coca out. During those years I learnt everything about drug trafficking, my new job. I learnt how to make the layers, put them in bags spread thinly, without air bubbles; I stuck them to my body, my legs or my stomach and I pretended to be pregnant. I put a swimming costume on to hold them in, I made a cloth belly on top and I stuck sheets to my legs. A thousand times I lived through the anguish of being searched or robbed by others.

After the agreement with the guerrilla and the decision to traffic in drugs, we never turned down a trip. We had lost everything. The last time we went from the farm to Villavicencio with the car and the lorry, we had another stroke of bad luck. We went past Puerto Arimena and the car broke down. We stopped after the

---

* an arroba = 25lbs

town and decided to leave the lorry, because it was risky to carry on without a car accompanying it. In Villavicencio we found out the guerrilla had abducted some DAS men who looked after don Pereira. He was the richest landowner in the region and was accused of forming paramilitary groups to murder Patriotic Union activists. He lived surrounded by thirty or forty DAS agents on the Lurina farm in Puerto Arimena, a stone's throw from where we left the cars. They were found when the reinforcements came in and combed the area looking for the kidnappers. The cars didn't have legal documentation and one still carried a Venezuelan license. We lost them because we couldn't reclaim them from the authorities as it would've identified us as guerrilla allies.

We went to Cali to hide, waiting for the repression to subside; then we went to Cúcuta and smuggled cheeses, chickens and gasoline. We went a few times a day with two cars, brought them back with full tanks and filled with contraband. We became wholesalers until we were bankrupted by a large chicken purchase which never arrived and we lost a lot of money. From one business to another, life went by, the second child was born and my mother-in-law died. We went back to Villavicencio for her funeral and stayed.

Our relationship had deteriorated because, in the city, he'd gone back to his life of bars and prostitutes. Although I wanted to be an outstanding wife, the moment came when I couldn't take it anymore. I wanted to be his friend and I tried with all my heart to understand him. Who was I to judge him? He was born and raised in that environment and it was the place where all the dodgy business was done. I told him we should treat each other as friends and I'd never hold what he told me against him as a wife. He confided many things in me, the orgies he'd been to, his relations with lesbians, the drugs he consumed and everything he enjoyed away from home. I made an effort to go out, dance, smoke and one day I ended up going to a motel with him and another woman. It was my last effort, because when he suggested that I go to bed with the other woman, I couldn't. He did and watching it broke my heart. I couldn't go on and I left him. He cried and said I'd tricked him by breaking the promise of being his friend and not using what I knew of his weaknesses as his wife. My first failure as a Christian began at home, I couldn't love my husband as he needed.' Socorro's voice is sad, she doesn't want to go on, but she knows she should. She took a deep breath and continued:

'For two months he pleaded with me to return home. He was the best father, my best friend, the bravest and boldest protector, and my children couldn't let go of him without a fight. I couldn't be his wife because it made me sick. I allowed him to have his sex life away from home, but when he came in, I demanded he set an good example. It was impossible for him to do it. The anxiety consumed him, he arrived at dawn, drunk, drugged and sad. In between the trembling, the guilt and the anxiety, he would promise it was the last time, but vice was stronger than him and his love for us.

I tried to keep him captive, as if having a passionate and strong man imprisoned was as easy as putting a defenceless bird in a cage. Amongst the traps I set, I brought his eldest daughter to live with us to inspire him and control him with her presence. It worked for a couple of days and then his addiction took over. Finally, we decided to go and live in a rural town, far from the city and its temptations. Rolando went back to being an activist and he took cars, uniforms, weapons and whatever else was needed into the plains.

I felt whole. I was back in the atmosphere I had loved since childhood and I trusted people. We bought a hotel in the port so I earned some honest money. I got to know a lot of people there and I was able to help people. I got involved in the community, we created projects for the children, we encouraged the men out of the bars and showed them life could be better without alcohol. I organised a weekly bingo, Saturday afternoon dances, theatre plays, choirs, walks, hikes in the country, swims in the streams. I fought for the children's playgrounds and people respected me. Everything was running smoothly again, until I fell in love with the parish priest.' Socorro went red and lowered her eyes. She was embarrassed in front of the group, not only had she lived with the devil, but she'd infringed upon God's domain. 'With this illuminating love and in the midst of my responsibilities, I regained my will to live, but as with Rolando's drugs, love was stronger than guilt and my desire to live and be happy were greater than my conscience. Rolando continued with his business and travelled all the time. I missed him when he wasn't there and I was relieved he didn't demand of me a married life I couldn't provide. The children waited for him excitedly and he continued to be a loving and sweet father.

On November 30th 1993, he came by the hotel. He told us he was travelling the next day and would be back on December 23rd to spend Christmas and New Year with us and he'd stay at least two months. He left at dawn, annoyed with me because I was home a little late. On December 8th, he called us to say he missed us, that he was sad he couldn't be with us on the day of the Virgin Mary to ask for her protection. He cried and seemed more upset than usual at not being able to be with the children on these important dates.

On December 23rd he didn't show up. The children cried and I consoled them saying I was sure he had a surprise for them for Christmas Day. On the 24th, we made chocolate sauce, fritters, sweets and cakes. We marinated a turkey and prepared ourselves to receive him as Father Christmas, but he didn't arrive. That night and on the 25th we still waited for him. On the 26th, his sister,

Herminia, came to visit him on his birthday and she was puzzled not to find him, as they'd agreed to meet there and surprise me.

Fernando, an injured guerrilla who Rolando had brought home two months previously, was staying at the hotel. I'd become his confidante and everyone thought he was a relative. When he saw my bewilderment and the sadness of the children, he said to me:

"Don't wait for Rolando because he's living with a woman in El Viento."

I was astonished. It was true our marriage had broken down, but his children had never stopped being the most important thing in his life. He had demonstrated that for years. Herminia was upset and said to me:

"Socorro, if you let him treat you like a fool, at least you shouldn't allow him to abandon the children. Get ready, let's go away ourselves and if he comes back for them, he can return to whatever has been keeping him."

I got my children's clothes ready and we went on holiday. We ate tripe, sausage, grilled pork, corn rolls, yucca bread, roast veal and yucca until we burst. The children played, swam in the pools, streams and ponds, ran through the fields, made fires and the days flew by. On the first of January, we went back and there was no sign of Rolando. Herminia went to Villavicencio and I went back to my routine until two days later she called me and said:

"Socorro, Rolando is not in El Viento, he's been disappeared."

I felt an electric shock run through my body, my heart beat furiously and my hands trembled uncontrollably. I refused to accept what Herminia was saying to me. But it was true. Rolando never appeared.

The pain of a disappearance is something impossible to express in words. Guilt consumed me. Conscious of my failure as a wife and Christian, I couldn't sleep, eat or think straight. I cried like a child. There's no rest for a lost soul and the nightmares, night after night, finished off my nerves.

I constantly repeated to myself I had demanded the impossible of him: I had forced him into the mountains looking to free him from a life which was incomprehensible to me. I thought I'd pushed him into the arms of death. Death was worse than his life in the brothels. Now I'd lost his eyes, his arms, his legs, his breathing. I had sacrificed him. To wash away his sins or mine? I asked myself endlessly. I idolised him. Had Rolando sacrificed himself for the good of the country? Or for his family? In this act, he had wanted to redeem his errors. I made him into a hero.

Would I ever find out what had happened to him? Had they caught him, tortured him, dismembered him and burnt him? He might be alive, crying for me or for the children, they might have been torturing him, maybe, during the time I was accusing him of being an unfaithful man or a bad father. Could I survive without knowing what had happened to him? No, it was impossible, I had to go out and look for him. They stopped me, his brothers were looking for him already and they wouldn't let me go to ask after him.' Socorro took a breath, her strong and decided voice became serious and her large eyes clouded over.

'A guerrilla commander from the area sent for me, but I was terrified, I thought they were going to kill me too and I didn't go. I became paranoid. I realised I knew so little of Rolando that anything was possible. Had the guerrilla killed him for not carrying out an order, or had the paramilitaries or the army disappeared him? At the time they disappeared a lot of people belonging to the Patriotic Union, many had been killed and others were in jail. The peace process had broken down. It was a free-for-all and barbarism spread like a fire in summer when the land is dry. Doctors, veterinarians, mechanics, butchers and chemists were disappeared. Everyone was in the sights of one side or the other. Doubt was worse than the certainty of death and I could trust no one.

I thought Fernando had lied to confuse me and cover for his comrades when he said Rolando was living with a woman in El Viento. I felt betrayed, lost and vulnerable. I thought perhaps they had identified him as a guerrilla ally because of Fernando's carelessness. He was seeing a teacher whom, I was sure, he'd been indiscreet with. The possible and the impossible went through my head and I was going mad.

"They tell me Rolando is in Vichada with the *muchachos*," one friend told me.

"We heard the DAS killed him after torturing him and he's buried near Puerto Gaitán," said someone from those parts.

"They told me he went to Venezuela fleeing the paramilitaries," another commented.

"He has a lover; he's commanding a front; he went off with the paramilitaries; he fled to Ecuador; he's buried here, there; he's in prison; he was kidnapped and they'll soon ask for his ramsom."

All versions seemed plausible and implausible. It didn't matter if he had been unfaithful or if he had gone off because of debts, if he was in prison or dead, what Socorro couldn't stand was not knowing what had happened. But, the one who nearly killed her was Pedro Sastoque, who said he'd spoken to Rolando in Saint Martin's Square. Socorro felt she couldn't take anymore. She went to spiritual healers, to witches and prayer groups looking for an answer to her uncertainty. The guilt would not let her rest and she spoke to no one so as not to raise suspicions. Her double life and double standards had set her a fatal trap. She hid her feelings and lied. How could she say she lived with someone who acted with deception and violence, while she preached peace and family and community harmony? She lost her husband, her stability and her happiness in silence. For someone who played the part as well as she did, there were no concessions or defeats. No one would find out what was going on or suspect the tricks she used in war to stay on the side of peace. Her life was going off the rails and she needed to hang on to her deception, to keep a firm grip on things and to keep playing the innocent.

It was possible her friends had lied to her. Some confirmed they knew where he was buried, others said they had spoken to him. Did they want her to lose her mind? The torture of uncertainty continued until January 30th, when Néstor, one of Rolando's brothers, returned from looking for him on the plains. He came with the confirmation of his death, knowing where he was buried.

'The pain was intense and my soul was shattered. I could never visit his grave or go and dig him up. Néstor said if we did that, whoever had killed him would come after us. The certainty of his death freed me from the uncertainty of having left him to his fate.' Socorro took a breath, exhaled, took the glass of water Laura offered her and drank.

She realised the uselessness of the war, how it doesn't achieve or resolve anything. Her war had been pointless, she had embarked on it without knowing how, where or why. What she did know was that it wasn't a holy war against evil. She wasn't sure who had killed Rolando, whether his friends or his supposed enemies. She understood that war only serves bad men, men of death, of deception and she had fallen prisoner to their charms.

She didn't want to lose what she had achieved. She was a leader and wanted to continue being one where she was known, but it was not to be. Going into the war seemed easy to her, to leave was practically impossible. She couldn't look for Rolando's body and she didn't report his disappearance. Knowing she'd never see him alive again was enough. Now, he wasn't the man she loved any longer. He was only a mutilated corpse, without a soul and without feeling. She would remember him as he was, vital, human, so much so he left a mark on her which was impossible to erase.

After a few minutes Alejandra's kind voice broke the silence. She brought a full cup of coffee, sweetened with sugar. Socorro, calmer, continued her story:

'When my children's exercise books disappeared from the nursery my world collapsed. A few days later I received a note which said: "Go, because it would be very sad if something happened to María Helena and Octavio, they're such lovely children." It was anonymous with printed letters which said nothing else, but it was enough for me to decide to up and go.

I didn't have anyone to confide in because no one knew the truth and those who knew it had lost my trust. I knew they whispered about me, they said nothing mattered to me, not Rolando or my children. "She's a hard selfish woman. Can't you see she doesn't even cry?" It was how I appeared. Those last days were horrible and I locked myself into the bedroom and barred the door with furniture. I cried when the children slept and saw how Octavio's life was slowly fading. The boy wouldn't eat and a fever wouldn't give him any peace. Money ran short to the point where I couldn't take him to the doctor or buy medicines. I felt trapped and yet I was so frightened of leaving, of separating myself from the town, of breaking the last link to hope.

One night Octavio was delirious with fever and at dawn, in the middle of a downpour, someone knocked at the door. It was a friend, anxious, his face contorted by panic. He came in, I gave him a towel to dry himself and he said to me: "Socorro, you know me well and you know I'm not mad. Listen to what I'm going to tell you without interrupting me. I've just seen Rolando. He was by my bed and he said: '*Compadre*, go to Socorro, she needs you, my son is ill.' I asked him, Rolando, where are you? and he replied, '*compadre*, I can't tell you, but go, please, they need you' and he disappeared." My friend borrowed a car and came at five in the morning, terrified and overwhelmed seeing how Rolando suffered for his children after his death.

I decided to come to the city. I collected what little I had and with the sale of the hotel, paid my debts. I suddenly understood how money which is dishonestly come by vanishes. Ten years of work and I had nowhere for me and children to sleep. The nightmare of displacement began: begging for a roof or bread, letting myself be humiliated and bowing my head, allowing my children to be embarrassed and pleading with them to put up with it, knowing I had nothing because I had risked everything on a fate which led to violence.'

Although it was late, no one moved. Socorro's story had come as a surprise. Nobody would've guessed that she, who appeared so sweet and fragile in her kindness, had been a brave and determined woman. Her sincerity with the group and about the past impressed them. Was it possible to love so much? Had Socorro forgotten her moral and religious principles? There were a lot of questions going through their heads and many times they interrupted her story to question her, even though they had agreed not to, but she made slight gestures with her hand to let her go on without losing the thread. She was frightened of stopping, losing her strength and her words.

Laura

They will not wipe out the seed

The following day was cloudless. The storm had left the sky clear and a fresh wind blew on the plain. The day before, Laura had wanted to let out everything which was crashing around in her head. She had interrupted, gesticulating, and no one had given her the chance to speak. She was sure she had suppressed a part of her childhood. Her arm hurt and although she tried to hide it, her smile had disappeared and her mouth, drawn with bitterness and suffering, hinted that she was in severe pain. She hated their pity for her, she could take anything but that. It was her turn to start and she was not, as in previous mornings, serving coffee or cleaning the tables. She arrived with the group, sat down and waited until everyone realised she wanted to speak. Then, exasperated, she raised her voice and asked them to sit down and she began:

'On top of the three daily beatings, my mother was capable of anything. When I was ten she dragged me along glass and gravel and she tore the skin and muscles off my arm. I shouted, cried, pleaded and she just hit me more without stopping.'

Her mother realised what she had done when her father, seeing her happy faced disfigured, took her to hospital. Laura had an eye half-closed, the other surrounded by a dark bruise, and her cheekbone was scratched and marked. When her father arrived and asked her what had happened to her eyes, she moved her swollen lips and said, weakly:

"My arm hurts a lot, father."

She tried to smile, but her split lips stopped her and tears ran down her swollen cheeks. She nearly lost her arm.

Her life continued on a desperate path. She married young and she didn't love again as she knew was possible. The myth of virginity drove her to leave her parents' home. She developed a strong and determined character which for years took her away from home, seeking validation. Fortunately, after suffering rejection and failed love, she went into a political movement. She had children, and she worked in a shop to support them. There she held her political meetings and made contacts. Whatever the need, for housing, paving, schools, she was always in the front line. Her husband allowed her to participate and because he was involved too, it was never a source of disagreement between them. Escaping poverty was their first priority, but backbreaking work was not enough to improve their lot.

'I worked with him for years. He did his thing, while I dealt with the crying children, without abandoning the neighbourhood battles. I let nothing stop me, and I learnt alongside my *compañeros* from the party who began to take me seriously when they saw I was capable of doing what any man could do.

He left us, terrified by accusations and fear. Fear, from my point of view, is the worst enemy of a revolutionary, but it's real and we all feel it. What we do is confront it in different ways, but fear accompanies the struggle, like percussion the guitar. Being frightened doesn't in any way mean you're a coward. I was a bit braver than most because I didn't have any attachment to life. I allowed them to hide arms in my house, I bought supplies, I received guerrillas, took messages and I did it with the children by my side, pushing our luck as though I were playing Russian roulette. I thought, either we all live or we all die; I never thought beyond my impulses. My *compañeros* admired me and thought I was a woman ready for the revolution. All I really wanted was to die. I didn't desire anything beyond releasing the anger of my unfulfilled dreams; the satisfaction of my political work kept me alive. I felt part of a family and I was capable of any sacrifice for them. If they arrived in the middle of the night, I got up, made them food, washed their clothes, gave them food to take with them and wrapped them up to sleep as if they were my own flesh and blood.

After my husband left I continued taking care of everything and even felt the flame of a new passion. I was happy for a time, too short to learn to love life again, but I cared so much for my *compañeros* that for years they substituted for my love life. Friendship is love too, it's a form of love. If, as a friend, I loved to the point of wanting revenge against anyone who harmed them, then I'd be wrong to question if I had ever loved and even more to have concluded I'd never loved anyone. I was frightened of loving, or rather, I was frightened of my incapacity to love.

The struggle was my salvation. Time passed and the intelligence services found me and the persecution began. They threatened me to my face and under cover of the night. They attacked me at home, when I left the market and in my shop, where they tried to kill me while I was serving. But nothing could stop me and in the end it was the organisation which ordered me to leave everything behind. I obeyed and began to feel a humiliation and an indifference which nearly drove me crazy.

My first displacement of many was terrible. I lost my friends, my *compañeros* and without them life meant nothing. I was never attached to material things and saw death as a respite. If I die, I thought, they should buy me a coffin and sing a Julio Jaramillo song and if they can't then they should put me in a black plastic bag and throw me into a hole. In spite of these feelings I began to move around to escape death. I was in two towns before coming to where I live now and the army found me in both places. I had to hide, run away, leave everything and start again. The hatred against those who persecute and murder us kept me in the struggle. I didn't stop going to funerals, although they tried to convince me not to go and I repeated, "there will be others and they will not wipe out the seed."

When I had nowhere else to hide, I crossed the country to Cesar to begin a new empty life, far away from everyone. I'd gone back to my husband and together we migrated to find new opportunities. We rented a tenement room. The children were still very small. The owner wouldn't let them out of the room to play in the corridors or the patio and they only left the room to go to school. I began to lose my mind, imprisoned between those four filthy walls and I vented my anger, exacerbated by my powerlessness, onto the children.

My nights were tortuous. I barely slept and I watched as thieves killed people by the drug addicts' small shacks behind the tenement. They hung them, strangled them, knifed them and I was helpless faced with so many deaths. Each night I felt a different torment and understood the fear I'd been so proud of not feeling. I was so frightened I asked myself if blood or fear ran through my veins and if my brain existed or if it had been replaced by fear. I thought I had managed fear in such a way that we were old friends and therefore I would never feel its symptoms. During those nights, I asked myself: will they kill me? Will I survive this confinement? Will I overcome this misery? At that time I was more afraid than in all my years in the clandestine struggle.

From then on, I could describe all of the symptoms of fear, I'm reliving them now as I tell you about my life,' she said and for the first time her eyes filled with tears.

She remembered how her throat had closed and her neck tensed, her womb went numb and her arm hurt intensely, her sphincters relaxed, her pupils dilated and her lips, exhausted and dry, gave her away each time one of the neighbourhood addicts passed by. Laura had been born into a neighbourhood where you grow up giving instead of receiving and this place devastated her. Madness showed in her eyes, revealing an unmanageable rage, her hands trembled and when she saw someone murdered, she fought with her husband and with herself:

"They're giving him a thrashing, they're going to kill him!" she'd shout.

"Yes they are," would be Manolo's response.

"Is it possible that no one will intervene?"

"It is."

"But everyone who lives here can hear his screams. Are they all deaf?"

"No, they're used to it."

"We should do something!"

"We can't."

"Yes we can! It would be enough to go and point a gun at them."

"They would report us."

"I can't stand it!"

"Try to stand it."

These conversations drove her mad and she poured her frustration over the children. When they didn't obey, she felt powerless again and destroyed anything within her reach. She broke things over the children's heads, hands, shoulders and legs.

'When these symptoms became routine, Manolo took me to the doctor. My physical pains, my fits and my bursts of rage were diagnosed as a step towards madness. I was more frightened of myself than of others and decided I had to get better, whatever it took. I left, found another room and went by the party's office to offer my services. I would take no more nonsense nor obey blindly. I signed up to a housing programme and participated in a land occupation. To deal with my apathy, I built a hut with planks and plastic sheeting. I began to accept I wouldn't go back to my land and I should rebuild my life. They evicted us a number of times, until our obstinacy forced the owners to negotiate with the housing co-operative. They legalised the occupation by buying the land cheap. There were no services, public transport didn't reach us and the heat under the plastic sheeting was unbearable.

It took me a few years to make friends, to trust anyone again and understand city people's characters. I yearned for the extended family of peasant activists: the comrades who risked their lives without protest, the smiles of the children with a guerrilla they admired, the families fighting for their neighbourhood and their party. The city activists didn't impress me. They were undisciplined, not as brave as our children and they ran like rabbits at the first sign of the intelligence services. They were more concerned about their jobs than the struggle and they didn't act unless they received privileges in return. No one sold the paper and they didn't pay the quota which I paid selling ice-creams, as I was unemployed. They didn't form brigades to go fly posting and, above all, they talked too much. I realised that without the work of the peasants supporting the party, they would be a long way from the positions they held and from the deals they made with the governors, mayors and corrupt officials.' Laura showed her irritation and her hostility was apparent in every phrase.

'My comrades were willing to die for their country and kill for it too. As good fighters, we dreamt of first class funerals as our country's heroes, like those we'd read about when we studied the lives of patriots or revolutionaries in other countries. When someone died and they had to be buried in a hole with rubbish and manure, we respected them nevertheless. I know we all dreamt of being admired and of the day when the revolution would be victorious. Our dream was to see ourselves in the Central Square with party flags, smiles on our lips and singing the International.

Our hearts needed nothing more than this comfort, to enable us to die happy for our country and our people.

As I'd been trained in rural areas I didn't really understand the labour struggle. The occupation of land for housing was the only thing which resembled my previous life and I remade my nest there. Finally there was light amid the darkness of my dementia. I worked for the women's movement and was able to share my life of displacement with others. In 1992, there was the biggest peasant exodus I'd seen.' Laura paused, her whole body ached.

They had a short break to stretch their tense bodies. On their return, Laura wasn't smiling and she didn't serve the snacks as usual. She sat down, straightened her skirt over her knees, took out a handkerchief, put it on the table and then she practically shouted:

'I'm going to go on, *compañeros*. When I rejoined operations we had to support the families who arrived traumatised by the killings. The families would split up during the journey and the children were abandoned with relatives or friends in the evacuation. The conflict took on dimensions we could never have imagined. Not one newspaper told the truth – they wrote about the Patriotic Union finishing off the peace process. I thought, of course, how could the comrades in the mountains think these city types were going to understand and protect a movement of the poor? They don't know rich people's greed and arrogance. Even when they apologise they're disdainful and even when they're in an uncomfortable situation they're arrogant. One way or another, they get what they want. They blamed all the problems on the poor, but they never saw the magnitude of the genocide and the newspapers hid it. They said there were guerrillas in the Patriotic Union, the labour movement was infiltrated with subversives and the Communist Party obeyed the armed organisation's command, but while these discussions were going on, three thousand five hundred leaders were killed and they still ignored it. The paramilitary groups carried out the dirty work the army couldn't do and no one saw or heard anything. Only now, ten years later, are people beginning to ask themselves what happened then.

The best union leaders fell, councillors and deputies were murdered on the street, or in their own homes, or in the capital of the republic. Anyone who reported a murder was identified as a guerrilla in the guise of a democrat and if anyone spoke of peace and laying down arms, they were disloyal comrades and traitors to the working class. Those who fled, terrified by their brush with death, always felt guilty. If they were silent they were accomplices to the system and ended up being persecuted by their own people, because, as they said: the working class doesn't forgive. No one knew anything else but lies and you began to see everyone had two versions.' Everyone looked guilty, hearing Laura's words.

They knew this story. New leaders took the place of those who had fallen and, in a few days, they were being replaced because they had to leave or were killed. They knew the killing reached incalculable ferocity and the newspapers said nothing. They knew people were displaced from one city to another and many fell to the death squads who were paid handsomely for their murders by the narcotraffickers' alliance with members of the armed forces.

'They were paid three hundred thousand pesos for each victim. Families arrived from Santander, Bolívar, Antioquia and other departments. Some women cried for their dead husbands and others looked for the disappeared. The older children took on the running of the home, working in construction, badly paid, shamed by their ignorance and with revenge whispering in their chests. The smallest children forgot their father's face and showed signs of autism while others had terrible depressions or fits as if they were anticipating what their future would hold. No one knew what to do.

The bitter life stories I heard in those months introduced me to people who say they're on your side when all they want is to screw you. Such duplicity led me to suffer the worst crisis of my life, a crisis of conscience. I asked myself if I'd been right to believe in the war and the questions I never thought I'd confront haunted me. The doubts I never thought I'd have tormented me and made me change from a trusting activist to a demanding woman who didn't believe everything she was told.

I wondered whether those who hated arms and uniforms were right. Should I be working alongside those who maintained we lived in a culture of violence and we must build a culture of peace? Had I been wrong to love the war, to respect it, to implement it, to say it was the purpose of my life, that it ran through my veins and gave me life? Or had I been wrong to believe any intelligent and sentient person made war? No, damn it, no! Enraged, I protested that surviving and existing are worthy of the struggle also. Animals devour each other to defend the herd, the fish and the insects eat each other to survive as a species, therefore, I had not been mistaken all this time. But doubts returned every time I saw a mutilated hand, an orphaned child, a woman widowed at eighteen, or a pregnant mother whose child first opened his eyes when his father had just closed his forever. Humans are not animals – I repeated to myself – we are rational beings who know we can reason, who create and know we are creating, who destroy and know we are destroying, who kill and know we are killing. Our mind is capable of finding different solutions than those offered by nature.

I ran around trying to help anyway, and when I hadn't found a boarding school for a boy or a post as a domestic worker for a girl, another family would arrive, a worse case than the previous one. The party gave me new tasks and I carried them out, leaving my doubts to one side. But the deaths of my *compañeros* in the city, whom I had finally learnt to love and respect, finished off my fighting spirit. In funeral after funeral I began reassess the phrase, "they will not wipe out the seed". It had become an empty phrase, faced with the contemptuous violence of those with power. Legal work won my heart, my resolution and my devotion.

Over time, I had regained my sanity and my fits of rage diminished until they disappeared. Working legally in peace projects was an effort for me, but I slowly got used to it. I'd still become desperate and my family bore the brunt of my outbursts. But I was moved by the displaced people who wrote with difficulty and made terrible spelling mistakes. They said they'd been to school, but they had rarely reached first grade of primary. The authorities asked for written proposals from peasants who had never read a book and they asked for documentation of forced displacement from people who had never before left their village. They were cast adrift in the chaos of the city. They'd never seen a transport terminal, a motorway, or an airport. To them, airplanes were huge birds which flew dead straight and which left behind a trail of smoke. They didn't know they could spend hours in a city getting from one place to another and that they should arrive on time to their meetings; they didn't think they had to dress differently to be respected. They ate food from the street which made them sick. They ran across the motorways and avenues, after they had waited for fifteen or twenty minutes for someone to let them pass, and they were terrified of dying like they'd seen dogs die on the country roads.

"Mother of God, what a city, oh, holy Virgin," they'd say, crossing themselves.

Five hundred thousand inhabitants, two million inhabitants, seven million inhabitants. The buildings, the cathedrals, the shops, the warehouses, the bright street lights and roads and more roads. In them, the thunder of cars, bicycles, lorries, buses and crowds of people walking fast. No one could help them to find an address. They didn't use their hands to indicate how to get there, instead they said: "turn right for three blocks, then, turn left for five blocks, then, keep going to the roundabout, at the first traffic lights go straight on and then ask where number 4522 is". They don't understand traffic lights and they set off whether they were green, yellow or red. They take forever to get to a meeting and the authorities tell them to come back another day or send them on to another place. They steal from them, they tread on them, they push them, they don't let them on buses and many times they're left behind anxious and petrified at the bus stop. They lose the little money they have when they take the wrong bus and then they have to walk for miles. When they have a friend who has figured it out, they're told to take the one with the sign which reads: "Centre, Quiroga, San Rafael, Santa María, a green bus with yellow stripes, *comadre*, don't mix them up." But the buses rush past their eyes, without them being able to read even the first word. "This is worse than the war," they say a few days after their arrival, "how on earth did we think we could survive here when in the countryside the only problem was political violence."

The poor, such as ourselves, don't know that violence is born of ignorance and ignorance is born of the neglect the State has subjected us to because it doesn't consider us citizens, except at election time. They want us to be understanding when they say, "look *compañero*, we have to forgive and find a new modus vivendi." "What's a modus vivendi, doctor?" "Well, it is the way of life here," "Oh, but I don't want to live in this chaos, doctor," "Think about it, you can't go back to your village." '

Laura had described so precisely the anguish, anger, grief and regret of the displaced. Displacement was no less of a torment than the living hell of a murder or a forced disappearance.

Each one of them knew what it was to be displaced. The only one who was still in the same place was Gabriela, but she had suffered a social, economic and painful psychological displacement. The story of how much the displaced suffer saddened them. They remembered their own distress and even though they hadn't included them in their tales, they were marks impossible to erase. They got up to leave and embraced Laura in an act of solidarity and gratitude. There was no one like her when it came to recounting the suffering of those who lose even the right to choose the place in which to live their misery.

Antonia

The only man who respected her was dead

Antonia had to continue this afternoon and she was nervous. She had so much to say about the story of her abused childhood, that it was impossible not to be anxious. It was painful to go back, but she had to do it because it was important. When everyone came back and got comfortable, she sat down, looked at the *compañeros* and said bravely: •

'The horror that I lived through to forget my mother was not the end of it. My father took me to live with one of his sisters in Bogotá, but my aunt insisted on shaming me and hitting me until I bled. She never bathed me, she dressed me in dirty clothes and she made me eat on all fours from the dog's plate, after the animal had eaten. I slept on a poor excuse for a mattress and she made me work for ten to twelve hours. Finally, my father felt sorry for me, took me home and my mother got me back.

I went to live far away with my mother and never saw my father again. She married again and she forced us to call our stepfather, father. He behaved well initially and we worked hard, planted coffee, yucca and banana. We were three girls and two boys until the youngest girl was born. The worst thing we could do was to play and so we would run away to the *conyubal*, a large shed where the corn and rice were stored. When they found us, beatings and screams soon followed, which we could never avoid. Playing was synonymous with laziness and rudeness to them, and it was the greatest offence to my mother, it was worse than sinning. She said if children were born and brought up working, they grew up into honest people. Day and night, she repeated: if a sapling grows crooked, its trunk never straightens.

The rigidity of my mother, the lack of respect of my stepfather and work were my company. When I was seven years old sexual violence came back into my life. My stepfather began to abuse us when my sisters and I were between six and eleven years old. He would touch one or other of us all the time. At night, even when my mother was there, he would put the hammock by the bed where we slept and we would go tense and fight not to be on the edge of the bed. We never spoke of it because it was a sin to even think it. The terror gave me a knot in my stomach which has accompanied me all my life. My fear of sleeping on the edge of the bed was such that later I would always put one of my children or my husband there.

"Children, put your bathing costumes on because we're going to the river," my stepfather said to us one morning.

"Yes, father," and we ran to change. When we were ready, he sent my siblings off and kept me behind at the door.

"Wait, Antonia, you can help me prepare something to eat at the river."

I immediately began to shake and I felt my body tremble, as if I had a fever. My heart was racing and my lips were blue. My head gave the order to run, run, run! He's going to rape you!

I stood paralysed and he was still too, watching them set off on the path. He turned around, grabbed me and began to take off my costume without saying a word and I began to struggle desperately. I kicked, screamed, cried and pleaded.

"Shout all you want," he said to me, "no one will hear you."

I kept screaming until finally he covered my mouth, he ripped the costume off and tried for a long time to rape me. Every effort exhausted him, I was dripping with sweat and his penis became flaccid and he didn't manage it. He was irate and smacked me. He beat me with all his strength and then suddenly stopped, snorted like an animal and his mouth dribbled. I thought he was going to kill me. He had already tried to kill my mother twice, in front of us. Panic took over and I don't know how I did it, but I got away and ran. I ran and ran, until I'd nearly reached the river and only then did I realise I was naked. I ran to a banana tree to hide and from there I watched as he looked for me and then went to the river. I went to the house, put a dress on and went to hide again in the banana tree, praying for my mother to come back.

I didn't tell her because my mother loved him and forgave him everything and I was scared they would take me away from her. I remembered what had happened with the tribe and at my aunt's house and I preferred to keep quiet. After all he hadn't raped me and besides, he was my father and he loved me, fed me, taught me how to work and sent me to school.

When they came back from the river, he took me by the arm:

"If you say anything to your mother, I'll beat you and say you provoked me."

"No, father, I won't tell her," I replied, choking, trying to appease him.

"If they ask you about the marks on your face, say I hit you for disobeying."

He abused us for years. He touched us, he made us touch him and he looked at us all the time. He didn't manage to rape me and I don't know if he did it to my little sister or not, but he did rape my older sister and then provoked her abortion. I didn't know what an abortion was until the day she wouldn't stop bleeding and the bed was soaked. We were all sent outside. He and my mother had a vicious fight. My sister bled all day, the haemorrhaging wouldn't stop and they had to take her to hospital to save her. When I studied to become a rural health promoter, I understood what had happened to my sister that day. She was in hospital for a month and from that day on, my mother distrusted us because she believed my sister had seduced him. She didn't speak to us and kept us away from her. She gave us to other families and ignored us for two years.

I was sent to the home of a sergeant and a nurse who didn't have children. She worked night shifts in the hospital and I began to live a nightmare worse than I'd lived through with the Indian chief and my stepfather. The sergeant drank nearly every night and when he was drunk he abused me, but I never allowed him to take away my virginity. I was so frightened of losing it that my body tightened up and penetration was impossible. He hit me, tied me up, tried to caress me and make me touch him, but I refused. I also screamed and kicked, but he was stronger and I had to allow him to do what he wanted with me. He entered me from behind, I screamed with agony and he always said to me scornfully:

"Does it hurt? Well, put up with it. This is what happens for not letting yourself be entered into that big and beautiful vagina of yours. It wouldn't hurt you there, you fool."

I preferred a thousand times the sharp, stabbing pain and the lacerations, rather than losing my virginity. I would go on my knees and plead with him, but the more I pleaded the more excited he became. It didn't bother him to see me cry, he didn't care that I was a defenceless child, he only thought about satiating his passions.'

Antonia ran out of breath, she felt she was drowning. She wanted them to know so perhaps some young girl could be protected as she had not been. A respectful and pained silence filled the room. The women cried openly and the men rubbed the tears from their faces. Antonia's impenetrable expression and her rigid body showed the effects of what had happened. The impunity of these events made them more painful.

'Every night was hell for me. In the countryside, I had friends who understood me. When we were little they taught me how to chew marijuana to bear the beatings, but I had no one here. The sergeant threatened to kill me each time he abused me. He put a gun on the night table and took out a bayonet, which he pointed at my neck and said:

"Damn bitch, I'm going to slit your throat if you don't do as I wish."

I lived with the trauma for thirty years. Every time I saw a bayonet or gun I was paralysed. If anyone had watched my body they'd have realised something was the matter.

One of my daily tasks was to take the sergeant his lunch at the station. One day I arrived and he'd left to deal with a strike and there were eleven soldiers at the station. They surrounded me and they put me in a windowless room. They gagged me and they all abused me. The sergeant arrived and when he saw me bleeding he was furious and he grabbed them and whipped them. He made them go on their knees and ask me for forgiveness. I was angry, not with them, but with the sergeant who did the same things and no one beat him. From that day on, I knew I was more helpless than ever, my shame was known. The pervert must have bragged about his exploits in front of his soldiers, otherwise they would never have dared. Strangely, I felt strong because I hadn't lost my virginity.'

To her, only vaginal penetration was rape. She had been spoken to so often about saving her virginity, she was so frightened it would be noticed if she wasn't a virgin and there was so much talk of no one loving her if she wasn't a virgin when she married, that she ended up believing it herself.

Mercedes passed her a glass of water. Everyone had a dry mouth and red eyes. They wanted to give her strength, tell her they understood and they respected her now more than ever. Antonia looked at them and a slight smile of thanks flickered on her mouth.

'The sergeant continued abusing me until one day, desperate, he cut my vagina with a bayonet.'

Her face suffused red and tears began to stream down her cheeks again. She made a effort to calm down in the middle of the silence. Again, everyone was moved, they wanted to run away, to not hear of such torment, but Antonia dried her tears quickly and with a broken voice continued:

'I was cut up aged eleven, and I carried the shame with me until I had my first child. Even with the painful incision, the sergeant couldn't penetrate me and he went mad, shouting, kicking and cursing. When he realised I was bleeding profusely he became frightened and asked me for forgiveness. Then he calmed down and ordered me to not say a word. He offered to buy me a dress and give me money, which he took out of his trousers and put in my hand. Then he left the room and came back with a bottle of surgical spirit, cotton wool, gauze and bandages. He forced me to lie back and let him clean the wound. I cried, but I could do nothing as my arms were still tied up and I had a handkerchief cutting into my mouth, I was choking.

"I'll take the handkerchief out if you don't scream. If you're good and obey, I'll let you go."

I nodded my assent, and he let me go. I got dressed and went to my room. Every day I felt more terrified and ashamed. I cried every night before he came for me and I trembled and hid in the patio, crouching behind the laundry basin. He left me alone for a few days, but I suffered all the same as all I could think about was when he'd come back. I stopped eating, sleeping, living. It got so bad his wife realised and asked me what was going on. She bought me vitamins, she told me to eat more and I felt worse by the day. The sergeant began to worry that if I continued like this, his wife would take me to hospital and everything would be discovered. He started to be good to her and said the best thing to do was to send me back home because I missed my mother.

"No, she's bigger now, if she didn't cry two years ago, why is she crying now?"

"That's it, two years is a long time without them coming to see her," he said.

"They mustn't love her. No one comes to see her," she said.

"When it comes to abandoned girls, it's best to send them back to avoid problems," he responded.

I heard them and my hatred for that evil man alarmed me. I realised the sicker I was, the sooner they would send me back or he would leave me alone, so I stopped eating. The nights were hellish, each sound made me seize up and it took hours to allay my fears. Some months earlier the sergeant's mother had come to live with them. She was an old woman who'd lost her only daughter and came to spend her last years with them. She had heard my shouts and asked the sergeant what was going on. He threatened to throw her out if she said anything to his wife. He began to gag me after that and as she didn't hear any more screams, she thought I consented to it, so she constantly pinched me and smacked me. Her brutality saved me from staying in that house.

One Sunday, my older sister appeared, who was sixteen years old. She came to the house and found me in a vest which showed the bruises on my arms. She asked me why my arms were bruised and I told her that the lady slapped me and pinched me all the time. My sister was angry. She spoke to his wife and told her she was taking me away because it wasn't right that they should hit me. Doña Martina said she didn't know what to do as it was her mother-in-law. My sister left and I was even more anxious, thinking of what would happen when the sergeant found out my sister and mother were going to take me away. But my fears were unfounded. On hearing what had happened he started to behave better and he didn't bother me at night. One day, when I took his lunch to the station, he took me into the back room and said:

"Antonia if you tell anyone what's happened, I'll make you suffer for it. I can say you provoked the soldiers and slept with them, which is true and your mother will kill you. She'll accept they did it because you're a flirt and it will be to your detriment. If you say nothing, I'll pay you your wages and a bit more and you can go to your village without anyone calling you a whore. As nothing is broken, no one will notice and you can get married without any worries and everything will be forgotten."

He didn't wait for me to answer, he thought that was that and opened the door and left. I waited for more than a month for my sister or mother to come. I thought they'd forgotten about me when my mother arrived one Sunday at midday and spoke with doña Martina. The sergeant paid me and gave me some extra.

"This is for your services, Antonia," he looked at my mother, "She's a good girl, but my mother took a dislike to her and we couldn't help it. She should be with you doña Mariela, it's a difficult age and it's best she's at your side."

I was twelve years old and felt I had lived forty. I felt destroyed, but within myself, I was happy to leave without anyone knowing what had happened. In the end, I thanked the sergeant for not blaming me for what had happened with the soldiers as my mother would've beaten me to death. And what about my stepfather? I had forgotten about him and the life I was returning to. My older sister was married and my younger siblings couldn't defend me. I packed my box with what little I had and went home with my mother.

At home, things had changed. My stepfather hit my mother constantly, my older sister had left and my siblings suffered watching how my stepfather mistreated my mother and she took it submissively. He didn't bother me again, the farm prospered and they bought a car. My mother's jealousy had been terrible ever since my sister's abortion. Lucía, my younger sister, and I, never went near my stepfather and if by chance one of us was alone with him, my mother would appear immediately and glare at us.

The torment of those years was watching her being beaten, seeing how she forgave him every night when he arrived drunk shouting obscenities. Not being able to defend her upset my siblings and one night they dared to confront him. They took me by the hand to help them, but my fear left me stiff as a post in the bedroom doorway. They took a machete and confronted Ramón. When he saw them coming with the machete, he shouted, "I'm going to kill you bastards!", but he was unnerved when they didn't back down. He stopped hitting my mother and walked out. Life was unbearable, my mother wouldn't throw him out, he was worse by the day, until they separated. He went off with a young woman, who was sold to him by her mother, which is how women were treated around there, given away to the best bidder. Ramón was well off, which was all that mattered.

Four years had passed between my coming home and their separation. The children had grown up, I was now a woman, studying to become a rural leader. Leaving home was painful, but it jolted me into learning a trade. I returned six months later and was nominated as the health promoter for four regions. I left every morning on my mule and I looked after a thousand people more or less. I earned their affection, but I couldn't be happy because of the comments made about me.

In town they'd say: "what a strange girl, so old, still single". Some said my stepfather was my lover and others, that I was gay. The boys bothered me and so I decided to accept one of them. Months went by and I wouldn't even let him kiss me. I wouldn't be alone with him and his friends hassled him, saying I was using him as an excuse to continue being my stepfather's lover. He asked me why I was so cold, and I told him quietly I wasn't going to give myself until I was married. The gossip in the shops and the bars offended him so he plotted with his friends to put an end to the speculation by raping me.

I met Esteban, who later became my husband, because he told me they were going to attack me. One day my boyfriend came to visit me and found me alone. I realised his friends were outside waiting for his signal so I ran to the door, pushed him out, closed it behind him and our relationship ended there.

My mother never knew why I finished with him. She looked for rich, older men for me and I avoided her pressure and blackmail and sought a friendship with Esteban who respected me and had loved me since I was little. He went to work in the town to make money so we could get married and we wrote to each other in the meantime. My mother found a man for me to marry who was twenty years older than me, but I refused. Instead, she forced my fourteen-year-old sister to accept him. I'll never forget the wedding day. My mother had bought the wedding dress in the city and brought it home for the final fitting. Lucía wouldn't try it on and I had to stand in for her. On the wedding day itself, my mother sent me to help her dress, but the more I pleaded, argued and reasoned with her, the less willing she was. Half an hour later, my mother asked if she was ready.

"No mama, Lucía doesn't want to get married," and I went to her room to see if I could convince her. It made me sad to see Lucía cry and she pleaded with me to run away with her.

"Mama, why don't you let Lucía cancel the ceremony?"

"What on earth are you talking about, Antonia. The harder I strive for your happiness, the more you exasperate me. This is the best man for her and she has to understand that," she came down and gave her a monumental hiding without touching her face, so no one would notice at the wedding. She beat her into the dress and dragged her out.

My mother was determined to marry me off to another rich man who offered her good business contacts. As I was older it wasn't so easy to force me, but she organised the wedding and I decided to play the fool and accepted the man's offer while I planned my escape. I asked my little brother, Pastor, to help me find Esteban in the city.

"Pastor, please say you're coming with me to Villavicencio to choose a wedding dress and shoes and I'll go and find out what happened to Esteban. It's over a year since he last wrote."

"Oh my God! The beating I'll get from mother when she finds out is going to be terrible," he looked at me, white with fear.

"Please! Pastor you have to help me!" He nodded with a stricken face which made me feel for him, but I had no other option.

I spoke to my mother and she looked at me suspiciously and asked:

"Why this sudden yearning to go to the city alone?"

"No, mother, I'm not going alone, it would scare me. Pastor offered to come with me and we'll be back soon."

Finally she acceded and my little brother and I took the bus. As we were leaving I climbed onto the bus with Pastor, in case she was watching. A short way down the road I asked the driver to stop and Pastor got off, pretending I was forcing him to. I arrived in Villavicencio, but I was so nervous I forgot my boyfriend's name and when I arrived at his workplace I didn't know how to ask for him. I was so shaken the doorman took pity on me and named a few security guards, until I remembered. When Esteban came out, he looked at me as if he'd seen a ghost:

"Antonia, what are you doing here?"

"I came to find you," I said.

"Me?" He said astonished.

"Yes, you. I came to see if you're married as they say in the village."

"Me? No, I'm not married. They told me you were about to, next month."

"My mother is trying to make me and I pretended to accept to be able to run away and find out why you'd forgotten about me. You haven't written in months."

"That's not true, I've written to you many times and you never replied."

"I've not received anything from you for ages," he looked around nervously because if they saw him talking during his shift he'd be in trouble. He took my arm and led me to the fence:

"Antonia, I'm on my shift right now. Tonight we can meet in a café, on the corner of the main square. Where are you staying?"

"In the Vistahermosa hostel. Don Augusto recommended it to me on the bus."

"I'll see you in the café and we'll talk." I agreed and I went off to wait.

We talked about our lives and how we still loved each other. He walked me to the hostel and I decided to give myself to him so my mother couldn't force me to marry someone else. Esteban returned to the village and my mother was dismayed. She didn't speak to me until she found out I was pregnant and about to get married. I stopped working as a rural promoter and he left his job as a security guard, so we could work our land together. My eldest son was born and then another but I was so cold sometimes my husband thought I was ill and at other times, that I didn't love him. I loved him during the day, but at night I couldn't stand him. To be able to go to bed with him, I invented a mix of liquor and crushed marijuana leaves which I would drink on the nights I knew he would seek me out. I told him it was a remedy the doctor had prescribed; often I fell asleep and he made love with what must have seemed a dead body.

We began to clear the land and build a home. Violence came to my family with the murder of my mother-in-law and two of Esteban's brothers, who were little. They had a barn from where they distributed goods to the farms in the area. One day they ransacked the place and took everything away on fourteen mules. We never knew why they'd killed my mother-in-law and the two boys who were with her. They said they killed the boys first to make her suffer. They deaths were the first atrocities we knew of. They cut their heads off, like hens; they killed her the same way. Ten months later, they shot my husband's older brother, Jorge, twice and cut him up with a machete. Those who saw him said he had nine machete cuts. He managed to live long enough to speak to one of his sisters. He told her who'd done it, that we were next in line and they were going to kill my son to wipe out our family from the face of the earth. Jorge's death shocked us and we decided to wait for the birth of our second child to move away.

We lost those years of work. We went to town, worked together to pay the rent and raise the children. Four years later we returned. Our best land had been invaded, about twenty hectares of flat land next to the river, but I prevented my husband from fighting the man who had stolen it, to keep the peace. We began to clear the land and plant coca, which was at its peak. But the violence found us again and one day, one of my brothers-in-law told us he was on a death list.

"They're going to kill me, but not because of the coca, Esteban. It's the army, they interrogated me and accused me of helping the guerrilla."

"They can't prove that," Esteban said to Camilo.

"No, but they asked me to collaborate, to tell them where the guerrilla are and then they showed me a list of twenty people, all party members. Even your mother-in-law is on it."

"What?!" I shouted anxiously.

"Just as it sounds, *comadre*. Your mother is on the list and it looks like they want to kill them all."

"Oh no, my God, not again," I said sobbing.

"I'm not going to rat on anybody, I'd die first, but the army is going to come back and they'll find someone who'll collaborate. They told me they'd be back in a few days, that I should think about it and if I helped them, they wouldn't bother me any more."

"You should go far away, although maybe they won't come back," I said.

"Not come back? Don't be so naïve. They're here constantly to protect your neighbour, don Pereira, the one who stole the land from you. He's the most important drug trafficker for miles around. Didn't you know? Hadn't you realised?"

"Well yes, but we didn't know they were protecting him," Esteban answered.

"Haven't you seen he pays them huge sums to let him keep his crops and send the drugs to Villavicencio?"

He stayed with us that night and we tried to convince him to stay, to avoid the town in case the army was still there. We wondered how best to protect ourselves and decided the best thing to do was to wait until the money for the next harvest came in and buy three lots of neighbouring land to live more safely, one beside the other. Time went by and we collected a good harvest. The children grew and Esteban played with them on the dining table where he had painted a checkers board and a Parcheesi board. They enjoyed themselves after work was done. My oldest son worked like a man, the second one was in the village school and lived with one of Esteban's sisters, my third child was only one year old and I was expecting another.

Esteban was assassinated two months after he and my brother-in-law had decided to go and buy the lots for the three families. He'd felt lazy about going, but finally one Thursday they left and said they'd be back on Sunday, for his birthday.

"*Mijo*, I'll wait for you to come back to kill the chickens, in case you can't sort everything out quickly," I said to him as he left.

"Yes, *mija*, wait for me. I promise I'll do everything I can to be here for my birthday. The children really enjoy the celebration."

They went to the village and saw the boy who was at school, returned to the municipal capital in the afternoon, picked up the money from the harvest and saw the lots they wanted to buy. I thought they would come at dawn on Sunday. I became a little nervous when a hen crowed because in the countryside we consider it a bad omen. I got up before dawn, tidied up and stood watching the path as the sun rose. From the house I could see a long way off. I could see as far as a bend in the road which was a good hour and a half from the house by mule. At about seven I saw the animals and Esteban. He was wearing a green shirt, black trousers and a dark hat. I started to sing as I killed the chickens and I made a start on lunch. The children were happy and we prepared the party. At nine o'clock I heard his voice saying: "Good morning!" and I went to the yard to hug him and was surprised when I saw nobody. I went back to the kitchen and thought: I'm going crazy.

Two or three hours went by and he didn't arrive. I thought he'd met a neighbour who offered him a drink to quench his thirst on his way. It was a summer's day and the sun beat down. I'd prepared him breakfast, but as it was late, I continued with lunch.

Five or six hours later, dusk was approaching and still no Esteban. The bad omen became a premonition. I couldn't help feeling something had happened to him on the path and I said to my eldest son:

"Hector, something has happened to your father."

"No, he's probably only drunk, with my uncle."

"Don't be daft, you know your father hardly drinks," I said to him.

"But it's his birthday," Hector countered.

"That's why I can't believe it, he respects celebrations."

Night fell and we lay down to sleep. The children dropped off and I stayed awake. At dawn I drifted into sleep and shortly afterwards, there was a knock on the door. It was my sister and when I saw her, I knew something terrible had happened to Esteban.

"What are you doing here?" I asked Lucía, who came with her husband. She held me tightly and said:

"Antonia, Esteban had an accident on Camilo's motor bike."

"Oh my God, Holy Virgin. Tell me the truth, Lucía, is he alive?"

"He's in hospital. Get the children ready and let's go."

I threw some clothes on and got a set of clothes ready for each of the children, while Lucía and her husband ate breakfast. I felt something strange in my bones and every other minute I asked Lucía if she there was something she wasn't telling me. My brother-in-law loaded the mules and we left. We went to his parents' house, where people were already congregating. They reinforced my nervousness, especially my friend Rosa who cried when she saw my recently-born child. I screamed at them to tell me the truth. Hector shouted with me and the *compañeros* took me to the kitchen and him outside.

"*Comadre*, we're not lying to you, but Esteban is in a serious condition."

"No, no, I know you're lying. He's dead!" I repeated.

"No, *comadre*, calm down and we'll go see him in hospital."

"Let's go, let's go now *comadre*, I can't stand it." I sobbed anxiously.

By now it was night once more and no one wanted to come with me on the dangerous paths. We waited for dawn, unable to sleep. The children slept a little and my sister prepared breakfast for us early so we could get going. During breakfast my father-in-law arrived. He didn't have to say a thing because I saw in his face Esteban was dead. He had not been able to bring the body because it was too decomposed.

It was horrible! I couldn't stop crying. I could hardly recognise his putrefied body. They had dressed him and I only saw his swollen face, half of which was cut open, his hair matted with blood. I'll never forget that moment. The aseptic smell of the hospital couldn't cover up the smell of death and I became hysterical. We held the funeral immediately, to avoid the bodies decomposing further.

When I asked what had happened, no one answered. They didn't want to explain; fear was transformed into silence, my friends withdrew and no one would talk to me. Activists were dying and silence was their survival strategy. After the funeral, the parish priest accompanied us to my brother-in-law's house and he told me what he knew:

"Antonia, I'm going to tell you what I know because I think you're in danger. The same day they were negotiating the lots they reached an agreement with the owner, and to celebrate, they had a drink and went to bed early to be at the farm by dawn. They were on Camilo's motorbike. I was with them in the bar until eight in the evening, when they left. In the morning they were shot on the main road in front of the cemetery. As I had to say mass in Costa Rica, I went by on my motorbike at six in the morning and I saw them sprawled on the ground. I wanted to go to them, but the soldiers stopped me" – he bowed his head, embarrassed, breathed deeply and continued – "they were alive." He saw my startled look and took my hand – "they moaned and I said to the lieutenant he should let me take them to San Juan: 'keep your nose out of this, Father, keep going, we're doing what we have to,' he said to me. I went to Costa Rica, celebrated mass and drove back at one in the afternoon. The bodies were still there and now they were silent. They were left to rot on the side of the road until five in the afternoon when they brought them in." He was remorseful and he looked at me as if he were asking for forgiveness, "I couldn't do anything, Antonia, they wouldn't let me near them, I can't go on," he sobbed. "This is terrible." I cried and he stroked my head as he might a little girl. I know he felt it deeply, they were his friends. Two months later he was threatened and he had to leave himself.

Justice was never done. We knew the name of the lieutenant who had threatened Camilo and we assumed it was him, because he was posted nearby. Esteban was not political. Our farm was far away from his brothers' and we were never part of a cell, but both our families had been militants for years. The party *compañeros* accompanied us all the time. The sacrifice of both families was great, as one after another, we fell. My mother had been forced to leave two months earlier because of the list my brother-in-law had told us about. I couldn't live in our farm any longer. Fear and Esteban's ghost haunted me. I feared my children would be targeted so I decided to take refuge in town.'

The only man who had loved and respected her had died and with him went the security she'd achieved in those years. Her nightmares returned and she feared every man who came to the farm. She had never told anyone about the abuse she'd suffered and it was killing her. She abandoned her life and years of work again. Not only ghosts followed her, but also real enemies, crouching and protected by uniforms and impunity. Now she had no one to protect her.

There was nothing more to say, and each one left with their thoughts, their omens, their premonitions and their infinite sadness of having lived in the heart of the war.

Marcos

What does our country mean to us?

Marcos was the next in line to speak. His face had been tense the day before and he was scared of telling his story, but the others' frankness forced him not to lie. His doubts were such he'd considered leaving the group. Stomach pains had been bothering him for a few days, but his commitment to the people, to the group, encouraged him. His experiences could throw light on many things about the war.

He battled with himself. If he could convey how much he loved his party, respected its principles and how loyal he was to the armed struggle, he would come across as a hero. But the truth was that the army he loved, where he felt he had found his roots and which meant everything to him, was also ruled by the authoritarianism of each one of its commanders. They had absolute power over the lives of militants. He couldn't forget how after having given them his all, they accused him of lack of discipline. He who was strict and had never spoken to his wife about what he did; he who always tried to keep her out of his illegal work; they blamed him for the persecution he'd suffered.

He was still committed to the struggle and he didn't want to feel a traitor. He felt indecisive and confused. Reason told him he should speak plainly, that mistakes became faults when they're not corrected and that, conversely, love corrects when anger is not invoked and the truth is spoken. His *compañeros*' reactions would hurt him. He knew the group well enough to predict how some of them would try to distort his point of view and they would no longer admire him . He came to the conclusion it was cowardly not to speak and courageous to do it:

'*Compañeros*, when I went into the guerrilla I was not a child or a youth, I was a fully-grown man. I'd travelled for years across the country selling bits and pieces, I was married, had six children and an enterprising wife, who supported me in whatever I did. I'd lived through the misfortunes a poor man's life presents and was still poor. I didn't have my own home or a stable job and I got by making harnesses for animals with other craftsmen at a stall in the market. My neighbour was a good craftsman and a man hardened by life. He spoke well and I admired him. He would rant on about politics during the breaks. He spoke about people's rights and he invited me to meetings to talk about what was happening in the country. I realised they were political talks, but I didn't want to become a militant, I had too many responsibilities to take another on. As we became friends, one day he asked me if I had my own house. I said I didn't and he sold me a lot in an undesirable neighbourhood, but on reflection, I realised it was my only chance of owning a home. Leonor, the children and I moved to the lot. We built a house of wood and aluminium roofing and I began my life as a militant not long after.

I enjoyed learning how to speak properly, knowing about politics, economics, poetry and everything they taught in the party cell. I was a communist and proud of it. I joined the Community Action Council and was supported by the guidance they gave me. We legalised the neighbourhood, brought water and electricity and later on we organised a protest to stop quarrying on the river bank as this increased the risk of flooding. I met councillors and deputies, I took courses in the Regional School and I rose in the party until I was on the Regional Committee, the highest authority in the department. My wife was committed to the struggle, but the six children didn't allow her the time to become a militant, although she supported my activities.

I knew what was what, until one day they asked me to run a special errand.

"Comrade, you're a trustworthy man," the political secretary of the front said to me, "therefore we want to ask you to carry an important message to a place I'll indicate to you."

"Of course, comrade, whatever you say," I replied enthusiastically.

"Look comrade Marcos, you'll go with comrade Ramón to the Santuario region and there, at a peasant's house, whose last name is Suárez, they'll give you more instructions. The message is for the commander of a guerrilla front. Ramón already knows," he watched for my reaction and as I didn't seem perturbed, he didn't offer any further explanations.

"How long will it take?" I asked him, "I need to know in terms of work."

"Of course, comrade, we'll give you money for two days' work and you tell your wife you're going to work on a farm," he reassured me.

My link with the armed movement began there. A month later, they invited me to a weekend hunt and some guerrillas stayed in the house with us. We spent the evening together and I was pleasantly surprised by their camaraderie. I was proud to be useful. I received some intelligence training, I learnt how to use a weapon and before I knew it, I was making caches to store ammunition and arms for the guerrilla and receiving comrades who came through and spent the night at my home. I liked it more and more and I felt important. It was during the courses that I fell in love with the movement. The camaraderie, the respect, the lively joy in the camp and seeing how they shared their food and their tents made me idealise them.

It was only once I was deeply involved that things turned ugly. We were helping an engineer put together a radio station so people would have an alternative to the government's version of events. The official news demoralised our supporters, so it was good to be able to communicate directly, to inform people about battles, casualties, what we thought about peace and many other things.

Ramón and I realised the work they'd assigned us was important and we'd been going to the mountains for months. To have a radio station was a huge boost to our forces. Test transmissions had been successful and we had managed to make the installation portable, easy to put together and take apart, light and protected in boxes which could be buried if necessary. The commanders of the southern fronts were very satisfied and we were proud and happy.

My comrade Ramón made a serious mistake, though, involving his wife in bringing radio parts from the capital. He didn't have children and serving the revolution was his only responsibility. She was young and he, an older man in love. He thought it was better to let her know what he was up to. He was so proud of what he did and wanted her to admire him, so it wasn't surprising he had a loose tongue. We were about to finish our work successfully, and had been asked to do the same in other departments to achieve national coverage. I remember how Ramón, the engineer and I, left the meeting glowing and we went to a café to celebrate with a few beers, even though we'd been advised many times not to be seen together.

We were only missing one last part and it had to be bought in the capital. Ramón sent Rosaura without suspecting they were already following her. While she was away, Ramón got a call:

"I've been arrested, Ramón. Please do something!" She shrieked down the line. He went pale, but managed to ask her if she knew why.

"No, they won't tell me anything, they only let me call you. They say you should come for me and they'll explain."

Rosaura was so innocent. She understood she was doing something for the revolution, but she'd never been told how to react if she fell into a trap or faced interrogation. Ramón felt guilty. The anguish kept him on the 'phone, trying to find out which station she was in.

"I don't know Ramón. They're not in uniform. They say if no one comes for me, I'll be in trouble," she said, choking.

"Don't worry Rosaura, I'm coming for you, but tell me where you are."

"Please, please, don't leave me here."

"Calm down and tell me where you are," at that moment the line went dead and Ramón understood they were tracing the call.

He ran home and buried his weapon and incriminating documents. He packed two sets of clothes and fetched his motorbike. When he opened the door the street was full of soldiers. They were searching don Joaquín's house, where he had received the call. Ramón, who thought Rosaura had betrayed him, realised they'd not come to his house which meant she hadn't. Instead, they had tricked her with the phone call. That's why they had allowed her to call, to locate him. If she had reported him, she'd have given their home address and they would now be ransacking his house. He calmed down and felt cowardly leaving her exposed. The damned soldiers thought she'd called him at home and they were smashing their way through don Joaquín's place systematically. Like good soldiers, they shot first and asked questions afterwards, which saved us. Ramón realised he had no other option but to drive right past them. So he set off on his bike. The soldiers, seeing him come straight towards them, let him go by. When they'd finished digging up the garden and terrifying the whole family, they asked don Joaquín about Rosaura and only then did they realise the call had been for his neighbour, Ramón. By the time they realised their mistake, he'd got away. They continued to search his house and then his mother's and the arms cache was found. When Ramón didn't turn up to help her, Rosaura told them everything she knew.'

The group was tense and eager to hear the end of the story. When Marcos said Ramón had got away, a smile appeared on many faces and when he told them of the discovery of the arms cache, their faces showed disappointment. Marcos was elated to see how he had captured their attention and he continued:

'Ramón went to see another comrade from a special cell and sent for me. He told me what was going on, to warn me to leave home immediately:

"Comrade, the truth is my wife knows about everything we do. When we began the work on the radio station, I made the mistake of telling her you were my colleague."

"Comrade, I can just about understand you telling her what you do, but to tell her who you work with is dangerous and stupid," I said in angry disbelief.

"I'm sorry comrade. I'm telling you because as long as they're interrogating her, you've time to get away. I'm going to the mountains and then I'll see what next."

"It's alright for you, you don't have six kids to worry about," I answered anxiously.

"I know, and I'm truly sorry, but we mustn't make any more mistakes. If your wife doesn't know anything, she can stay, that's what the leaders said, I spoke to them a minute ago. But if they've found out your first name and everything, you're not going to be able to come back. The *compañeros* will take care of your wife and children," he apologised, head down, embarrassed.

I rushed home looking for Leonor. The pain in my stomach had me doubled over. I felt sure my ulcer was going to burst again. I breathed deeply to subdue my dizziness. My hands trembled and I didn't know if it was fear or distress at having to leave my home, my wife, whom I loved so much, and my children, the little ones who hadn't even started school.

"*Mija*, come here, we have to talk." My voice was so anguished she dropped the plate she was holding. "Tell the boys to go for a drink, and to take the little one with them, so we can talk." She looked at me as if she understood already. She shared with me the secret of the comrades who came to the house and the cache, which had been built in the yard, but she'd never asked any questions. She was a good peasant woman who approved or disapproved of things with her actions. She sent the children out and sat with me.

"Some one informed on me and I have to flee!" I said without thinking of the impact it would have on her. She went pale, but didn't reproach me. "It may be forever. We may not be able to see each other again." The words stuck in my throat. "I'm going to the mountains, the only place where I can be safe and as soon as I can I'll be in touch and send you some money. You're going to have to face all this alone. The comrades will give you some money to get by," I spewed out. I told her everything, everything I'd kept inside for years, I told her in fifteen minutes. I didn't have any longer and I loved her, but my life was at risk. Now I had to disappear. Tears rolled down my face and I couldn't stop them. Seeing my distress, she said:

"Go and don't worry. I'll take care of things. We must give our all for our country. *Mijo*, don't feel guilty, you know I share your ideals. Take care of yourself and when you can, let me know you're alright." She tried to give me courage with her strong voice. If she was ready to confront life alone, I'd be a coward not to continue in the struggle.'

Marcos felt calm and excited, but the time had come to not lie, to be straight about the hard truths.

'Years later, I began to see I had been deceived. I was taken in when they first involved me, without any consideration for my family. I thought I knew the movement inside out, but really, before I was living in the mountains, I didn't have a clue. All the camaraderie, respect and democracy was for show. When the commander said it was all our fault, there was no way to discuss it with him, no reasoning, no room to appeal.'

The group seemed uncomfortable and the first to jump in was Alejandra:

'I don't think it's like that, they respect people's opinions. Most of the time, though, one makes a mistake and doesn't want to admit it,' she said with conviction.

'Well, I'm going to show you that's not always the case. How can they say a comrade is undisciplined when his wife has to know who comes to the house. How do you keep her in the dark when people in camouflage appear in the middle of the night, speaking in whispers. How can you not tell her who they are when you ask her to prepare food for them. How do you hide the fact they come from the mountains, armed, covered in mud and exhausted. How do you justify the presence of the wounded or those convalescing from an operation? Let's see *compañeros*, what do you say to your wife inside a home measuring four by four or eight by eight, if you're lucky? Do you tell her they're guardian angels disguised as men to confuse us while they tell us about Jesus Christ? Come on, *compañeros*, how do you keep a secret in a poor home?' ranted Marcos sarcastically.

'Well of course it's difficult, but why did you involve her in the arms caches?' questioned Daniel.

'Of course, it's easy to go out in the middle of the night with a box weighing sixty kilos, swing it on your shoulder, take the pick and spade in your other hand and walk to an isolated spot to unload the box. Then, while you spend the whole night digging a hole you also assemble the wooden planks, hammer, nails, tools and other materials needed to make a cache, which you've brought in your third hand. It's no problem at all to open the cache and keep watch or ask the local guardian angel to help you. After making the cache, putting the weapons away, covering the hole and gathering up the materials, you then tell your wife you were making harnesses at three in the morning or planting trees for the future.'

'Don't exaggerate, *compañero*, it's not that bad. You could have found a comrade to make the cache with instead of your wife, surely?' maintained Angela, irritated.

'It's easy to see you've never been asked to make a cache. In my neighbourhood, the only safe place was the yard facing the river. How do you explain to the commanders if you lose the arms? If they're buried far away and someone discovers the cache, who'd believe you could be so stupid?' he said, irritated.

Everyone laughed, the tensions had relaxed with Marcos's irony. They nudged each other, wanting to tell their anecdotes. But Marcos had not forgotten how he'd felt when they hadn't listened to him.

'Order! I know we're going to be able to discuss things later on,' he said, quieting the laughter.

'I know what comrade Marcos is talking about,' said Daniel.

'I don't,' mumbled Angela, scandalised.

'Let's see *compañeros*, let's not rush to object to something. If we go over our stories and remember the times you said or did something which they didn't believe or the times they criticised you and didn't let you explain. I propose we examine our consciences, without competing. Let's remember how we spoke of our childhood originally: 'I had a happy childhood. My parents loved me very much. I was always respected. Nobody abused me,' said Marcos leaning his small body forward. They waited eagerly.

'I don't deny it, *compañeros*, I admired the fraternity of the guerrillas, and I still do. I saw how they shared everything, down to food and I liked many aspects of the life. The army says people join up because they're paid a wage and it's not true, but neither is it the case they go entirely out of conviction or because they've been browbeaten by life. Things aren't black and white, utterly bad or utterly good. Today I see them as a group eager for power, fighting against another group, which holds power in its hands. It turns out that in both groups, the ones giving their lives are the peasants. When the army comes, they take the boys into forced military service and if the guerrilla comes, they take the youngsters who are left or the minors, who the army can't take legally. In both cases peasants pay with our children's lives.

I ask you: pay for what? Why? Pay for poverty, illiteracy, unemployment and bad health? Let's think about what the country provides for us – it's a strange land where we don't even have a place to die, let alone a roof over our heads. Why should we pay them, I ask myself and I find no answer. I'm not just thinking of the guerrilla, I'm thinking of the soldier, who tomorrow may be my son and who confronts a *compañero* who'll kill him to defend what? He's not going to stop to think if he's going to kill Marcos's son, who has served the revolution so well, or if it's Alejandra's or Daniel's son. They kill because they have to kill. They say it's in the name of principles, but the truth is they kill to save their lives, from fear and duty.

When I speak to the policemen who die like rats, in the cage called the police station, sprayed by rockets, machine guns, and grenades, surrounded by two hundred guerrillas who shoot against eight of them, as though they were doing target practice, then I ask myself: what principles are these? In the name of what principles do you kill eight young people with bullets, who are María's, Rosa's, Jacinto's or any of our children, only to make a point. Has anyone stopped to think that the boy in the station hasn't had access to education, didn't find work and therefore ended up in the police. They kill a man who's frightened, so terribly frightened it can only be controlled through hate. If they survive, they're left mutilated, wishing they were dead. How can we ask them not to defend themselves or not to hate the guerrilla. The guerrillas, on the other side, shoot thinking only that the enemy is in the station, not a young person the same as themselves, who feels, thinks, loves, eats and hates because he was taught to hate. We sacrifice our lives for an idea and we kill an enemy, who tomorrow may be our friend, whilst we are with a friend who we try at all costs to save and defend, a friend who tomorrow may be our enemy.'

'I don't understand all this about tomorrow my friend may be my enemy or my enemy may be my friend. Explain it to me Marcos, because I'm clear about who my enemy is,' said Ana Dolores.

'*Compañera*, it's not so easy to know who the enemy is and who the friend is, even here we've seen it. Socorro lost everything because of the guerrilla who kicked her father off his land tearing the family apart, but later she happily worked with the guerrilla of the plains.'

'You can't generalise from that,' Angela jumped in.

'There are many other examples. Sometimes in the same family you have a member in the DAS and another in the guerrilla, or one with the paramilitaries and another with the guerrilla. I think if we get to the bottom of the problem, no one was fully aware when they chose what they did.'

'I think Marcos is right. One sees how in the same house a daughter can be married to or in love with a member of the army or the police and another is the guerrilla or the other way round. But it's not just the children, we ourselves may come to love or live with a man or a woman who hasn't been on the same side as us,' Mercedes intervened.

'Yes, the soldiers are soldiers until they come down from the mountain, dress in civilian clothes and walk down the road in our neighbourhood. They're the lifelong friends, or the children of friends and we know they're good people' said Antonia.

'In war, we the poor are cannon fodder for all sides,' said Alejandra.

'Ever since the rich discovered the country could be run from an office in the capital, they never returned to battle. Armies of the upper classes are history in this country,' replied Marcos.

'Also, in the country's official history we find generals such as Bolívar, Santander, Ricuarte, Córdoba and others who weren't common people. The people's warriors were the lancers of the plains who went to battle naked and the army cooks, called the Juanas, who didn't include any mother, wife or daughter of a general,' explained Socorro.

The discussion began to take shape. They were going beyond feelings, primary emotions and unquestioning prejudice, deeper than fear, than hate and the desperate conditions of their day to day life. They seemed so tough, but at the same time, so vulnerable. They wanted to find out why they had chosen the path of violence. They wanted to know how to live in peace and how to be happy when they still did not know much about themselves. They wanted to become the protagonists of peace, to tell the world the horror of being and not being; of wanting to defend their people, but hating the ways in which they had agreed to do it. They let themselves be filled with desperation, which later would become a passion for saving the world.

It was harder to think than to be blind and obey, cursing with the authorised hatred which allows you to sleep like a log, because it doesn't generate doubts; more difficult than following a straight path, without ups and downs, to instead remember that the stony path doesn't lead to heaven, but to hell. They wanted to submerge themselves in lakes of forgetting and rivers of ecstasy, but they had no chance of forgetting or intoxicating themselves because they were uncomfortable, dissatisfied in ways they were only now discovering.

Marcos emptied his lungs with a loud sigh. He seemed to be holding down a cry which arose from his soul, as something clicked. He remembered his wife, an enticing statue of flesh and blood, in whom his hunger and his thirst were never satiated. He didn't know when he'd lost her or if he had never had her, but he knew he'd left her, even though he loved her more than his life, and left her at the mercy of people who could harm her. God, what pain! He would have preferred to die and in some ways he had truly died, because he had destroyed the chance of loving her and being loved by her. He regained the woman who had sweetly ironed his shirts, who prepared his favourite food, who held his hand, who chastised him. He recovered the woman who swung her hips, her shapely body and roared with laughter when she was happy, but he never got back the woman he left to save his skin. He had betrayed her security and when he returned, she was the security for her children and for him. She was the head of the family. She never stopped treating him as if he was, but it was not true and it never went back to the way it was because now she could live without him.

Marcos looked around him to see if anyone guessed what was going through his head and seeing the respect with which everyone observed his silence he calmed down and continued:

'I was in the mountains for more than three months and my ulcer wouldn't give me any peace. The medicines they gave me were useless and I spent the entire time vomiting and passing blood. I lost fifteen kilos and my skin went a greenish colour. Finally, seeing they hadn't arrested Leonor, they let me go to a nearby town to see a doctor and spend a few days recovering. I sent for her and she came immediately. When she saw me, she hardly recognised me and her expression revealed to me the lamentable state I was in. She couldn't stay for more than a day because the children were alone and the shop was closed.

Six months later I was able to go and settle in another town, a long way from anything I knew. I took work as an assistant in a factory where they exploited me shamelessly. They gave me the hardest and most unpleasant jobs and I lost the little faith I had left. I knew Leonor was a tough woman and the *compañeros* were supporting her, but I also knew that making ends meet with six children wasn't easy. I sought every means to solve my problems without disobeying my superiors, but each day I felt more forgotten and my strength deserted me. My ulcer reacted to each badly-prepared meal. I didn't sleep well and in my nights awake, I reflected. When I was near despair I sent for Leonor again. She found me sad, melancholy, discouraged, in a dirty shirt, shoes without socks, a beard and yellow eyes. She chastised me gently: "you cannot let yourself die *mijo*, I keep going and I believe more than ever in the ideals of the struggle. The *compañeros* help me and I serve them in any way I can." That made me panic, because she could be the next to be persecuted and then who would take care of the children?

"I don't know *mijo*, but I can't stop to think. Someone will keep them going," she said to me, sure of what she was saying.

They had won her over to the war and the children would pay the consequences. She said goodbye and I thought I was losing her forever. I couldn't face being a widower. Every day I feared they'd kill her and it all contributed to my illness.'

Marcos ended up in hospital. He had learnt that life doesn't end when you lose a loved one, but he didn't want to live without her. His manic need for love kept him alive. He already knew no love can overcome neglect and he had left her. He repeated to himself that love could not be substituted for and she could pretend, but she couldn't fill the empty space he'd left. The time to think in hospital heightened his agony and made him feel as he had on the first day he left her.

'I asked if they'd let me go to another, bigger town where I could practice my trade, earn a decent living and in time, be reunited with my family.' Marcos continued with his face hardened by the emotion. 'They gave me permission. They sent me to Magdalena, where I couldn't settle down. I don't know if it was the people, the customs, Leonor's absence, the memory of my children or the militants who were so timid. I went into a special cell and kept doing my work for the revolution, but it wasn't the same. I was burnt out, as they say in the guerrilla.

One fine day, courage awoke in me again, but courage born of love doesn't take danger into account, it doesn't reason and tries to move mountains, which at times it's capable of. I went to an area full of danger where the killing had been worse than where I came from, but, much as I tried to forget, I was desperate to go back for Leonor and my children. This time I didn't ask for permission, I informed them I'd made the decision, which they didn't approve. I proposed to continue as an activist and asked what I should do once I settled in. They told me to go to the party headquarters for further instructions. I did as I was told but they never called me. Months of suffering and neglect went by, which I'll never be able to erase from my memory. Guilt mixed with anguish and uncertainty stopped me from moving forward. I felt paranoid and on top of that I was treated as a pariah and a traitor by my own *compañeros*. The pain in my stomach was acute and my solitude became unbearable. I had to ask for help and love from someone and again I sought Leonor, my children, my family. I brought them back with me and little by little, over ten years, I rebuilt what I'd had before I began my adventure. Leonor put her duty as a wife first, but I know I deprived her of the revolutionary life and in her soul she's never forgiven me. She resigned herself, she struggled, sought support from the party and was demoralised to see so many *compañeros* killed without knowing if their deaths would be in vain. We both love our people. We gambled on violence and we lost. Which is why today we pin our hopes on peace.'

He couldn't go on. His memories took over and he cried. The silence filtered into the hearts of those who might have wanted to judge him. No one broke it until he started to speak again:

'I'd like to take a break before going on so each of us can think about how conscious we were of what we were doing. Was it clear it could lead to the destruction of your family? I want you to tell me, in the name of what principles a person should abandon his family and hand over his life? I'd like to know whether you ever once thought you were shooting at your own homes, at your own family and brothers and sisters of your own class, that is, shooting yourselves. It's best to have time to mull it over, to let your heart express itself and feel the shame and rage for what we've done and what's been done to us.' Marcos watched them intensely as he spoke. The group agreed.

'We behave as in the biblical saying "we see the mote in the stranger's eye but we don't see the beam in our own." ' said Socorro, 'we shouldn't forget the fights, the killings and the disappearances which we've applauded or even contributed to.'

They felt a tremendous exhaustion and an ever greater need to make sense of the senseless and understand what passed understanding. They asked themselves if they had been taught at school to have compassion for the enemy or to look honestly at the slayings in the name of god and country and they reached the conclusion they had never been taught to wonder what those on the other side think or feel.

'The circumstances are not equivalent,' Antonia said.

'It's the same sacrifice, so, they are the same circumstances,' Mercedes responded.

'I think we should leave these discussions till the end,' said Daniel, swinging his legs.

They agreed and Marcos finished, saying:

'To wrap up, I lost my family and years later, I had the fortune of being reunited with them. My sisters were not so lucky. Two of them lost their husbands, accused of aiding the guerrilla. My younger brother died in battle, as he'd taken up arms to defend his ideals. My father watched his family disintegrate and he died a little as he realised his daughters had lost their security and his grandchildren were orphaned. By the time I became aware, it was too late. Our lands ended up in the hands of others. The region, which was devastated by bombings and fumigation is now an arid waste which only produces basic subsistence foods.'

Marcos saw his extended family disappear and the women, born to carry on the line and take forward their efforts, left sterile. He saw how those who still inhabit the region die in hunger and ignorance and are forgotten.

Alejandra

The saddest part of the war is getting used to it

After the break, hot coffee and some cheese tasted heavenly to them. They sat down to listen to Alejandra, who, with her characteristic signs of anxiety, crossed her legs, squeezed a handkerchief and began:

'The saddest thing about war is losing your fear of death and brutality and no longer trembling when they tell you they're coming for you.'

Alejandra had appeared calm, but when she spoke of the war and shared her opinions, her hands betrayed her, and she had to make great efforts to compose herself. She knew that when you lose your fear you face barbarism unprotected.

'Perhaps what I'm going to tell you will seem absurd, but I want to finish my story. As I said, I failed many times, but from the first, I didn't respond as I should've and I left my daughter in my parents' hands, knowing how hard life could be for her. I didn't want to take care of her and I went into my second relationship, where love came and went like the April breeze, brisk and silent, and cruelty came like the hurricane winds of August. I had to leave the house with my children and go back to the damn town and my parents' disdain. They didn't want to take responsibility for my three children, so I decided to flee from everything which broke my heart and look for something to break my body. I'd come across a peasant organisation in the town where I'd lived with my partner and I'd linked up with a military organisation which sought support from the poor, working people. A combination of my wretched life, their initial speeches, feeling that I wasn't alone and that they would protect and support me, moved me to say "yes" to the guerrilla.

I don't know how I lost my fear of them because I'd heard they were bad, atheist men who hated God, killed children, raped women and even gave their own mother away if necessary. I saw them first in my brother's house, who was a peasant leader, although I'd known of them in the eighties when the land occupations took place. Those were the last occupations because the killings and the paramilitaries destroyed fifty years of the peasants' struggle for land. As I got to know them better I longed to disappear and give my life over to their cause instead of continuing to waste it looking for love. When I separated from the father of my children, I decided to take them to my mother, but a little later I left them again with their father and disappeared.

I still don't know how I had the guts or where my motherly instincts went, to be able to do what I did to them. I left not only my town, but the region where I was born, I forgot the past and felt young and strong, far away from any links to my miserable childhood. For the first time, I thought I was loved by a more educated and less sexist man, who gave classes in the regional rural school. I gave myself over to a sweet and gentle love. I received military instruction and the *Basta Ya* which was our catechism.

I began working for the movement. I learnt it's more dangerous in the towns because there are so many informers. I learnt their methods, not only to protect myself from them, but also to collect intelligence and investigate those who wanted to join our ranks. They had checked me out thoroughly. Other comrades travelled to my home town and to Bucaramanga to make sure I wasn't an infiltrator. I worked for a few years until the army came to find my front. Just as I was regaining some happiness, I was frightened again and I decided to go before they found me and killed me.

I loved Jaime, my partner, and the separation was hard for me. In the first instance I went to my mother's, who treated me as badly as ever:

"I can't believe I gave birth to someone as callous as you," she said, "to leave your children in the hands of that awful man who hits them, lets them go hungry and worse still, shames the youngest and has him tied up naked so as not to have to care for him. What have you got in your heart Alejandra?" my mother asked and I didn't reply, but guilt was eating me up. I didn't remember how she had treated me because I felt so bad. I decided to fetch my children. The comrades from the movement gave me a plot of land in a shanty town and I felt a little better even though I had no shelter. Tins, cardboard boxes and plastic containers were strewn around and winter transformed the floor into pestilent mud. We put the ripped and mouldy mattresses in the sun each day, but at night, we slept again with the damp soaking into our bones. The roof, reconstructed from rubbish collected after a storm, was tied down, but it would blow away regularly. I didn't cry any longer and neither did the children. The solitude, the sadness and the routine of poverty overcame us.

The first job the *muchachos* helped me to get was making cloth shoes, for which they paid me between two thousand five hundred and three thousand pesos, when it was going well. I paid for the materials and the travel expenses there and back and sometimes I was left with one thousand or one thousand five hundred pesos to satisfy my four children's hunger.

When they asked me to work with the movement in the city, I didn't know I would confront worse brutality than I'd seen before. I thought I'd seen it all. Executions, torture, humiliations and other despicable acts which you begin to accept as normal when you're involved in the war. But I hadn't seen it coming from the guerrilla before. For the military it was routine, but the violence inside our movement consisted of punishments and executions with prior warning. I didn't know there were other types of movement which recruited any youngster who said yes. In the city things are very different, I saw such cruelty I never went back.

One Sunday, I went along happily to one of those meetings where we all looked at each other with the complicity of those in the know, but the army fell on us and took a few boys away. They had a list. When they left there was an ominous silence. All of a sudden some *compañeros* from another group singled out a girl who was dancing. They were from a group we called "the epileptics", a play on the acronym of the organisation, which we used to signify our disgust at their behaviour. They pulled the woman by the hair, hitting her and shouting she was an informer – minutes later we heard the four shots which ended her life.

We asked ourselves why they were executing people without evidence. Even though they were from another group, what they'd done seemed crazy to us. From that day on, I felt insecure again. The city militants were not trained for war and we could end up eliminating one other. The girl they killed was known in our neighbourhood. We eventually found out she hadn't informed and they had killed her on the strength of a rumour.'

'But that happens very rarely, *compañera*,' replied Angela.

'Not that rarely. Let me tell you what I've seen and we can discuss it more later. The second atrocity they committed was against a boy who someone, maybe even an army informer, said was an infiltrator. They claimed he'd ratted on some *compañeros* who'd fallen prisoner at the time. They killed him without trial and to teach everyone else a lesson, they cut off his head. Then, while we were in the park, they came with the head, they put food, a fizzy drink and liquor in his mouth and shouted: "Do you want to eat now, you bastard, informer son of a bitch, here you go!" It was a terrible spectacle, but even worse was seeing his mother and sister pleading with them to give him back, while they played football with his head. They were drugged and drunk. Later, they flung the head together with the rest of the body in the rubbish dump and told his sister where she could collect him, as the rubbish he was.

This event changed my perspective about the militants in the city. Our command was called together immediately and the majority of us old hands took a radical and hardline position. The commanders of the front were informed and three days later they came down, listened to what had happened and assured us, "it won't happen again comrades, we guarantee it! You shouldn't leave the movement because of this event. We'll sort out the problems and in a few days you'll see how everything has changed."

Eight days later they'd executed seven of the lads who'd participated in the murder. They thought executions would restore people's faith in them again, but now it wasn't one upset mother cursing the movement, it was eight mothers screaming for revenge:

"They're cruel, savage, they don't deserve our support, executing boys who they themselves have armed and whose heads they've filled with hate;" the women repeated in every corner.

The movement began to crack. The fathers and mothers, the brothers and sisters, the cousins, the uncles and aunts, the grandfathers and grandmothers all wanted revenge. This was the first big disaster, and informing became widespread. The army didn't have to infiltrate the movement again because every day, to avenge a death, someone killed, denounced or raped someone's wife, mother or sister and the circle grew until it was impossible to know who was friend and who was foe.

Boys without any political training abused girls, boys, youngsters and even tried to abuse their own family. A boy of eighteen, who I knew well, climbed into my bed with a gun and tried to rape me. When I reported him to the family and the organisation, *I* got into trouble. They had pardoned the boy's life over the decapitated man, but as he was the son of a militant he was sent to the mountains, to a difficult area and his parents blamed me.'

'I don't understand,' said Angela 'how did he manage to get into your bed?'

'In our neighbourhood, the houses don't have doors and we sleep without any security. Now, six years on, we've managed to build some brick houses, but we didn't have enough money to buy doors. The only way to survive is with the neighbours and guerrilla keeping law and order. I don't like the fact we would be defenceless if we didn't have the backing of the guerrilla. The police and the army stay clear and certainly don't protect the honour and goods of the displaced.'

There was complete silence.

'First I was frightened of my mother and later of my daughter's father. Later it was the bosses and the military. But the worst is fearing our "liberators", as the *muchachos* call themselves, being frightened of contradicting them and that they will single you out, frightened of the protectors and defenders of our honour and goods, because if we don't do what they want, they can also harm us. Fear, a fear which is like a sticky sweat you can't get off even if you wash in bleach. I've only been able to get rid of it by confronting reality, facing the fact I obey out of fear.

The first day I confronted fear was when I stood up to Jaime. I loved him deeply, but he hurt me. It was very tough. I had to decide between the love I felt for him and my love for my daughter. Thankfully, I had some scrap of self-esteem left and I felt I was beginning to break the cycle of violence in my life and in my family history. You'll wonder why I'm so sure. I know because my mother's response was immediate and utterly different from the criticism she'd subjected me to all my life. I had her complete support and since then, she's never left me alone. It was late, but the day came when I earned her love, my daughter's love and everyone's respect.'

Alejandra felt the fresh breeze pass through the room, taking with it her dishonour, the neglect and the desperation. The paradox is she had to lose the man she loved in the process.

'When Jaime said he loved me and came to live with me, I was in seventh heaven.'

Her marriage was the consummation of her repressed dreams of being faithful, submissive, without being exhausted, persecuted or jealous. She thought she could be the perfect wife and live for pleasure. She would overcome any difficulty and she would conform to whatever he wanted. In exchange she would give all of herself, so they could build the nest she longed for, her home. Life smiled upon her. When she looked at it from a distance, her little house seemed to her the best in the world. She dreamed how its wooden walls would become solid brick, with an aluminium roof over those sleeping below. She saw the wide, resistant door through which broad solidarity would come, not the turbulence of betrayal. She had never felt so loved as she had in those days, months, nearly years.

But instead, what could be heard was the oldest cry in the history of man and woman, a cry of betrayed and lost love. She dried her face with the back of her hand and remembered her daughter, who had inherited her beauty. She saw her budding adolescence and relived her growing sensitivity and the enveloping tenderness of motherhood and shouted:

"Damn you Jaime, not with her, not with her!"

In those days of joy she discovered that in her rush to work and to do her best to build a future with renewed hope, she had forgotten about the duplicity of men who've been brought up in the shadow of the whip. Jaime was abusing her daughter. The man, divested of his kindness, gave her daughter tranquillisers to take advantage of her. The girl was permanently drowsy and her body became strange and hunched. When Alejandra spoke to her, worried, the girl told her what little she remembered from the drug-induced state, which she thought was a dream, although it made her feel both scared and guilty. Alejandra was enraged and her soul darkened. She had never before felt so weak and so strong at the same time. Nothing was worth it, now, working herself to the bone while he had wanted to possess all the women in the house. She lost control of herself, she cried and this time Jaime did not manage to break her with his pleadings and lies.

"Don't waste your time, if you loved us, you would've controlled yourself."

"Your daughter wants us to quarrel because she's jealous," he defended himself.

"I trust her as myself. I haven't brought my children up with lies and you're not going to make the pain worse by sowing doubt."

Alejandra thought life was settling the score with her. She began to realise how much she loved those children she had neglected. Her character, which appeared submissive, became its natural unyielding self and she would not give an inch. Jaime exhausted all tactics and even arrived at the extremes of humiliation, he cried all of one afternoon in Alejandra's lap. She would have sold her soul to console him, but she did not give in and he had to leave.

We began to see that peace was not a formality. It was born from the desire to end the lies, to condemn the injustices and to go back to being men and women with the status of human beings. Nothing more.

Ana Dolores

Sleeping with your eyes open to remember

After Gonzalo's death, Juan left the house for a while because he thought they might kill him. Life was difficult in the neighbourhood, where violence appeared without the warnings you get in the countryside to ease the anguish. In the city, bullets awaited in any shop, around every corner. The men met to air their worries. They spoke in whispers around tables and in the muggy heat of the night, soaked with sweat and liquor, they tried to distance themselves and pretended not to fear death.

'We women were more alone than ever as we waited for exhaustion to overcome us and for our husbands to return drunk, shouting they were willing to die there and then and we women could never replace them or, kicking and hitting us, they'd demonstrate their bravery and manliness. I understood how Juan must feel, having lost his position as head of the household. He never thought his wife and daughter would work in strange houses and that our food, clothes and the children's education would depend on us. The more he drank, the sadder he became and the less he could understand what was happening to him. He was hard on Matilde and his anger against her for replacing him grew each day. He was looking for someone to blame for his impotence. When Matilde arrived and gave me the entirety of her wages for food, Juan would frown and his silence foretold a fight. He wouldn't eat and immediately he'd ask me for money to go out and drink, knowing nothing offended Matilde more. One day she couldn't take it any longer:

"Mama, I'm leaving if you keep giving him money for his drunken binges!" she shouted at me, flying off the handle.

"Ana Dolores, give me money. I'm going to buy half a litre of liquor to not kill myself or kill her for being ungrateful," Juan ordered with a look of hatred which surprised me because I understood that, such was his confusion, he'd come to hate Matlide.

From the day we had to sell the boat's engine to subsist, he began to die a slow death. He couldn't go back to the swamp or the river and feel useful. So, I decided that even if we all went hungry, we had to buy another engine or the family would be destroyed once and for all.'

Ana Dolores was not working so she could take care of the children and Guillermina, and Matilde shouldered the burden, including bearing Juan's helplessness and feelings of failure. Matilde had kept watch during the nights in the mountains when they fled; before she was ten, she had handled weapons and her fear. She could not endure one more responsibility on her skinny pre-pubescent shoulders.

'I had to work and I finally confronted the problem of Guillermina. If I had to take care of her girl, then at least she'd have to care for herself. Guillermina left home, I left the children in Rosa's care, who was ten years old, and I went out to work, without being able to help how this upset Juan. With both jobs we were able to save and buy a secondhand engine so Juan could go back to fishing. Life improved, not so much because of the income, but because he stopped drinking so much.

Juan never stopped feeling persecuted. We were all activists in the party and life was precarious for all of us, nobody was safe.

The war reserves a slow death for us women, one of terror and of eternal grieving for our dead, one after the other, a rosary without a crucifix which repeats itself eternally. Juan survived due to fear and by forgetting the dead. His desire to be remembered by his family, to not be forgotten, gave him the will to live. He preferred to hide his convictions, rather than let himself die or be killed or worse still, allow his convictions to be forgotten.'

Ana Dolores knew there were great dangers in the swamp, but in the city Juan would end up mad and maybe death would play him a bad hand and persuade him to seek it.

'The activism in the city had given me more security and I was happy when I could go out and help the *compañeros*. Life seemed less hard when I could take my dignity out for a while. I felt dignified when we organised fairs, raffles, demonstrations and marches in the name of the people. Lethargy and poverty never got in the way of these activities. No one can take away one's dignity even when faced with the most atrocious fear. Reminding myself of this allowed me to confront death and persecution again without being ashamed of the fear which sometimes made me hide my ideals.

What affected us most was the helplessness. The enemy had us under siege, they were so strong and powerful. Matilde would grind her teeth in her sleep and I became more and more scared by what we were living through.'

Ana Dolores knew this was how hatred, revenge and retaliation were born. She heard *compañeros* speak of wanting to torture the torturers, assassinate the murderers, disappear those who disappeared people, that is, become what they had so wanted to destroy.

'Fortunately we were peasants trained in the old ways of the party. We had an ideology, we firmly believed in what we did and our training was stronger than our instincts. We never sought to react with the Law of Moses: an eye for an eye, a tooth for a tooth. We responded to hatred with political work and we managed to involve many peasants and workers in Puerto Berrio. The party really was a party of the masses in 1977, when you could feel the strength of an organised society. Then the persecution began. First, if we got votes through our work with the masses, they countered us by buying votes, but the time came when they couldn't buy the consciences of a people who began to understand. In the 1982 elections we won the majority of seats in the Municipal Council and even though the fight was biased, that confrontation was not a patch on the cruelty unleashed afterwards.

The worst thing to happen to us, with the corruption generated by the buying of votes, was the idea that what we needed was a lot of money and the guerrilla began to get mixed up with the legal party. It was not clear who had to pay "war taxes" and all the big, medium and small farmers were charged the levy. The situation became more complicated when they refused to pay and, to show their authority, the guerrilla began to execute them. They fell into the game they were fighting against, the lethal trap of equalling the enemy's brutality. The response was not long in coming, the paramilitary groups were organised and the dirty war began.'

There was no way to protect oneself from a shot in the back or in the face, at home, on the street, or in the offices. The legal struggle could not protect itself. The confrontations were not between the guerrilla and the army. Instead, people were disappeared or were murdered, defenceless. Later terrorism reigned with massacres and impunity.

Terror became the inseparable companion of activists. They killed all the councillors and later the leaders of the Communist Party and forced disappearances began. They sent a few leaders from Bogotá to close down the party's office. The rumours of how they tortured the communists for days, weeks and months and the constant sensation of falling into their hands, made them flee to the mountains and later to the capitals. As this went on, the newspapers, the radio and the television showed nothing. The first displacements took place, the activists went underground and inevitably became part of the guerrilla.

The women left their beds to replace their husbands and the orphans were forgotten. The children grew up nurturing hatred. Their impassive eyes looked at death with the incomprehension of unconsciousness, but the brutal form in which it appeared allowed them to legitimise their revenge, which was securing its hold.

'The children and adolescents who witnessed the horror are the hundreds of dead, the prisoners and the militants who today surprise us with their cruelty as they kill, torture and mutilate their victims,' Ana Dolores states sadly.

'*Compañera*,' Daniel interrupted in a thin voice, eyes shining with rage, wider than ever, 'isn't it worse to see them die of hunger than revenging their dead?'

'No, I think it's worse to die with the certainty that the sacrifice changes nothing,' she replied.

'The dead will never know,' Daniel retorted.

But the living did know and she knew the wounded, the mutilated and the displaced and nothing indicated to her that one of those deaths had made a difference. She wanted just one reason which would justify what had happened to them to be able to continue with a lighter heart. The only justification was dignity, to say with head held high that they fought because they believed in it. But what about the victims, who suffer all kinds of humiliation and who live without solutions to their most pressing needs, what to say to them? That the struggle for their "dignity" is the reason for their humiliation today?

Daniel looked around at the faces, looking for support, but all he could see was uncertainty. They wanted to agree, but they couldn't see how. He took a deep long breath and asked:

'Do you know what the most painful death is? That of a son or daughter. It's not possible to accept the death of one's child and even less so if everything they fought for is lost. With their death, there is so much rage, hatred settles in and revenge digs its trench in the heart and stays there because justice cannot be done and it's not possible to have a moment's rest. When the hatred has to be concealed, when you have to deny one child to save the others, when the decision is between one or another, guilt saturates the body and everything hurts. When you cannot die although you want to, when the relief of death is denied and the sentence is to live eternally with the rage and when helplessness is your faithful companion in bed and neither hunger, nor fatigue from work which becomes exhaustion, nor malnutrition are able to make you close your eyes, you sleep with your eyes open to remember. Memories play themselves over and over again. When the anxious tightening in your stomach is not because you're in love or because fear makes you alert, but because you cannot kill the person who killed your child, then you understand you'll never accept their death was pointless, because if you do, you would kill everyone you love and then yourself afterwards.'

His sobs stopped him from continuing. He felt an acute pain return to his chest and the guilt rampaged through him again. Silence, like a sharpened knife, causes numerous wounds with any small movement of the soul.

No one looks, they don't want to feel, each of them has brought their dead, their wounds and their abandonment into the room and the air is thick with pain and hatred, mingled with their grief. Daniel's sobs are a torrent which threatens to drown them all in a sea of revenge.

Faced with their experience, peace was disintegrating. The remedy they were trying against revenge and hatred had no effect. Their anger was deeper than they had dared to imagine. They knew they had not defeated their enemies and those building peace today, were still not their friends. They saw themselves in their adolescent children, they heard them talking with their voice.

They were tired of uncertainty, of the vicious circle of an eternal war which was still in the same place, except each time they stopped to think about it, they were older, more exhausted and they still asked the same questions that were asked centuries ago: why, how and until when? There was always someone who said they knew the answers and said everything was going well. It was the most appalling aspect of the struggle, that nothing definitive ever happened.

The pain in their hearts seemed to win the battle against hatred. However, they looked for a refuge from the heat of the last battle, where they could recuperate lost energies and their youthful souls for the fight against cruelty. They had to abandon revenge.

Angela

I brought up my sons to be men

Angela began to speak as she always did, with a commanding voice. She had cried listening to the others and she wiped her eyes, which had turned grey. She seemed to be looking into infinity.

'My life at my mother's side was one of work. I was happy to live with her until the local gossip implied I was my stepfather's lover. He was my half-brother, and it wasn't true. I decided to look for a boyfriend and Pascual showed up at the farm once we'd cleared a large area, were raising animals and were harvesting yucca, banana and corn. Pascual was twenty years older than I was, but his body was firm and muscular. He didn't have much money, but enough to take me to live with him. I was fourteen-and-a-half and I thought of myself as a grown woman. He'd grown up among rubber workers and learnt all he needed to know about the job. He worked for a rich man, but they paid the rubber workers a pittance. Although rubber made a good return, the job was for Indians and poor peasants who they treated as slaves. I didn't know anything about rubber production, but I learnt to keep his accounts because he was illiterate. I was good at mathematics and Pascual was proud of me. I had to write down the amount of rubber milk which each worker brought, what they requested from the company store and the food and clothes which were given to them. Rubber tapping is done far away from the

towns and we had to take everything we'd need for a minimum of three or four
months while we were in the forest.

The first two years were good because we loved each other. Nothing bothered
him and I was compliant and dutiful. We didn't have children. He'd been around
and we had to wait a few years for him to clear a venereal disease. He was tormented
by jealousy and he came to control me to such an extent that when the workers
arrived, I had to shut myself in our room. Once, I had to cook for them because
the cook left and I had to serve them walking backwards, without lifting up my
head so he wouldn't be irritated.

When the work was finished we ventured off to look for rubber on our own
and got lost. We were saved by monkey meat and wild fruit. Then we found the
juansoco, the tree which produces the most rubber and which is only found in
abundant copses. Our joy renewed us and we found the way back. We marked the
trees and we were able to make good money from them. The *perillo*, that is, the
rubber paste, was of good quality and when it was processed, it yielded enough
money to buy a motorboat to transport it. By paddle boat it wouldn't have been
possible because the plantation lay between the Yari and the Caguán rivers, near
Vichada and a long way from the port. By the time the trees were dry, we had our
own farm and a brick house. Pascual worked as a contractor at a sawmill in the
cedarwood boom. I cooked for the workers and we made improvements on the
farm at the weekends. We kept poverty at bay because we didn't have children.

He began to hit me after two years of marriage. He made me work hard, but I
was used to work and didn't mind until one day Pascual appeared with a thirteen-
year-old nephew who was gormless and lazy and no help at all. One afternoon,
Pascual was cooking the rubber in large pans to extract the *perillo* and the wood
ran out before he'd finished pressing the plate. I was chopping wood to cook and
he shouted at me to pick him out some sticks for him to finish off his work. I was
exhausted. I'd begun my day at four o'clock in the morning, making the workers'
breakfast, their lunch, washed the dishes, brought water from the stream and the
nephew was sitting comfortably by the stove, watching his uncle work. So, furiously,
I shouted back:

"If you want wood, come and chop it yourself or get your lazy nephew to do it.
He does nothing apart from warming his balls in front of the stove." He didn't
reply, walked over and took the wood I'd piled up.

"If you take that wood there'll be no food," I protested. He looked at me
angrily, took the wood and I swore at him. He came back and looked at me,
surprised. The submissive, obedient fool who allowed him to do as he liked with
her, was blowing her top.

"You stupid cow," he shouted as he took a swipe at me. I went at him with the axe and he dodged the blow.

"Who the hell do you think you are? You'll see what I'll give you for your trouble."

He stalked off to get his whip and that day he hit me for the first time. I told him I was leaving. I packed up my clothes and headed for the river. I knew how to run the boat. He caught up with me in the yard and he hit me, kicked me, dragged me by the hair and if it wasn't for a neighbour, he'd have killed me.

Six years of beatings and fights went by. Love turned into disgust and when I least expected it, I got pregnant. In the beginning Pascual said it couldn't be his because he was sterile and he nearly finished me and my child off with his beatings. But when my son was born he was exactly like Pascual, the same Indian features and dark skin. Pascual was happy to have a family and stopped hitting me, but I had a long list of grievances by then. If he came into the house, I left and if he went out, I came in. I couldn't stand his presence. A few months later our son died of meningitis and I was pregnant again.

Time went by and wood became scarce. Pascual looked for new wood and marked trunks, which was what was respected on the plains. He contracted labourers and worked to cut the cedar timber until the last branch was gone. Then they came to build the road and he was contracted to manage the teams of workers.

I had a big, empty house. I helped to bring up two nephews with my small children. In between the jealousy and beatings, I had two more children. I worked hard because Pascual would go away for three or four months and he left me credit at the shop, but no cash. If we needed medicines, clothes or anything else, there was no way to get them and he didn't care. On his return, he'd accuse me of having a young lover and tried to turn the children against me.

Again, I had to go back into the wilderness to help him, cooking for the teams of workers. I had to take the two little ones with me, leaving the older ones with my sister-in-law and a friend. I struggled to protect the little ones from the insect bites, the dirty water, the soured milk and the rotting food. On one of those trips I met my second husband, Duncan. He was eight years younger than me, he respected me, admired me, was a good worker, strong, bright and very poor. We met doing the accounts and we fell in love. Pascual never suspected and when he finished the roadworks, he brought him back to the farm with us. For the first time I entertained the thought of leaving Pascual and starting my life anew.'

Angela still struggled. Every time Pascual hit her, she defended herself, but he was stronger and she always came off worst. Her new love was the incentive for her to lose all those years of work, economic stability, her brick house with its terrace, aluminium roof, the yard, the crops, the animals and the marvellous stove where she baked bread and cakes to sell in the market to pay for her children's clothes and education. She didn't appear to be a submissive woman. She was never satisfied and money became a need stronger than love. She thought that love lasted a brief time and the only thing left was money. Only the revolution plucked her from her routine of buying and selling everything that passed through her hands, whatever it was: crops, animals or human beings. She gave her sons to the revolution without searching her soul and she married off her daughters, who came later, to whoever she wanted, not to who they wanted. She gave them to older men who provided her with business and money to fill her pockets. Being an illegitimate daughter, and always distant from her mother, marked her forever. She never felt secure without money. She tried to be a strong mother and to offer her children security and protection, without counting the cost.

Her second husband gave her love, children and more work for many years. When she left Pascual she fled far away, so far that the children never saw their father again and they learnt to call Duncan father. He endeavoured to give them what they needed and he made them work with him without allowing them a minute to play. He educated the girls to be submissive, hard workers and tough like their mother.

'I brought up my boys as one should educate boys: to be as hard as rock, calm when faced with danger and brave, not like little girls. They were good workers and were never daunted when presented with problems. They defended me when Duncan hit me and when they grew up they confronted him. Their disagreements were so bad I told them it would be best for them to go into the guerrilla and I would defend myself. Facundo, the eldest, began to drink and I agonised thinking he might be killed in town in a drunken brawl. So I decided to ask Commander Pedro to take him to the mountains and reform his bad habits. They did as I asked and took him for a few years. In the beginning, he suffered, but little by little he left his vices behind and became a responsible man.

It's not true what's been said about him after his death, they don't even respect the dead. Today, young people are given weapons and they feel big, brave, terribly macho, but at the time my boys joined up, it was difficult to get in and impossible to get out. Life was given over to the revolution and if only it had continued that way, we'd already have triumphed. But, no, now any idiot thinks he's a warrior and they want an easy life, to work in the city and have good food and meanwhile their exhausted mothers are washing strangers' clothes and cooking on the street. There's no discipline, no obeying of elders, no money for the family and from the time they become men they have a lover and they forget their duties,' she said angrily.

Sitting at a desk with her gloomy thoughts, captive of another terrible moment of her past, she knew she had given her sons up to be sacrificed, but she had made men of them. She was proud when the guerrilla told her they were real men. She was tough and couldn't help it. All she knew was that those who killed were respected and no one was ashamed by the red glory of having a murderer in the house.

Yet she was unable to sleep at night because of the horror she had sent her sons to. Jacobo bled to death and she was not able to give him a Christian burial. This offended her principles, which were deeply rooted in her spirit. But, she also lived with the distress of having lost those principles and of having lost her sense of belonging and for the rest of her life she would be one of the many who had been marked by the violence, that tragic number of people who feel they can only achieve justice with a gun. She had no other option but to comply with her destiny, from the day she gave her sons over to wield a weapon, she had to accept what the weapons demanded of her.

'Facundo, my eldest son, was assassinated in town. A combined patrol of DAS and the army killed him. He'd recovered from his drinking problem and he was good at logistical support for the guerrilla. In his last year, he was bringing in supplies regularly and money too, and he'd also set up a factory to produce uniforms for the guerrilla. The commanders appreciated him, and the children loved him because he bought them bread and soft drinks and played with them. He appeared to be a rich businessman. We think a high-ranking official had him killed. He had just bought a thousand uniforms and a thousand pairs of boots from the army. It was the last purchase he was going to make from them. They probably killed him to avoid having to hand over the uniforms and to steal his money. They knew about the factory he was setting up and knew they were going to lose their profitable business. He used the runway to come and go without being seen in town. He tended to travel with a comrade who was a veteran and provided security for him, but on this trip he was posted elsewhere. He was walking along the runway with his replacement, when they saw two jeeps approaching. One had men from the DAS and the other had soldiers. He saw them and kept walking, calmly. The patrols got closer and the comrade who was with him got scared and started to run. They say Facundo managed to grab him by the shirt to hold him still, but the boy tried to flee anyway. Facundo realised it gave him away and he tried to save himself by running towards the mountains. The patrols were already shooting and they riddled their back with bullets.'

Angela wiped away some involuntary tears. Laura passed her a glass of water and Alejandra offered her a box of tissues. She took the glass, the tissue, and carried on:

'It was the best thing that could've happened to him. When they take them alive it's much worse. I knew the boys might not come out alive. I thought I was prepared and it wouldn't be so hard, but it's not true. We buried Facundo and it was the hardest thing I've done in my life. They said he was my favourite and that I had spoiled him and allowed him to drink. It's true I took care of him when he was drunk and aggressive; he reminded me of Pascual, his father, who had always set them a bad example. So when he slipped out of my hands, the only thing I did was ask the guerrilla to get him off the bottle. I went to collect his body and as I was his mother, the soldiers allowed me to. We buried him in Mesetas, the region which we helped to found and of which we were largely the owners. I cried over his grave but said goodbye calmly. I knew he had enjoyed the last years of his life.

The party had trained me well. I was on the Zone Committee and then on the Regional Committee. I participated in the meetings with councillors and deputies, getting to know the peoples' problems in depth, their real needs and if they were lacking roads, schools or desks. I knew everything a leader should know. I had good teachers and when it was my turn to represent people, I did it well, following the political line which the party had outlined. Those were times of discipline and we peasants were aware and obedient. We followed orders, the work was hard and we had to go around all the regions of the municipality, speak to people, have meetings and keep our promises.

At the time, the military wing was bound by the political wing and the injustices and brutality of today didn't take place. Everything was clear and as Socorro said, if there was theft, the people involved were called and confronted with their actions. If they carried on they were forced to pay and if they wouldn't, they were asked to leave the region. If they disobeyed, they were killed. They were given three opportunities before being killed. If they took no notice, it was their problem, not the guerrilla's. Honest people were grateful for their support and felt protected. They called them to act as judges in their disputes and they settled problems from infidelity to land boundaries. The people really loved us communists. We tried to teach them about their rights, we organised a farming union and we worked for the good of the community. Busy in my political activities, I lost interest in my businesses. A place I had, which came to have the best custom of the area, with its jukebox and more than six hundred records of tango, boleros and the songs by Julio Jaramillo, Alci Acosta and Daniel Santos, was full every night. The only thing left from that famous bar are the records. The *compañeros* and commanders were very good to me and gave me money for transport, food and drink and when I went with my small girl, they gave me money for her sweets. Sometimes they helped me with a little money for the household costs because a councillor is required to spend time visiting people in their homes, talking to them and finding out what their needs are. I enjoyed this work.

I became a militant because of Duncan. He was the one who took me along. My enthusiasm and bravery were put to the test a few times. My children went into the guerrilla years later: Facundo was forced, as I've said, and Jacobo, despairing of my submission to Duncan's beatings, took the decision when he was a young boy of fifteen. Many years later he told me he was desperate and tired of suffering in the mountains. He had to fight in the Guanía and that jungle is terribly fierce. The climate is unhealthy, the mosquitoes bite through any netting, the swamps, snakes, crocodiles and river piranhas are as fierce as the human enemy, who you also have to defeat. It's a wretched life. There's no proper sleep, bath or meal to be had. Before he died, when he was the commander of a front, I visited him in a Mapiripán downpour. You see, my boys turned out to be good for the struggle.

The day I saw him he said to me: "I can't put you up with any comfort, don't come again, mama." I replied, "Where would a mother not go to see her son?" He was paler than the last time I'd seen him, a little taller, lonelier and sadder than ever. He said to me, "Mama, I made the decision to join the guerrilla and I have to live with it. I don't want you to feel guilty and suffer. Don't come back to visit me." I cried seeing him so ill. "I have to stay here until the day they kill me and I'm not going to lose heart." I've never stopped thinking it was my fault he joined up. Jacobo was close to the family, especially to his sister Rosmira. When I sent her to study in the capital, he became desperate at home, watching me fight with Duncan. More than anything because I always ended up making up with Duncan after the beatings. Even I don't comprehend why I stayed there, getting old, waiting for him to leave me. I asked my son many times why he had chosen the military life, he sighed, and said: "Because of a cruel twist of fate. There's nothing to account for me making such a mistake."

Jacobo was killed in combat. The comrades in the movement never told me how and the doubt of whether he really died and how, has stayed with me for ever. I heard informally it was in a battle on the river. He was the leader and normally they don't go into combat, but the comrade who told me about it said the army was wiping them out and he wouldn't abandon his men. "We live through such hell only for fifty damned soldiers to kill us! No, and a thousand times no! I won't allow it!," he told me Jacobo shouted. He jumped into a boat, shooting at the banks to bring the enemy out and relieve the pressure on his men so they could escape into the jungle. He and two other men got into the boat and turned the engine on full throttle. He managed to force the army to cover its back in case they were attacked from the river, which allowed the guerrilla unit to escape. They shot Jacobo in the legs and as the army gained on them, he made his men row to the banks and leave him there because he couldn't walk. They wanted to carry him, but the soldiers were at their heels and he told them to leave him hidden in the foliage and go on. He gave the order and the men obeyed. When the battle was over a commission was sent to find him and they found his body. His clothes were torn, his hair was tangled, his beard was covered in dust, he was barefoot and had bled to death.'

Angela felt a terrible desire to cry and she let out a wail which echoed coldly in her soul. She felt that without children to embrace, her arms were superfluous. Waiting for the revolution to come, she had lost the strength in her thighs and her breasts. Her hour of sweetness should be approaching, but she had nothing left to understand. It was too late to realise that men, as the children they are, are frightened of death. The only feeling which remained intact within her was her affection for the party. The same feeling she'd felt when she was an activist in her district and it was not founded on love, but on complicity. She felt forgotten, not because of lost love, but through the cruel forgetting death brings with it and she said:

'This bloody violence finished everything off!

They told me later Jacobo was buried with hero's honours. His name is invoked as an example and many have wanted to take on his alias.

When he went into war, he took on Duncan as his alias, his stepfather's name. Duncan was the man he most admired and hated at the same time. The man who had pushed him to take up arms. Jacobo, the man who loved his family and gave his life for his men, didn't die, because a man who is capable of risking his life for others is not a murderer, but a hero who survives in the memory of those whose lives he saved.

The *muchachos* said that he wasn't scared during the battle, nor when he was left alone. They told me how in the boat he was shooting and shouting: "Finally I'm going to be free of you, you bastards, come and get me, I'm not scared of you!" The fear which had accompanied him since childhood had disappeared.'

It was not to be the end of her suffering. Her granddaughter had gone into the guerrilla, reviving her guilt anew. She understood why the girl took to the insurgency and she was proud someone followed her example. But she was not happy, because she had gone due to abuse at home. María de los Angeles enjoyed the war for a time but then she began to complain that life in the mountains was tough and they would not let her leave. Angela tried to use her influence and the memory of her sons to help her, but nothing worked. They told her she had to stay in the guerrilla for eleven years.

'I desperately tried to help her but my status as the mother of two dead guerrillas meant nothing. They help you when they need you, but not when you need them,' said Angela in a defeated voice, tired of life and of so much struggle.

'My granddaughter was beautiful, slim, with deep eyes and jet black hair. She had long hair and an enviable body. In war, she was a woman prepared for combat and she learnt so many bad words she resembled a labourer herding difficult mules. She got a hernia from carrying heavy loads and she was operated on twice because each time she exerted herself, the hernia would rupture. She knew it could free her from the eleven years of service and she overdid it until she was left permanently crippled, but still she was trapped. They sent her to cook and serve food. She finally got pregnant to break out of the prison which the guerrilla had become and went into the prison of a guarded room. I'm so angry about how they treated her. They won't tell me where my son is buried, which I cannot forgive them for, and they destroyed my granddaughter's health.'

'Why won't they tell you where Jacobo is buried?' Antonia asked.

'They keep it a secret because they don't like the death of a commander to be public so the enemy doesn't gloat. They also say it's not a good tactic of war, if the enemies dig him up, his soul will be set adrift. I respect their beliefs, but a mother suffers eternally if she can't accompany her son on the earth which will embrace him forever.'

'You should try to forget. You can't live with such resentment constantly remembering a life which you've renounced. You'll feel more and more bitter.' Antonia pleaded.

But every time Angela tried to forget, life took it upon itself to remind her. She tried to recapture her leadership with her dominating ways she'd always used with her children, her grandchildren and her electorate. Her work never daunted her, but she was tired of failures. They persuaded her to work in the party and she suffered another blow: she did not find the respect she expected from her compañeros.

'Although there were wonderful people in the cell, people who like me had suffered the rigours of violence against the party, the city activists, as Laura said, are different. The treasurer didn't report back, even the leaders didn't pay their regular quota and the jobs were done by the most humble, the most disciplined. It's not sustainable when they're killing us one after another, without hope or glory. That's why I left. They called me to be on the Regional Committee, but whoever works there is murdered within the year and I'm not going to die riddled with bullets, like a dog, for no reason. In the city they trade votes and privileges and the posts are for the friends of the leaders. One of these days I'm going to look for the muchachos and I'm going to tell them what I think. If an old woman like me challenges them, we'll see if they're capable of finishing off those bloody rich people!' She looked at the group and felt they regarded her with curiosity and pity, which enraged her and with her old, booming voice, restored by her deep self-disgust, she spat out the hatred her heart could no longer contain.

The death of her sons, sons-in-law, friends and now, perhaps, her grandchildren, did not make her feel sorrow, rather a blind rage, aimless and frustrated.

'We can't even die when we wish. They've even taken that away from us!'

She, as all of those present, was subjected to the daily indignity of petitions, pleadings and reports, to the "come back tomorrow", "almost there", "we are studying it", and "your programme is very good, but there is no money". She was resigned to the war of eternal postponement. She did not feel any more dignified than those who still waited for the government's help. This government, which called upon them to be prudent and peaceful, which had called them compatriots when they would not guarantee a return to their lands but had never treated them as citizens. They were the displaced, surviving on public charity.

Her lucidity and her ability to take care of herself made you forget she was sixty three, but because of her failing health, provoked by being unable to satisfy her most basic needs, she suddenly looked her age. She preserved a dignity and control which saved her dignity. She wanted, at any cost, to maintain her poise, which only faltered when her feelings overcame her and she showed how much she hated being confined in a house. She finally understood that in her comrades' deep silences there was solidarity, not disdain.

They were going away for a couple of weeks to reflect on what they'd heard so far. They would return to seek answers to these two weeks of work. Being with their families again, knowing how the work was going, listening to the newly displaced who were arriving by the thousands to the towns and cities, would confirm the need to keep going, to avoid the living death of believing in nothing. We had to try and prevent more people from dying convinced their actions were for the better, that they were exempt from punishment for killing an enemy who tomorrow could be a friend. We had to prevent the war from coming round to the same point time and time again.

Part Three
Creating Our Country

Two weeks later we met again. Everyone had deliberated and put down in their notebooks their ideas, disagreements and their contributions to a culture of peace. Now, more than ever, no one was there to judge the other. Each would offer their point of view and thoughts, along with their feelings. I thought the analysis would benefit from no interruptions and so I asked them to take that into account. They agreed.

Bringing back memories of school days, the notebooks appeared on the desks and their worn covers showed heavy use. I proposed that we organise our ideas first. There were too many themes and I was sure they would all have something to say. In the end, they proposed that each person should intervene on each subject and those who wanted to speak again could do so after the end of the first round.

We all went back to the first page of our notebooks and read quietly for a few minutes. Alejandra, without taking her eyes off her notes, raised her hand and asked to speak.

Hatred doesn't end with the signing of peace accords

'We've been killing each other for more than fifty years. The story of Gabriela's mother made me realise war is not recent. The powerful have always tried to finish off any progressive party or movement. The problem is power. The working people have never had power. But, what is power? To me it's about control and I ask myself: who rules, over whom, and what are they ruling for? For example, in my life, the first ones to exercise power were my parents, my grandmother and my older brother. Then, it was the employers, my partner and later, the commanders. There is always someone who wants to rule and someone who obeys. I've always bowed before authoritarian people,' she looked to Laura and Angela, showing with her gesture that they, because of their age and their manner, frightened her a little, 'only very recently I learnt how to say no without shouting, because as a girl I learnt to overcome fear by emulating those who made me feel afraid. Now, when I'm listened to, I don't feel the need to attack, but when I'm not taken into account, I still feel angry and react badly.'

Gabriela looked at her notes and as if she thought she might forget her ideas, she spoke quickly and in a clear voice:

'Looking at our childhood, we've discovered what is hidden behind parents' authority. How it affected us and how much we've suffered through our upbringing. If we relate the forms authority takes we can find some answers. In politics, *cachiporros*, communists, or the Patriotic Union were all the same to the killers – what mattered was showing that social change was impossible. In the history of

Colombia, the way I see it, every time a group rebelled against established power, they were exterminated. Without knowing much about history, I think peace negotiations are too exclusive. Accords are signed but working people continue on one side or the other of the dividing line they've drawn to decide who's with them and who's against them.'

Ana Dolores had her notebook closed and she had a small piece of paper to take notes. She scribbled and underlined as she spoke:

'My family belonged to the Liberal party and I know the liberals spent years seeking power and were persecuted dreadfully. My grandmother told me Magdalena was owned by rich landowners, conservatives to a man. The rich families put their sons in the military or tried to make them priests because these two powers, the military and the church, were feared by the liberals. When they were killing each other and no one was winning, the leaders of each party got together and negotiated. That's how the National Front came about and us women could vote for the first time.'

'We see that behind every struggle there's something else,' Marcos intervened, 'do you see what I meant before? Today's enemy could be our friend tomorrow. Years ago the *cachiporros* were the heretics. Years later, they're the heroes who fought for their country. Today, the "problem" are those in the new parties called "the left". It comes full circle, the demobilised are today the liberals' and conservatives' allies.'

Angela responded with the speed of a mountain cat:

'They've lost their ideals, they sold out, except those in my party. As soon as the demobilised enter the world where everything can be bought, they sell their dignity, freedom and life. They forget the peasants who died for them or their families. Their lives are no longer important. The majority of the intelligent, capable and brave men of my party have been assassinated.'

'Class hatred doesn't end by signing accords. In the previous wars the liberal peasants and the conservative peasants killed each other and since we've known about socialism, we decided to fight allied with our class,' Daniel intervened, 'but during our break, I've realised we continue to kill other peasants. The guerrilla groups, the paramilitary and the military are made up of peasants and peasants' children. The rich keep us uneducated and busy fighting for ideologies and we don't realise.'

'So then we must ask ourselves, what's our country, whose is this country and what is this country for? Is it only for them, for the rich? They defend the country's sovereignty to protect their interests, but they hand it over if their privileges are endangered.' Marcos excused himself for having spoken without awaiting his turn. They all looked at me, as if requesting an open discussion. Socorro asked the group if they would prefer to leave formalities aside and each intervene as they wished, but with moderation and respect. They agreed.

Changing our outlook is not easy

Gabriela raised her hand to remind us of what she had said about power and authority:

'It's obvious that the violence in my mother's childhood changed not only her life, but mine. Children are always worst off. When she got lost, she suffered a great deal, but what she never recovered from was her family abandoning her to her fate. Even though they couldn't help it, but to her it felt they didn't love her. Till the day she died, she resented them. In the life stories we saw the break up of families,' she said, licking her intensely red lips which made her face look darker and her eyes shinier, 'I doubt the authority and power parents have over their children is bad. Look, if the family breaks up, that's terrible. So I ask myself, wouldn't it be better to live with the authority of the past, as our grandparents exercised it?'

'Tell me about it! I lived through Juan's loss after we were torn from our land and he stopped being the head of the family. I saw his intolerance with the children, my anguish watching him seek oblivion were terrible. The children lost all respect for him and even now, fifteen years later, we've not managed to get them to respect him as they did before.' Ana Dolores said, passing her hand over her linen skirt, looking at it without lifting her eyes. But then she lifted her head for a few seconds and said out loud 'I don't mean to say that authority as we know it is good. My children respect me for who I am, because I've learnt to treat them well, to understand them, to face up to myself too. If we decide to fight for our rights we should responsibly accept what comes with it, even if it's painful. That way we'll secure true authority, true power, which I believe to be healthy. The rest is authoritarianism.'

'Ana Dolores is right. Now we defend ourselves by talking. In my town I go to the peace negotiations and there they don't allow me to express a point of view if it contradicts what has already been agreed. They bring us to working groups to express what we think, but they've already come to an agreement and they impose their ideas on us. If you don't agree, they come at you with such aggressiveness that you avoid them. However, I make myself go back and each time I'm more sure of what I say. Although I never manage to get them to listen or discuss what I propose, I hope that sooner or later they will. At the end of many years of perseverance I've made friends for peace,' said Antonia enthusiastically.

'We repeat what we've known since childhood so easily: shouts, beatings, frowns, bitter faces and an aggressive manner. My father never gave an order without shouting or without a threatening tone, so I do the same. When I married Fausto, he did the same to me as my father had and my children were learning the same. They obeyed him because they were frightened of him and each day I felt more lost. I began to do the same and when he went, I took it out on the children, hitting them, shouting at them and humiliating them.' Mercedes hung her head, embarrassed, 'the authority I gained by force and imposition got me nowhere. I couldn't imagine a different authority until I recovered my self-esteem and gave new meanings to my life; I say "recover" as if I'd ever had it, but you know I had to create self-esteem, and I've done it through the process we've shared. If I hadn't forced myself to look inside, I'd never have known I could value myself as I do now. I think that to overcome authoritarianism, we must know ourselves first. That's the first step. Up until that moment, my children lived a harrowing life and I was terrified Fausto would leave me. That's why I allowed him to buy my love with any present after he'd beaten me. Fortunately, by looking at my life and examining my childhood, I began to understand where the fear came from and I managed to leave Fausto. In the beginning I lost my children but now we're together again. I've stopped treating them badly, they love me so much that my greatest joy is coming home. They're good children, they love me and are proud of me. I didn't believe that one day I'd be able to express my feelings and retain my authority.'

'I've changed with my children, but not as much as Mercedes. The subject of authority confuses me even though I have relived my childhood. When I look back, I realise how much I hate weak characters, like my father. My mother harmed me, but I reserve my resentment for the weak. I used to think I loved my father more, but it's not true. When kindness means the inability to protect a child, it's a dirty trick, cowardly and stupid,' said Laura without a smile on her lips. She didn't want to hide her feelings now, 'that's why I still believe in authority even if it's based on fear. I appear to be a docile woman, but I'm not. I now recognise that and I doubt authority can be based on good faith. In my home, I represent the moral authority and make the most important decisions. Since I was left alone and the children were small, I stopped being a housewife. I've stopped feeling like a victim and I don't feel obliged to be a slavish mother for them to love me.'

'Of course not Laura. Our training process and the recovery of our life histories, has changed us. In my house, even though they're men, they help me with everything,' said Antonia. 'I've only borne boys, and when I looked into my past, I realised how behind my apparent love, I resented them as I did all men. Only now can I hug the older ones, because once they became men, I felt too angry with them. I'm helping the youngest to overcome the fears I imposed on him. The older ones left before I could talk with them about what I did. I haven't asked for their forgiveness yet, for not having loved and protected them when they needed me. I'm afraid because they're violent and they might say it's because no one ever loved them.' Her agony about her children was palpable.

'It's not possible to be a good parent without knowing who one is beforehand, without knowing how abuse is reproduced and how, for many years, the chain of authoritarianism teaches us to order and obey, without thinking. There were times when I wanted to kill my children and then kill myself. What horrifies me now is that a few years ago, it was normal for me to think that way. I can't deny I miss a man's love, but I'm happy to have prevented my daughter from being abused and I hope my children will not need violence to live. Now I let them play, run and even laugh at me. I'm proud and I could even say I'm a little envious of them. I'm respected and when we're done here, I'll continue working as a leader in my neighbourhood. I've managed to influence many people through my example. I help them to work out their hatreds and resentments so they can learn to forgive and move on.' She laughed, as she heard herself speaking words she never thought she'd utter.

'I see you're all happy with who you are now and that's great, but where is the analysis of authority? I don't understand where you are going *compañeros*,' murmured Daniel, with a severe look.

'You don't understand how for us women, our attitude to life has changed. We were authoritarian, aggressive and used punishments for everything. You cannot imagine the number of horrible things we said, how we humiliated those we felt were inferior and how we emotionally blackmailed the children and elderly. Now we know such education backfires. I've changed to the point where sometimes I don't recognise myself. The change was long and took years because I didn't know how to challenge my assumptions. Through training to help others, I began to see myself in a new light, and I acknowledged my pain. I learnt to express my feelings and not project them onto those around me. Now I understand psychological abuse better, the pedagogy of humiliation and manipulation. That's why we've been able to initiate changes in our homes, in the neighbourhoods and with our children. Changing the way we think is not easy, but we're getting there,' Ana Dolores insisted.

Authority and relationships between equals

'We're living and building a new way of life,' Antonia said to clarify to Daniel what they learnt through participating in the training workshops. 'It's not easy because habits are deeply rooted. We were like stunned mules, closed up inside and obstinate about changing paths. To accept I had problems greater than economic ones, I had to force myself to trace my fear. I couldn't accept my past. I'd invented a happy childhood, but the abuse and the violence were never far from the surface. Facing my demons allowed me to regain my will to live. Accepting who I was has made me feel secure and stronger. Now I know a child is not stupid, as I'd thought before. The child is a person who feels too. He learns and can make mistakes interpreting his feelings and blames himself for everything. It's painful to go back to one's childhood when one has suffered, but if I hadn't done it, I would never have been able to help myself or my children, as I also help hundreds of other children who are displaced or have experienced violence.'

'It's wonderful to hear you say that, Antonia. As a man, I've felt ashamed for what you've encountered at men's hands. I'm glad you can reclaim your dignity without hating us. As girls and boys, we were told being a child was no good: we had to obey, take whatever came our way and we felt useless because we believed we were an extra load for the adults and a curse upon our mothers,' Marcos reflected.

Daniel was hanging his head and he didn't want to speak. Remembering his childhood disturbed him. As he listened to the others, he realised how their children suffered and he thought of his children, of the girls who had left and he asked himself where they might be. He thought of the errors he had made. He had to say what he had done, he was disgusted with himself.

'*Compañeros*,' he said with a broken voice, without lifting his eyes, 'I have to confess something to you. I abused my daughter.' His sobs shook him and stopped him from speaking. He left us all reeling. He lifted his head with a tremendous effort and said. 'The truth is that two men live within me and one of them is very bad. I apologise, I only told a part of my story, the heroic side, but not how despicable I've been, a man who took advantage of his daughter's innocence.'

'Now she has a son of mine and I'm jealous because she lives with another man. I'm a miserable coward and a bad father. Even though I have sacrificed myself for them, I'm lower than my enemies. I thought my daughter wouldn't suffer, that by being her man, I would prevent her being taken away by men like Jacinto. She had mothered my youngest children, I loved her and I forgot I was her father. I didn't want her to be anyone else's. I did it time and again,' he bit his lip and a thread of blood ran down his jaw. 'She was frightened of me and she didn't reject me until the child was born. Then she sought help and left home. She went to live with a man who humiliates and mistreats her because she allows him to. Listening to Antonia I realise how my daughter must suffer because of me.' He went quiet and Angela passed him a tissue whilst Laura gave him a glass of water.

'Don't be so hard on yourself, Daniel. We all make terrible mistakes, but others help us to overcome them,' said Socorro, matter-of-factly, and added, 'if we killed Christ, what are we not capable of doing? Our passions are stronger than our soul.'

'I don't want to justify myself before you, but if someone had helped me, I wouldn't have continued. I hope one day my daughter will forgive me,' he tried to smile but could not stem his tears.

'If she had participated in these workshops, she would have forgiven you already. Emotional recovery passes through hate but does reach forgiveness,' Antonia assured him.

'I don't want to leave the subject of authoritarianism to one side,' Marcos declared seriously, 'it's the problem which leads us to search for someone to obey, and means we end up in the armies.'

'But it's not only the military groups which exercise authoritarianism. They always say the military are ignorant and arrogant, as if civilians were, by contrast, cultured, intelligent and straightforward. Authoritarianism is rooted in fear. Thought begets tolerance,' emphasised Socorro who lived among cassocks, authoritarianism in another guise.

'There's nothing worse than giving a fourteen-year-old boy authority when his life has been nothing but fear. When they're given a weapon, their fear dissolves and they feel powerful. All they know is danger, and fear has accompanied them from birth. Violence and authoritarianism are ways of dealing with both, which in turn generate the hatred which strengthens vengefulness,' Alejandra mused.

'If parents, priests, the military, the landowners and in general, adults, didn't exercise authority, do you think there would be no violence? I don't think so. Let's ask where the problem of authority stems from,' said Angela impatiently, 'I think the young do as they like and need a good hiding to stop them becoming lazy and cowardly!'

'It's not to say they shouldn't respect their parents or other adults in authority. The problem is how it's imposed,' Mercedes spoke from her own experience, 'if it's imposed, and they don't understand or don't agree they obey against what they believe. If we don't have the patience to explain to them why we want them to do it, they do it against their will and feel angry with themselves for obeying. If they obey because they're afraid, they feel humiliated and if they feel humiliated they seek to get their own back. If they cannot avenge themselves, they hold the anger inside and at the first opportunity they bring it out and the chain begins to form, link by link.'

'Yes, a chain which makes us prisoners of hate forever,' echoed Angela.

'How are we going to break this chain if each one of us contributes to it every day. Is someone, one day, going to put an end to child abuse and this war?' Gabriela asked.

The discussion was achieving greater depth and Marcos whispered to Alejandra and asked:

'What can we contribute to the problems of State power, of class and of equality? How do you think the war benefits the powerful?'

They looked at each other nervously as if they were being examined. They did not understand why Marcos asked in this way. He noticed their reaction and quickly added:

'I'm only trying to ensure we don't forget important themes which you all know well. Don't you think now it's an everyday occurrence to kill thousands of people, it's important to ask these questions publicly? How does the desire arise to exterminate millions of human beings in order, for example, to maintain the power of one country over another? Remember how nearly every time a child is punished we say it's for their own good and the same happens between countries. The strongest applies sanctions on the weak, arguing that it's in the name of democracy.'

'Like the case of Cuba,' Daniel agreed, 'the United States have forced an embargo on Cuba for more than thirty years which has impoverished them, only because the men in power in the US need Cuba to serve them.'

'Don't they say they violate human rights in Cuba?' Socorro asked.

'Yes, in Cuba human rights are violated, but they are here too and in greater numbers, according to the United Nations. But, we don't have an embargo because we don't have a socialist government which puts people before profit,' said Alejandra remembering what she'd learnt in recent years.

'But Cuba doesn't want to be democratic,' insisted Socorro.

'Do you know, *compañera* Socorro, how many dictators the US has defended? How many countries which violate human rights they trade with? You know they supported the coup against Allende in Chile, who was a democratically-elected president and approved the killing of left-wing people just so a socialist country wouldn't succeed,' countered Angela.

'Double standards often cloud our ability to understand history in its complexity. Each side claims to defend their principles, but the principles depend on their interests and they're very flexible. Power everywhere is most effective when it learns to hide its methods. Obedience is the supreme principle. Disdain and harassment of weak countries, as well as suppressing aid for a country's development if it attempts to determine its own path, are well-known tactics. But, if we continue to unveil the rules of the power game and how it is legitimised, we'll be able to bring about change,' Marcos tried to explain what he thought. He knew he sounded as if he'd had a speech all worked out and this worried him, but it made him feel important all the same.

'It's not easy to understand that social relationships are power relationships. It took me years to see it. Now I feel that social relationships involve power because of the possibility to influence and at the same time, be influenced by others. Our life stories belong to the social and as such, and it's clear how we have been subjected to power, and wielded it, also. We thought power was a political concept, we thought of the dominant class, the landowners. But power relationships are human relationships, whatever they are, that is to say, love, work, or community.'

'So when are they not relationships of power, or are they always?' Socorro interrupted Marcos.

'They're not power relationships when they don't try to influence or direct the behaviour of the other. But the problem is dominance.'

'And when are they not relationships of dominance?' Socorro asked, interested.

'When they're based on equality. When they're between equals they're balanced, reversible and negotiable. We have lived through unequal relationships throughout our lives, without the freedom to alter them, even though we know we should have had it.

The idea that a society can exist without power relations is false. However, one can work for a society without relationships of domination, where freedom is real,' Marcos stated.

'Relationships would be less unequal if we had access to education, health, housing and above all, to an upbringing which is not based on violence. With those resources, and if we were educated to be free-thinking, we'd be much clearer about which party to affiliate with and how to be influenced by their ideology,' Angela added.

'Our formative years are the key to the relationship we have with ourselves, the way we develop morally as we become responsible for our actions. Freedom means taking responsibility for our actions. People want not only to change the history of their country, but to transform themselves. It's difficult to have healthy power relationships while we perpetuate the same practices of social domination. When we act, we should be conscious of how acting changes our position from victim and object of history to social actor,' Marcos said without lifting his eyes from his notebook.

'For example, dignity, as Ana Dolores showed in her life story, implies having moral courage. Although actions may not result in the desired outcome, the courage to try to change a situation we consider unjust is what I call honour. I understand her when she says she continues to go out to the demonstrations to fight her corner. The fact we now use peaceful methods doesn't mean they don't require dignity and courage. More so perhaps than we hid behind the power of a gun,' added Alejandra, who had highlighted "dignity" in her notes.

'Going back to the land, which gives us life, might reconcile us. I feel most hatred when I feel most powerless. While you spoke of dignity and courage I went over my life, step by step, realising that, with all my mistakes and failures, I've held on to my dignity. I remember the question Marcos posed about what our country means to us. We can say "our country' when we've helped to create it, when we've fought for it. The traitors are those who don't care about their country. The powerful may be in control, they may be here, but it's not their country,' Daniel said, with an obvious pride in his thoughts.

'I lost everything in the violence, but I felt I was working for my country,' said Socorro, looking at him warmly. 'I hear Daniel and I feel satisfied. I'm clarifying what I think about my life. The war taught me that violence does not lead to peace.'

'There's an idea of group solidarity which only applies to immediate loyalties, and which we haven't expanded to cover the whole country. It manifests itself in the solidarity the army shows their own to cover up their brutality,' Alejandra expanded on Socorro's contribution.

'When a child has been subjected to an adult's inflexible will, he or she can live through any political subjugation later. With Angela's forgiveness, I ask you to consider how her children complied with what she wanted. They were only allowed to develop the capacity to obey orders. Faced with this type of family relations there's nothing easier than transposing obedience to the military, for whichever side,' Antonia said fearlessly, although she was eager not to offend anyone.

'The family or the concept of the family is another deception,' said Socorro with a tinge of sadness in her voice. She remembered the way she believed don Fabián words were gospel truth.

'I fought for my family, convinced everything I did for them was valuable. I didn't mind trafficking, stealing, deceiving or cheating others. I never thought of the children and young people who were going to poison themselves when I planted coca. I justified all this because I was looking out for my family. What would a priest say to me now? That I did well because the family is, after God, what is most important. When we talk of will, I ask myself about the predestination they went on about in catechism classes. If our free will is able to influence God's plan for us on earth, then we are not helpless before the horrors of war and we must not allow them take our will away from us, in the name of religion. But the more I think about it now, the more I feel everything is manipulated by external forces, by a badly understood God or by what we call destiny.'

'The *compañera* has picked up something very important. Every day I hear people say: "if God wishes", "as God provides", "with God's will". Our people are too submissive and that's why we say religion is the opium of the people. We don't believe God has placed us in a vale of tears. With that concept of Christ we are justifying murders, kidnappings, extortion and torture,' Angela murmured, as if speaking to herself.

'Family, tradition and property are the bywords of the enemies of equality, of those who want to impose their ideas by force and who want us to sing to their tune. They think they provide order, but with those concepts they've justified authoritarianism to keep themselves in power. You're a good person, but they deceived you with that tale. The Church is too full of its holiness.' It was Laura, unsmiling, responding to Socorro. She got up, poured a coffee, came back to her desk and said: 'We have to understand the deceit behind the kindness, we have to lose our fear of facing the truth, we have to learn to respect one another and not try to inculcate false ideas in others. It's not an easy thing to do.'

'Laura, you've said the guerrilla is the law in some places and you justified their removal of people from the countryside. It's a deception equal to or worse than religion, it's a false idea of patriotism. They think it's ethical to displace entire families because they don't agree with their methods, as they did to us when we didn't march for them,' Mercedes replied, looking Laura in the eyes.

'You're right, but now I realise how much a displaced person suffers and I understand I was mistaken. I carry many prejudices, which go back a long way, like how women should be, the ideas of virginity, marriage and submission. For years I worked fourteen or eighteen hours a day without complaining; but the worst thing was that I laboured without feeling important or valued or knowing I had any rights. My response was to be aggressive, hardship gave me the right to shout and humiliate others. No one keeps everything inside. Now I see how hard life is when you're displaced from the land, I know how unjust all of the armies in the conflict can be. I'm not going to deny I sympathise with the guerrilla,' responded Laura with a laugh, 'but now I can judge them by what they've done. The war has given us the chance to confront ourselves. Perhaps, if I hadn't suffered persecution and displacement, I would have never asked myself why. If another path had not been shown to me, and made me examine my life, I'd continue to support the war. What I did was not ideal, but it was honourable.'

'I don't have anything to add to this long history of obedience, but little by little I'm overcoming it, at least my body is changing and reflecting how I feel. Submissiveness made me suppress all of the brutality I've told you about.

Authoritarianism, fear and not being able to talk are the greatest enemies of peace,' Antonia spoke openly of her fears.

'Every time Antonia speaks, the shame is overpowering,' Marcos said, this time without lowering his head. 'I don't support extreme positions because they're authoritarian too and I don't think everything can be judged in the same way. The context is fundamental when examining the facts. For example, when there's no justice, someone must wield it, but what matters is how it's handled. If the guerrilla was less arbitrary and didn't favour their own people, it would be much easier to find peace. Approving of the barbarity of guerrilla acts while disapproving of the barbarity of the military makes no moral sense. If we want to build peace, we have to combat violence, injustice and impunity wherever it comes from. If we were impartial, we'd judge an act according to its nature, form and circumstances and the war would not have degenerated so badly.'

'We're no worse than them,' Angela interrupted angrily.

'We can't keep up this tit-for-tat mentality. It's a chicken and egg situation. What came first? First came abuses of authority, injustice, trampling of the weakest, and helplessness. Now we have to uncover the ways in which they have us poor people killing other poor people to defend those who wield power.' Ana Dolores was irritated. She wasn't happy with Angela's disqualification of what Marcos said for no reason except years of accumulated hatred. 'Excuse me *compañeros* for intervening in this tone,' she added quickly, 'but we should look impartially at what the other is saying to find the best path to peace. We must try to overcome what happened to us, and there's nobody better than us, who've lived the violence, to seek peace with all our strength. All of us here have lost much and we can't get stuck in competing over who lost more or less. We should see we've all lost things and ensure others don't. We have to help them see change can be achieved peacefully.'

They realised that if they did not steer the discussion, they could lose sight of their proposed aim. The difference between them was that some had freed their repressed feelings and had rationalised what had happened to them while others had not. Working through grief, that is, transforming a feeling of hate into something constructive, was fundamental to tackling these kind of discussions. Those who held onto extreme positions were directed by the blind rage caused by unresolved pain.

'First, God gave freedom to humans, but he prohibited them from eating the forbidden fruit and they, by disobeying, condemned us to exile from paradise. They disregarded their only restriction. We continue to disobey; if we observed the commandments, there would be no war, hunger or injustice,' Socorro said, a dogmatic tone in her voice.

'That in itself is one of our problems: the authority imposed by God. But who did God give power to rule over us? To parents, to the family, but to a family expelled from paradise, displaced and helpless and lost. Within the family began the chain of injustices: by preferring the older son and naming him heir, Cain killed Abel, because an injustice was committed against him and no one understood him. Instead of killing his parents, who were unjust, or protesting against the divine law, he killed the person who had done nothing to him, but who represented his loss. The chain continues and in the name of this authority the military threaten, humiliate and torture unarmed peasants, like Daniel, retaliations come and the chain continues,' Marcos said quickly and confidently.

'How do you correct without punishment?' Socorro asked.

'By setting an example,' responded Antonia.

'Good examples are not enough for us to be good,' replied Socorrro, 'just look at me. My upbringing was steeped in God's law and love, yet for love I committed every kind of outrage.'

'I think you're mistaken,' Marcos said. 'Everything was always imposed upon you and what was important to you was to work and earn money, and not tolerate those different from you and much less allow them to express themselves. Your father seems such an authoritarian man that, today, twenty years after your first displacement, you've not told him his daughters had to prostitute themselves to survive and you say it's to protect him because it would kill him. You are very considerate towards him, but not with them, who've died in life. The father, like God, judges what is good and bad. The mother, a pained martyr, whose suffering nobody eases, gets her own back through the girls, who are all repentant Mary Magdalenes shouldering the blame for what they did. But it was your father who is to blame. When he chose to stay, he sought a solution by force by inviting the army to come in with the Yanks to finish off the guerrilla. While they were doing that, they finished off the peasants. Full of himself, he believed and continues to believe he's in the right.'

Socorro was quiet. It hurt her that they spoke this way of her father, but Marcos was right. It is an act of arrogance when we do not try to comprehend another's cause. It is acceptable not to share the cause, but between tolerance and imposing one's way of thinking, there was an abyss. She wanted to convince them that the problem was not the religion predicated by Christ, but the Church's interpretation, and that was changing. At the end of the day, the Law of Moses was in the Bible and the doctors of the Holy Mother Church did not refute it. Socorro thought for a few seconds and answered:

'Marcos is right, you're not who you say you are if your life is not a testimony to what you think. If we don't live our beliefs, it's easy to deceive ourselves. We must do as we think and not think after we've acted. I think that would be my feeling about authority, authoritarianism and arrogance.'

To show we're courageous, we behave like cowards

'Fear is what pushes us to justify everything. To show how brave we are, we behave like cowards. To hide our fear, we abandon our families believing we're heroes and because of cowardice, we hide behind a gun and think we're brave. It's all a lie and behind it is the fear we've had since childhood, the fear we'll be ignored when we speak and contradicted, and that's why we only tolerate those who think and act like us. I ask you all to unmask this lie so others don't lose their families. Losing our families kills us. Let's destroy this war we've all escalated. Let's accept our responsibility and move on from thinking of ourselves as victims. The only true victims are the children and our families, when we drag them along regardless.'

'Marcos has touched on something I feel strongly. I have to acknowledge I wanted to be a heroine, but a heroine who abandons her children, who doesn't care if they live or die, who hides her frustrations behind an alias and believes she's an avenging angel, is not a heroine. If we'd fought to protect human beings, we'd never have fallen to the army's level. We were trapped when we decided we needed money to triumph, then we bought more weapons, bombs and we began to kill others peasants, like ourselves. We'd become so indistinguishable we had to tie a handkerchief around our sleeve, to know who we were shooting at. Both sides in uniform, frightened, torturing, violating the agreements – war has become our best friend.' Alejandra took a breath to go on, but Angela interrupted her.

'We fought for land, for a better future for our children and the methods we used were the only ones open to us at the time!' she shouted, furious.

'I don't agree, *compañera* Angela, and with all due respect, what have you achieved in thirty years of struggle using these methods you say are so acceptable? Do you have more land? Are your children better educated? Have your grandchildren seen more justice? I know it's hard to face the truth, but we must do it.'

'*Compañera* Alejandra, I've lost everything, I already said that, but I don't regret it, my principles are intact and I make others respect them,' Angela answered, calmer now.

'But you said they've not allowed your grandchildren to get out of the obligatory service imposed by the guerrilla,' Antonia intervened, 'you said you've lost your land and you can't go back to live with your family in the country. Have they given you means to live elsewhere? Have they supported you in your town? How can you go out and fight for your beliefs hungry and without protection?'

'I fought for what I believed in. If it didn't work out, at least I'm satisfied I lived according to my convictions,' said Angela, banging the desk with her pencil.

'I also fought and continue to believe change is possible, but now I see it's not through war. The armed struggle had its moment, everyone joined it out of conviction, or at least that's what happened where I'm from. The workers and students joined the guerrilla to change so much injustice. Many died and others continue to fight. We, the displaced peasants are fighting without guns to achieve a better world. Life is more difficult, but it's real,' Alejandra responded with her soft voice, worried that she had offended Angela, who now looked so vulnerable.

'Everything I did using violence and deception came to nothing,' interrupted Soccoro, 'I lost love and losing Rolando is worse than being dead. His death crippled me.' She recalled this painful event out loud again to show Angela that everyone had been mistaken, that it was possible to change, and not feel vulnerable. 'Later, little by little, the memory diminishes, it fades and if you don't cling to it, it finally fades. You're never the same again, even though you manage the pain. You've learnt, suffered, died and been reborn. I couldn't change Rolando, but I've been able to change others and live according to my religious convictions.'

'Angela, the price we have to pay is high, if we want to change in the midst of war,' Laura said in a conciliatory tone.

'What price do we pay if we have nothing?' replied Daniel before Angela could react.

'We still have the most important thing, our children, and that's the payment they demand of us,' responded Laura loudly.

'Our children shouldn't pay for our mistakes, not because they're our children, but because they should be able to decide how to live their lives. Today I'm a long way from the conflict and my children don't run the risk of being forcibly taken away, but peasants come to the parish fleeing to save their children from military service and from serving in the guerrilla. I believe we should resist the recruitment of minors into any army.'

'Socorro says many peasants come to her parish, but I wonder how many they really amount to because in recent times the majority are fleeing from the paramilitaries. The displaced like us, who live in medium-sized cities, don't suffer the war with the intensity of those who live in the remote countryside and isolated villages. I agree we should take a stand against our children going into any army, but I think that as well as organising groups in our areas of influence to do it, we should set an example. We're the ones who get them involved. It's not only that they're taken away, they go because of what we teach them. If we believe the solution is by the gun, sooner or later they will take it up.'

'Ana Dolores has pinpointed a painful truth. My children, for example, wouldn't dream of entering the armed conflict. I think they suffered enough when they were small while I was persecuted and attacked. Furthermore, I never speak to them about war, but about peace. I hope my absence while they were growing up and the abuse I submitted them to don't lead them to this,' Laura said with a nervous, guilty smile.

'The majority of boys have to do their service in the army and that's very difficult for them. I've always said that although they do wrong, soldiers are human beings who suffer and they are our people. I confess I'm frightened to death every time I think one of my children may pay for my mistakes when they're called up and they investigate their father's background.'

'Don't worry, *compañero* Marcos, they take thousands of boys, the army cannot afford the luxury of checking up on everybody's relatives. Even though our past may be far less violent than our enemies', we're never at ease with the law,' Laura said, laughing.

'If our children decide to join an armed group, they're free to do so and we should respect them,' Angela defended what she had done again, with new arguments.

'Do you agree with your grandchildren being forced to join the guerrilla?' asked Socorro.

'I'm not happy it's under duress. I find it even less acceptable when they get them drunk to sign their inscription papers. These methods are unacceptable to me. One should join up convinced of the need to fight. If they're forced, they'll only fight to defend their lives and for their country and then they'll lose their dignity like any other mercenary in the current professional army.'

Equality is to be treated as human beings

'I feel my life has been wasted. To be born, to die for what?' Angela asked.

'To be a woman and belong to the human race rather than being a tree, an animal or an inanimate being. The point of life is to get involved, as you have done, in the search for justice,' Mercedes responded quickly.

'We have no justice, there can only be justice between equals,' interjected Daniel.

'Then we must fight to be equal,' replied Mercedes.

'How can we be equal if we don't have the same opportunities,' Gabriela intervened.

'Equality should not be based on whether we have a university education, money, or own a lot of land. Equality is to treat every human being the same' Ana Dolores said.

'How do you mean human beings?' asked Antonia.

'It's about treating each other with respect, fundamentally. Many who have known me for a long time know I was a submissive woman who trembled at anyone's insults and believed in force. Since encountering respect, I value myself and value my ideas, I don't let myself be humiliated and I respect others, because I feel equal to anyone. I know what I'm saying every time I do stand my ground, I feel stronger, equal to any professional, priest or soldier,' explained Ana Dolores.

'To feel that whoever listens to you respects you, understands you or tries to understand even though they may not share your ideas, gives you the opportunity to be yourself. That's how you discover your possibilities and qualities,' said Laura, following on Ana Dolores's idea.

'I'd say this is the path to justice. The important thing is to keep fighting, looking for justice. Justice can be created and the important thing is to live and die on the right side,' stated Marcos.

'We have to turn to God and ask Him to show us the way.'

'I beg to differ, *compañera* Socorro, I think we must turn to people and demand they respect us. We also have to fight for them and, sometimes, we must die for them,' replied Daniel.

'I'd like to say to the military, the paramilitaries and the guerrilla: let's negotiate an agreement, for pity's sake, let's prevent any more blood from flowing. Let's be humble, let's be courageous: one needs courage to be humble. But I don't know how to reach them, how to speak to them and if we don't find a solution, the tragedy will continue.' Marcos spoke with quiet intensity. 'I'm a realist and I don't see an end to this war in the short term. There are too many people who stand to gain by continuing it. Many speak of peace, but no one really wants it.'

Marcos's expression was sad. He hid his face in his two hands and stayed that way for a couple of minutes, which seemed to go on forever. We thought he was crying, but when he took his hands away we saw his eyes shone with passion. His reddened face showed the strength of his determination:

'I've seen many attempts to return to peace and they've all disillusioned me to the extent I now believe in nothing. I think good deeds always pass unnoticed, while the bad are decorated for their crimes legalised by a rag they call the flag. Other times I think of those who died without giving up in their defence of the poor, of those who've been true and have withstood torture without betraying anyone.'

Angela wanted to speak and raised her hand:

'Look here *compañero* Marcos, the gravest danger is to resign ourselves. One should never give up. We must think and rebel.'

Socorro jumped in:

'I think those who are resigned have no memory. They don't think. They pretend they're not in the midst of a war. They have no notion of dignity. We should pity them.'

'Why pity them, they're so much happier, they live very well.'

'Don't you believe it, Mercedes. Not only do they not live well, they don't live at all.'

'What do you mean? Death doesn't find them because they don't compromise themselves – is that it?'

'No, I mean death takes those people by surprise, they have nothing to hold onto. They can remember nothing except the emptiness of their lives. One cannot but appreciate those who fight, if only because they fight for their own and their children's dignity.'

'Dignity is not enough. It's not enough to die or let yourself be killed, because the dead can do nothing. I'm a widow, my children are orphans and the Patriotic Union was obliterated. Martyrdom and dignity are not enough,' intervened Gabriela.

'I believe it's enough to live in accordance with one's principles, to believe in justice, but for everyone. We must fight, but for everyone, for everyone's human rights, for international humanitarian law. Let's not applaud if they burn young soldiers after an ambush,' said Marcos mulling over his idea of justice.

'How do we know what's right?' asked Antonia.

'It's impossible,' responded Ana Dolores.

'We must be patient. If we make a mistake we should rectify it and start again. Anyway, we have to live and be aware of this war. We should live our lives as best we can, making our mark, shaping our history, dreaming of people's equality, being on the side of justice, not allowing ourselves to forget. If we let our memory go, then we'll have wasted our lives.'

'How do face the fear of making mistakes?' Alejandra asked Daniel in response to his vision.

'We mustn't be afraid of making mistakes because doubt is like nerve gas. Fear paralyses us. To be afraid to do the wrong thing is a luxury for people who believe they can play god, it's an excuse, a way of avoiding criticism for not fighting, for not trying,' Daniel dried his sweat with a handkerchief and carried on:

'For years I've had nightmares where I see my daughter berating me for having denied her. I don't know if I denied her because of cowardice and then justified it, arguing it was to protect the little ones. The fear, as I've said before, was terrible and doubt has tormented me until, working at your sides, I've learnt I'm not perfect, I have a great love for my country, but I'm simply a man. We, the poor, are faced with death and mistaken or not we must act, live or die. That's why in these few days I feel I've finally forgiven myself. I am reconciled to my children, I want to keep fighting and I want to correct my mistakes. I want to start by trying to stop children from entering the war, by making sure the young don't become informers and by preventing them from becoming torturers or members of paramilitary groups who massacre our people.'

Daniel moved us all again, making us understand him and respect him more each day.

Holding out your hand to help another is not enough

'We must recover solidarity to find the way to peace,' Angela proposed as the only response to the silence which reigned after Daniel's contribution. She looked one more time at her notebook, looked at us with her gaunt face and continued: 'Solidarity is a group feeling, as has been said here, but it's a feeling of love if we see it as solidarity for change. All of us, in the telling of our lives, have named solidarity and comradeship as part of what attracted us to join parties, movements or political groups. Holding out your hand to help another is not enough and it's not enough to point out their errors, we must have solidarity with them, we must love them.'

'We must understand solidarity in positive terms. We could fall into the danger of supporting the "group solidarity" which leaves no room for critical thinking,' said Marcos putting his finger on a familiar problem.

'Of course we must have solidarity. The rich and the army protect each other with it, why shouldn't we? We should foster group loyalty as we did before,' Angela said.

'It did us no good,' Marcos responded looking at her, 'defending the indefensible, lying out of loyalty and covering up the barbarities of our side is what has brought us to have the same moral stature as the enemy. If we think that they brought us into the conflict with their solidarity and comradeship, we should analyse if it was a good enough reason. We felt good, protected by a big family and secure, but when they started to murder and violate fundamental rights we let them continue because of "group solidarity", and we lost credibility with the people.'

'What do we care what they think, they don't care about us because we're poor. What's important to the middle class is that they have a car, a house and a scholarship, as the propaganda says, and the rest of us can go to hell,' said Gabriela irritated.

'If we don't believe people can change, it's going to be difficult to change anything and the war will continue forever,' Ana Dolores sentenced.

The next day, at dawn, Daniel and Alejandra arrived early, to speak to me before the group met. They were uncomfortable because they thought they had gone too far in their interventions the previous day. They had spoken the truth and, yet, they had not slept well.

'We came to see what you think about our honesty,' and they remained quiet waiting for my reply.

'I can't see a problem with it,' I replied, 'we're at a moment when everything you say may be an important contribution to peace. Knowing ourselves is sufficient for us to accept ourselves as human beings, that is to say, as beings who can make mistakes. To correct them we need to reflect and change the way we think, there needs to be a true change of mind.'

The others began to arrive and we sat down. They were quiet and I took advantage of the silence to emphasise the importance of respect for others, of not judging and above all, of remembering truth would lead us to peace.

'The subject of solidarity is so delicate I thought I'd bring in some definitions of *solidario* and *solidaridarse** – Ana Dolores kicked off the session, 'may I read them *compañeros*? Solidarity is the "circumstantial support for the cause or ventures of others", while *solidario* is "an obligation or responsibility shared by various people in such a way that it corresponds to each of them, not just in part, but in its totality", and *solidaridarse* is to "show conformity with the attitude or actions of others and being ready to partake of the consequences." '

'I still think we must have solidarity to save this country from misery,' Mercedes broke the silence, 'Solidarity can be for commitments and duties in accordance with the morality and ethics of each of us,' she looked at the others, who were quiet.

'Does solidarity mean we approve everything they do, not just the things we'd be willing to participate in?'

'Exactly, *compañero* Daniel,' responded Alejandra, "having solidarity with a group means we accept everything.'

'I don't agree with the participation of children under eighteen in the war, but I do agree we should fight for the land, decent wages and free education; I don't agree with massacres and other acts of violence either, so I can't go along with that definition,' said Gabriela.

'Supporting the armed struggle is to approve the use of force to dominate others. It is to approve the means as well as the ends. The fight to recover land can

* Spanish: 'Solidario' (to be supportive), 'solidaridarse' (to support).

involve killing your neighbour, or driving the peasants from their lands saying the paramilitaries are coming,' replied Mercedes, 'it's true we need land, it's our life, but the struggle for land reform began to bleed us to death a long time ago. The rich have always expropriated land by blood and fire. When, on the other hand, the guerrilla extorts, kidnaps or kills a rancher or a landowner, they're doing the same: expropriation or recuperation by blood and fire.'

'That's true, but Mercedes, you know how hard we work to clear land for cultivation, to plant, tend our crops and when it's ready to produce, the owner appears or the violence returns,' said Laura.

'The agrarian reform in Colombia has been done with violence and to benefit the few,' Angela noted, 'each time we abandon the countryside, we play into the hands of those who started the war. The guerrilla in Colombia was not made to fight for territories, if they had more than half the country would be ruled by them. But overseeing a freed territory is hard. By not declaring the guerrilla a belligerent force the government has managed to keep it a low-intensity conflict.'

'I agree with the *compañera*, but I propose we return to the discussion of solidarity. According to the definitions, we cannot go on approving only part of the armed struggle. We should state clearly we oppose it, that we support groups who work for peace and if we ask to negotiate, it's because we don't believe in armed solutions.' Daniel seemed pleased to speak and above all, to understand what he was saying, 'Now I understand what solidarity means. We should have solidarity with the negotiation of the conflict, with a new agrarian reform, with education for all, with health for the people, but through peaceful means.'

'That sounds great, Daniel. Do you think it's truly possible?' asked Antonia.

'I don't know if it will be possible, but we must try,' Daniel answered.

'We should have solidarity with the children, the families expelled from their lands, with the widows and the *compañeros* who lose everything. We must be open and we should invite them to build the ways to peace,' added Alejandra, sure of what she was saying because she had been doing it for some years and she wasn't frightened of being called a 'traitor' any longer.

'Where does that leave the problem of the paramilitaries who follow people from their lands to the city to kill them?' asked Laura expectantly.

'It's our most serious problem of late. Now, we don't know how to defend ourselves. The paramilitaries, supported by the armed forces, have reached such high levels of belligerence, they're now expelling entire communities. We don't know how to confront this problem,' reflected Marcos.

'I ask you, what are we going to do to offer them solidarity? Does it imply we approve of everything displaced people think, or do we only show solidarity with the right to live freely in an area and not be forced to leave?' Everyone wanted to speak and Ana Dolores made a gesture so that they would let her continue, 'the paramilitaries are now threatening the people who support the displaced. Years ago, when I was displaced, no one would admit to it, we were frightened and maybe that's why no one knew we were thousands of displaced peasants. Now, the displaced are in the press and even the government recognises the problem.'

We must oppose all the armed groups

'We have embarked upon finding new ways to fight for peace. We should be part of the negotiation of the conflict. We should recognise the mistakes made to lower the levels of intolerance and retaliation,' Mercedes said.

'The road will be long, *compañera* Mercedes, and many of us may be left by the wayside,' Gabriela countered, 'I'm frightened of helping you because those on the right will kill us before they work out what we mean. I don't want to die, I want to raise my children and rebuild my life.'

'Abandoning the struggle doesn't guarantee leaving danger behind. We must find courage in the events we've lived through. If we don't the violent will win. They want to terrify us, to crush us so they can take what is ours through violence. Fear, as we said before, is the biggest obstacle to peace. We must overcome it and keep going forward,' replied Antonia. 'I've been terrified for most of my life, and know there are better ways to live. The majority of peasants want to fight for their rights and support one or other of the armed groups without realising that, as unarmed civilians, they pay the consequences. You all know what I'm talking about. If we speak of this in each of the communities where we live and encourage them to understand our position, we might create a new awareness. We must change minds, for them to learn, like us, that the change to peace is a way of thinking and acting differently.'

'How could we organise them so they're not manipulated?' asked Gabriela.

'By telling them they can oppose any armed group which enters their region demanding support. We need to support those who have participated directly because, if we shun them, they'll continue down the same path,' Angela spoke, enthused by feeling useful and able to contribute a little of the vast amount she knew, 'we should struggle to save the children and the young people from the violence and organising them, break the chains of violence.'

Moving on

Daniel still doubted whether they would achieve full rights through peaceful methods, to live as they deserved or at least, to have a dignified life. At times he wanted to continue to hate and fight with the guerrilla methods and at others he wanted to fight with the instruments of peace. He opened his arms in a gesture of doubt, did not lower his eyes, but instead looked straight at me and asked: '*Compañeros*, what should I do with my doubts? Will we be able to achieve justice?'

'Powerlessness, Daniel, does us much harm,' Mercedes said. She looked like she was about to cry. 'I know you wish you'd killed the person who killed your daughter. But you thought of your other children and this made you reflect and come to the city to save your lives. It was not that you didn't dare. Your act was one of responsibility, not of hatred. You took the first step without realising it. You're a man who thinks and feels. You're not a killer.'

Daniel was crying; he felt understood in his most intimate thoughts. He understood he should not feel helpless, he did not need to kill to be a man.

'I understand what you're saying. If I hadn't had the little ones and was not so marked by the immense pain of being an orphan, maybe I'd abandoned them and I might have become an informer or a guerrilla. I could've been stupid and played the same game as Jacinto. In the end, out there, nobody cares why you make a decision,' he sighed, blew his nose and proceeded, 'I would have have pretended to be bought and the day after informing, I'd have waited for them with a guerrilla column. Then, that bastard Jacinto would have died with all his soldiers. I didn't do it because of my children. I want a peaceful life for them and the home I never had.'

'What is despicable is their method of buying informers. It's a double-edged sword because they assumed with so much money around, the first to fall would be the commanders of the guerrilla, but it hasn't turned out like that. No one has betrayed them, but corruption did spread and many, instead of informing for money, did it for revenge. The famous "faceless justice", organised to protect judges, became the best tool of injustice. Many witnesses are thugs who'll say anything for money. Our justice system is failing to such an extent that levels of impunity are 98 per cent for political crimes. The cure turned out to be worse than the malady. How can we protect our children and grandchildren?' asked Socorro anxiously.

'I'm not going to give up, *compañera*,' Daniel answered calmly, 'but I needed to overcome my guilt because it's eating me up inside. I also ask myself, night and day, how long is this war going to go on for? I ask myself if I'll have the guts and courage to continue to fight to the death for peace. I'm afraid of making the wrong decision.'

'What you feel is very human, Daniel,' Socorro replied, 'we all feel it, but God will give us enough strength. Think how strong you are that you've lasted so long in the heart of this conflict. Why then will you not last as long, or longer, in the struggle for peace?'

'*Compañera* Socorro, when I was in the war I didn't entertain any doubts and such blind faith gave me courage. I have questioned myself now, and it's much harder to act,' explained Daniel.

'We must be patient and above all, accept our responsibility. It's so easy to start a war and so difficult to end it,' answered Socorro, who was attentive to each question or doubt in the discussion.

'Not knowing for sure when this war will finish makes me anxious. My children and my grandchildren have already paid the price. Yet it seems we never stop confronting this war, which I began in my family and which I blame myself for now.'

'You mustn't blame yourself, Angela. You didn't start this war and your grandchildren are not there because of the side you were on. It's the circumstances: living in a zone of guerrilla influence, the injustice, the impunity and the lack of opportunities for young people all contributed to them deciding to join up.'

'But *compañera* Socorro, I did start the struggle in my family,' Angela remonstrated strongly, 'I was the first one in my family to join a revolutionary group. Didn't you hear how I pushed my children to join up and later I felt proud that my granddaughter did too? I also trained the children as messengers and taught them how to protect themselves from the bombings. I thought it was only right that we should all go to war: women, men and children. My eyes have seen many injustices. I'm responsible for barbarities committed against others.'

Daniel listened to her and when she mentioned the children, he put up his hand to speak. When Angela stopped speaking, he said:

'Unlike Angela, I always suffered for the children. Watching them run anxiously, being silent and risking their lives, left alone to face the army, while the adults hid, is something I'll never forgive myself for. We're irresponsible. We're so stupid that we exposed them to death, while they kept quiet out of loyalty to us. Now is seems despicable to me that the armed groups use them and we, the parents, expose them to die in our war.'

'I don't want my other grandchildren to join up,' Angela agreed, 'we already have enough dead. Now we should try to help the family survive.

'The most important thing we've achieved in all these years was discovering how power works. As soon as I understood it, I was free. Finally, I have my own memories, I accepted the real story of my life and new feelings appeared, which I had suppressed, because of fear,' Alejandra was happy to move with certainty towards harmony. Her face showed a happiness which revealed her sweeter side and it moved the group, sowing in it the seeds of hope, which gave new stimulus to the meeting.

'What should we do to develop such respect?' Gabriela asked.

'With the displaced and with the community in general, we should follow the same steps we've taken. Accept their feelings and be sensitive to their needs and the humiliations they've suffered. We should show ourselves as we are and tell them our truth,' reasoned Mercedes.

'It sounds wonderful, but how do we do it in practice?'

'I was working with Daniel,' Marcos said, 'and we agree with Mercedes, we should be open to understanding the hatred each person carries. If we don't achieve this small but crucial beginning, not millions of pesos, training, micro-businesses and other tried formulas will save us from continuing this conflict. We may achieve negotiations because the killings and the displacements bring the armed groups to negotiate, but in ten years we will be seeing the rebirth of a new war or the same war postponed. Our true needs are for our voices to be heard, for our wounds to heal, not to be humiliated any longer and the recognition that we are a dignified and hard-working people.'

'As *compañero* Marcos says, we are most offended by being treated as if we were imbeciles.' Daniel's passion gave his voice new spirit. 'Who gave the powerful the idea that peasants are beggars? In the countryside we're not used to being given things. I ask myself, what do they expect from us? Do they expect peace to come from the kingdom of heaven, when the war has been made in the realm of men? I remember how important a Truth Commission was in the negotiations in El Salvador; moral reparation of those who'd fought in the conflict is central. Truth and respect, I'd say, are the roads to peace.'

'The world should know what we've been through and in our stories see a reflection of the lives of thousands of peasants, so history doesn't continue to repeat itself endlessly. If they can feel what we've lived and why we expressed our most intimate needs through violence, maybe they will help us to change. We feel so insignificant, but we're a true war machine. Peasants, collectively, together with the powerful, are the protagonists of the conflict. We should let the world know the war is terrible for everyone in Colombia, that the war is waged to satisfy desires for power and revenge and that, rich and poor, workers and unemployed, peasants and city dwellers, we've all lost out in this conflict,' Marcos said with passion.

'How do we move on?' Ana Dolores asked.

'We must forgive the injustices suffered, but words are not enough. We must ask ourselves: where do we start to build a path towards true forgiveness? I think first we must know the truth, to see who has to be forgiven and not let anyone treat us as mere pawns in this conflict. We should become subjects of this story and accept our responsibility to be able to forgive and be forgiven. It's two-way process which must not skirt around the anger without touching it, but pass through it. Looking to all the armed groups to accept their responsibility is the first step. There must be moral as well as economic reparation,' Socorro proposed, and they all nodded their assent.

'Telling the truth hurts us, but it allows us to change,' Angela said.

'It's precisely the opportunity of living the grief, as we learnt to call the pain and our own virulent feelings, which deals a blow to guilt. Accepting what has happened to us, knowing we cannot change the past and cannot seek to blame others when we're all to blame, helped us to understand we don't have to seek forgiveness without conditions, because it would give us only the illusion of reconciliation,' Mercedes said, more passionately than she had ever spoken before.

I felt happy, after so many years of work with them, seeing them freed and sure of their proposals. As they left the house they talked amongst themselves, listened to new ideas, as if from one minute to the next, their lives had gone into an open field where they could shout out their dreams. Tomorrow was the last day.

We have to defeat fear

At six-thirty in the morning, the day was fresh, there was a breeze and the sun rose in the east, lighting up the plains. Laura came early and helped to prepare coffee; she fussed over the refreshments and lunch. She was radiant and had slept well and wanted to contribute to a future she saw with optimism for the first time. She spoke to me of her children, of the joy of being able to continue to work in the land where she was born; the place she wanted to return to, to work for her family and for peace. We had to forget the past to live the present and she was willing to search for the paths to freedom.

'Yesterday we left it that we wouldn't support those who use arms to impose their views. We're going to preach as Christ did, not only with words, but we're going to live according to our values,' Socorro said, who had arrived full of enthusiasm.

'It's not going to be easy. Go and tell the good news to someone who's just been beaten up or, a relative of someone who's been assassinated or to the soldiers whose friend has been killed. Tell them not to return a blow with a blow, that we must live in peace and you'll see what they say, *compañera* Socorro,' challenged Daniel.

'Nothing in life is easy, not even living it. It will be even less easy to build over the ashes of death. But we're tough! Were we not willing to give our lives for the freedom of our country? Well then, we have to fight for peace with the same strength, the same feeling and the same passion. We're not the twelve apostles, but we're ten warriors for reconciliation.'

'That's the spirit! We have to go forward with passion. Intelligence must win in the end,' Marcos agreed, excited.

'It's time to be true heroes. I still believe that underneath it all, that's what we want. We'll be heroes of peace. As Socorro says, if they kill us, at least we'll be on the right side.'

'What is the right side for you, *compañera* Alejandra?' Antonia asked.

'Now I'm clear: it's being on the side of peace, it's saying no to anyone who wants to impose their will with weapons.'

'So what are we going to do with the fear? You said when you lose your fear you're unprotected from cruelty,' Daniel asked Alejandra.

'I don't think one ever stops feeling fear, but it's human to feel it. Security, trust and responsibility will give us the strength to fight on the side of peace. It's not going to be easy, Daniel, but neither is it impossible.'

'The opposite is to give in to fear and stay silent,' Ana Dolores insisted. 'Doing that is to agree with the violence. They know we're frightened and that's what they base their security on. The best example I can give is the thief when he goes in to steal. He's frightened, but he shelters behind the gun and the terror you will feel when you see him, but if we come out and face him, even with fear, he will run out nearly every time, terrified. Is it not like that?'

'Living among the violent and confronting them unarmed is true heroism, but I'm sure many others will accompany us and it will be easier.' It was Angela's voice, echoing in everyone's hearts. She proposed to defeat the invincible with respect and truth.

They had come this far because they had accepted the strict rules of the game. Discretion and confidentiality were fundamental and above all, they had the will to reach a consensus, calling things by their names, without evasions or lies. In their own setting, they would use these same rules to build roads to peace.

When the meeting ended they closed their full notebooks. With hugs, farewells and tears, we separated. They went back to their homes with new hope and a great responsibility. Now they were free. Life and death, war or peace were in their hands and they knew it. The future did not worry me. Now it was not important to me to calculate if peace would come and how long it would last. It was not that I trusted in God's justice or in the justice of

I had to believe in the human condition, in the moments of happiness, the partial progressions and in our efforts to change. I remembered Hadrian, the Roman emperor whose thoughts on war and peace encapsulated my feelings:

'Catastrophes and ruin will come; disorder will triumph, but also, from time to time, order. Peace will reign again between two periods of war; the words liberty, humanity and justice will here and there regain the sense we have tried to give them. Not all the books will perish; our mutilated statues will be remade and other turrets and pediments will be born from our pediments and turrets; some men will think, work and feel like us; I dare to count on these continuators – born at irregular intervals over the centuries, with that intermittent immortality. If the barbaric end up taking over the world, they will be obliged to adopt some of our methods and in the end will resemble us.'

Other books from the Latin America Bureau
relating to Colombia and children

Colombia In Focus
Colin Harding

The authoritative and up-to-date account of the political, economic and social situation in Colombia.
ISBN 1 899365 01 X
1996
£5.99
75pages

Hidden Lives: Voices of Children in Latin America and the Caribbean
Duncan Green

'This book should be read by anyone interested in taking children seriously.'
Orbit, Voluntary Service Overseas

Duncan Green travelled to Brazil, Jamaica, Peru, Colombia, Honduras and Nicaragua. He talked to children, watched them at work and at play, on the streets and in the home. He interviewed teachers, welfare workers and other adults involved in their lives. His conclusions are refreshing and thought-provoking.
ISBN 0 304 33688 2
1998
SPECIAL PRICE £10.99
192 pages

Born to Die in Medellín
Alonso Salazar

A riveting insight into urban violence in Medellín, Colombia's second city.
ISBN 0 906156 66 1
1992
£5.99
130 pages

LAB is an independent research and publishing organisation. It works to broaden public understanding of issues of human right and social and economic justice in Latin America and the Caribbean.

To order the above books, please add 10% for postage and send a cheque or credit card details with your order, name and address to:
Latin America Bureau, 1 Amwell Street, London EC1R 1UL
Tel: 0207 278 2829 Fax: 0207 278 0165 Email: books@lab.org.uk
Contact us for a free copy of the Latin America Bureau's latest books catalogue